NEVER FORGET
TO LAUGH

ISBN: 978-1-889642-21-5

Grateful acknowledgment is made to the following for permission to use copyrighted material:

Robert Skutch, for excerpts from *Journey Without Distance: The Story Behind A Course In Miracles* by Robert Skutch, copyright ©1984.

Prometheus Nemesis Books, for excerpts from *Please Understand Me, II* by David Keirsey, copyright © 1998.

Neale Vahle, for excerpts from *A Course In Miracles: The Lives of Helen Schucman & William Thetford* by Neal Vahle, copyright © 2009.

The Gangaji Foundation, for excerpt from *You Are That* by Gangaji, copyright © 2007.

James Bolen, for excerpt from "Interview: Judith R. Skutch," *New Realities*, April 1977, copyright © 1977.

James Bolen, for excerpts from "Interview: William N. Thetford, Ph.D.," *New Realities*, September 1984, copyright © 1984.

Cover design by Kathryn Van Aernum
Text design and layout by Cathy Sanders

Printed in United States of America

NEVER FORGET TO LAUGH

Personal Recollections
of
Bill Thetford,
Co-scribe of
A Course In Miracles

CAROL M. HOWE

Also by Carol M. Howe

Healing the Hurt Behind Addictions
and Compulsive Behaviors
(English and Russian)

Homeward To An Open Door;
Exploring Major Principles of
A Course In Miracles

Emergency Procedures for Regaining
Peace of Mind
(English and Spanish)

Children As Teachers of Peace
(Co-editor)

Table of Contents

Foreword

Many of you will pick up this book because you know Bill Thetford by reputation or as a co-scribe of *A Course In Miracles*. Others may find it simply because you are meant to do so. Because of her close personal relationship with Bill during his years in California, and her clear and eloquent voice, we know of no better person to offer insight into Bill's life than our good friend Carol Howe.

My journey (Jerry) with Bill and Carol began in 1978 when she first visited Tiburon in the fall of that year. I was still practicing psychiatry and Bill was new in town. I could tell after the first time all of us were together that he was impressed with her. I was not surprised when he started visiting her in Denver and know that being there was a kind of escape for him. I (Diane) met Carol in 1982 when she was in Tiburon and also recognized that she and Bill had a unique relationship. Little did any of us know at that time all the ways our lives would be intertwined over the years or just where our work would take us.

This book is not simply a biography, but a body of work that integrates the facts of Bill's life with *Course* teachings and the personal reflections of more than thirty friends in a way that creates a unique and meaningful experience for the reader. Bill was a man of opposites and contradictions who did not fall neatly into categories. He was also a very private person and in reading Carol's account of his life, we discovered many things about him that we did not know despite our close friendship and all the years we spent together. That was a heart-warming experience for us. As those of us who were there in the beginning of *ACIM* history continue to age, there is a sense of urgency to put our experiences and insights on paper so that others may learn from them. We are grateful Carol has chosen to do so in regard to Bill's life.

After reading this book, we found it hard to imagine incorporating so many details about Bill into one document. Carol has accurately expressed the impressions and impact that Bill had on the many of us who loved and appreciated him so deeply. In many ways, it is a love story about Bill and his many friends, from comfortable close associates to casual acquaintances, whose insights and experiences with him are included throughout. It's also a love story about Bill and the *Course* and, finally, about Bill and God.

The offering of this book about Bill's transformation is a gift for those who choose peace of mind. Many of us feel a need to own our thoughts and attitudes, heal our split minds, and thereby heal the world we see. We take an important step in our journey when we become aware that it's only our own thoughts that hurt us and offer forgiveness instead. Bill's story is one of giant steps taken through willingness to forgive. Bill was a partner in the original transcription of *A Course In Miracles* and a true practitioner of its teachings. One of his favorite phrases was "celestial amnesia" and he suggested we all practice forgetting everything unloving about our past. His continual practice of forgiveness, his kind presence, and wonderful sense of humor all led to his ultimate release.

Carol's love for Bill and the *Course* shines deeply in every line she has written here. With this book, she brings a balanced perspective about his life so others can have a better sense of what motivated him. It is a window into his heart and soul, a gift of love she has created for us all. We feel certain that Bill is blessing her with his wit and smiles wherever she goes, with every *Course* workshop she teaches, and with every word she has written within this book. We are grateful that you, the reader, have chosen to share in this love as well.

With boundless love and peace,
Jerry Jampolsky, M.D. and Diane Cirincione, Ph.D.

Preface

In a few short years all who knew Bill Thetford personally will have exited the world stage. It would be unconscionable for this first generation of *A Course In Miracles* students, those who were Bill's friends, to leave without recording our collective witnessing of his transformation.[1] Humanity expends much time and treasure seeking any scrap of information about the teachers, philosophers, and avatars who have gone before, lighting the path for us throughout all cultures and ages. Bill was such a light.

Drs. William Thetford and Helen Schucman were professors of medical psychology at Columbia University's College of Physicians and Surgeons in New York, eminent in their field and known for their research into personality theory. The preface to *A Course In Miracles* states that the scribes' names do not matter and, therefore, are not listed on the cover. True though that may be, as the *Course* continues to become more widely recognized for the life-changing curriculum it proposes, more people are interested in knowing about these two who considered themselves most unlikely candidates for the job.

In beginning this project, I originally intended to simply write about my own personal memories and recollections of Bill, perhaps with input from my family and some friends in Denver who also knew and loved him. The writing project took on a life of its own, however, and grew to include recollections from a number of his close friends, as well as input from archival records. In time, even though we are never objective about anyone and see them through our own individual filters, a common view of Bill emerged—and what a picture!

In some extant publications on *ACIM* and from information on the

Internet—some incomplete or actually incorrect—Bill's role often seems marginalized as the typist or as Helen's helper. In most of these accounts, one does not begin to fathom Bill's *presence,* his greatest contribution. As for *A Course In Miracles,* his gifts were twofold: as Helen's unwavering partner and co-scribe and as its most dedicated and accomplished practitioner.

The *Course* lays out a specific plan to liberate our happiness and peace of mind, and Bill's commitment to it personified the process of forgiveness. For more than ten years, a number of people had the good fortune of watching a master teacher in the making, as Bill's ego steadily dissolved and his gracious presence—the same presence that exists in all of us—became ever more radiant and unencumbered. My intention is to pay homage to Bill for the gifts he gave us, to provide a more complete portrayal of his life, and to show how his awakening process can illuminate our own.

Introduction

And thus are two sons made, and both appear to walk this earth without a meeting place and no encounter. One do you perceive outside yourself, your own beloved son. The other rests within, his Father's Son, within your brother as he is in you. Their difference does not lie in how they look, nor where they go, nor even what they do. They have a different purpose. It is this that joins them to their like, and separates each from all aspects with a different purpose. The Son of God retains his Father's will. The son of man perceives an alien will and wishes it were so.[1] (T S I 7)

And so begins Bill's tale, like ours, a double story, a parallel story. On the one hand, "our own beloved son," the ego mind—the sense of a personal self that presumes it is in charge, alone, and always wanting something—develops slowly as we "mature," striving endlessly for security and recognition. Our initial purpose is to protect and promote this "son," and Bill certainly did that with complete dedication in his earlier days.

Simultaneously, however, the eternal spiritual presence, the I AM, is always moving deep within the psyche, knocking at the door of awareness to be acknowledged as what we are at the most fundamental level. Thus, "divine discontent" or "spiritual deprivation," to use Mother Teresa's phrase, becomes more pronounced as our worldly goals and our budding spiritual inclinations begin to clash. Consolidating our lives under the guidance of one thought system rather than two and adopting a single purpose of forgiveness allow the discomfort and uncertainty to diminish and finally disappear. Ultimately we awaken and recognize we are forever our "Father's Son." As we shall see, by the end of his life, Bill had accomplished this mission.

Like most people, Bill presumed he was organizing his life according to his personal priorities, but as I assembled the details of his life, it became clear he was being led inexorably, step by step, to his own awakening. His personal story, with its trials and triumphs, waxes, wanes, and finally closes, but not before he demonstrates how to lay aside the quest for the "best of both worlds"—that unsatisfactory mix of love and fear—to pursue the single goal of peace of mind. He also makes it clear that you can be "in the world but not of it" and accomplish the only feat that really matters—waking up.

Bill was a shy and private man, and all those who knew him are very clear that he would not and did not seek publicity. Once *A Course In Miracles* became the centerpiece of his life, he always preferred to focus on its teachings and not on his personal life. In any biography about him, he would want the transformation of his personal life to be "exhibit A" of what is possible when one chooses to practice the *Course* teachings. Therefore, in order for his life to illustrate some of its major principles in action, this biography provides some details about his "time and space" history. His life is representative of everyone's, and the steps he took reveal those we must take, if we would be healed. This document is less a traditional biography than a guidebook for learning to leave grievances behind, replacing them with grace and peace of mind.

Of all forms of recognition, Bill most objected to being sanctified or put on a pedestal. In the early days, some *ACIM* teachers were inclined to do just that. He used to laugh about his response to situations where he thought he had been unduly elevated, saying, "When they started that, I'd just have to smoke cigarettes and say 'shit'!" Now, he would want people to know his shortcomings and not evade issues he found challenging. Although he insisted on seeing himself as ordinary, most of his friends did not. Therefore, to honor what would certainly be Bill's request, I present him here as a beloved equal, a dear friend, and unwitting mentor to so many.

One wonders if he ever totally realized how greatly he touched others. In discussing this gift with him, in true egalitarian fashion he would ask us to apply that same question to our own lives. And so we should.

It is, of course, unnecessary to know anything about Bill Thetford and Helen Schucman to benefit from the lessons of *A Course In Miracles*. Some students are unaware of his existence and others may not be particularly interested. However, many are curious about the daily life, habits, and interests of the two persons who made available one of the world's most important psychospiritual works. For those who are not curious about the particulars of Bill's life, there are suggestions throughout this book that can help ease the burdens we often carry and move us toward a happier, more lighthearted experience of life.

One time years ago, when Bill was at my home in Denver, he indicated that he felt we were to do some work together, but at the time neither of us could imagine what that would be. *ACIM* was still fairly new, so more writing didn't seem called for. With his extreme introversion and my general extroversion, a project suitable to our different modes of being in the world seemed a mystery, so we agreed to wait and see what would happen. Years later, in the days after Bill's passing, I felt the mantle being passed to the next generation, so to speak, and that it was imperative for those of us drawn to the *Course* to increase our dedication to "walking the talk." I spent a great deal of time contemplating my experiences with him and presumed the obvious, that our "project," whatever it might be, would still happen even though we were on different sides of the "veil."

During his ten years in California, the last chapter of his life, Bill often told the stories of his youth, his career path, and the circumstances surrounding the scribing of the *Course*, almost always with a humorous twist. He used to say he would probably tell those stories until he was finally comfortable with them, as if telling and retelling them was a sort of soul-liberating confession. In particular, he often commented that if we thought studying and practicing the *Course* was difficult, we should have experienced the complications of scribing it. Therefore, we will read his tales from our current vantage point, which allows a more fleshed-out picture of him. I have also included firsthand accounts of his impact on those who knew him, the healings that occurred for so many, as well as my own experience of a precious friendship with him.

I have gathered information about Bill before his last ten years from secondhand sources—persons who knew him in his earlier days, archival records, and from Bill's own writings. In addition to his many academic publications (see Appendix Two), he wrote an autobiographical essay when he was fifteen for a school assignment and an unpublished autobiography, originally created through a series of taped interviews with Frances Vaughan in 1982, now held under copyright by the Foundation for Inner Peace. Although he could report what he did and what was important to him, he could not accurately portray his life as others experienced him. Therefore, those who interacted with him must say what that was like for us because his legacy is too important not to share.

In addition, as I spoke with old friends who were also some of Bill's closest companions, we reaped an unexpected dividend. We are coming back together with renewed appreciation for and delight in one another's friendship and company—and probably a common wish that we all had used tape recorders back then, not realizing the import of what we were witnessing. Now with this book, I hope to honor him, not to put him on that pedestal he abhorred or make him "special," but to allow him to be helpful still to anyone drawn to his presence. I have to believe Bill, wearing a big smile, is at the heart of this process. His energy was so present during this writing that I believe this is truly our joint project, offered to you with happy memories and many blessings.

Part I

CHILDHOOD THROUGH

RETIREMENT

Many students of *A Course In Miracles* are familiar with the oft-quoted statement,

Into eternity, where all is one, there crept a tiny, mad idea, at which the Son of God remembered not to laugh. In his forgetting did the thought become a serious idea, and possible of both accomplishment and real effects. Together, we can laugh them both away, and understand that time cannot intrude upon eternity. It is a joke to think that time can come to circumvent eternity, which means there is no time.[1] (T 586-587)

If ever there was one who learned to joke about the absurdity of the human condition, it was Bill Thetford. He was graced with a superb sense of humor, delighting in the antics, large and small, of both himself and his fellow human beings. A prayer in the liturgy of the Episcopal Church begins, "Almighty God, unto whom all hearts are open, all desires known, and from whom no secrets are hid, . . ." Bill was a mortal version of that omniscience; for him his fellow man was deeply transparent, an open book—and often a comic book. His lighthearted touch was his hallmark as he saw the comedy in the ego's serious postures. He laughed not at people, however, but at our treasured notions, beliefs, and practiced self-deceptions.

He had his own issues, of course, times that seemed depressing or fraught with difficulty, but sooner or later, his emotional equilibrium would be restored, the twinkle returning to his eye as he told his hilarious stories.

When we can laugh at the dramas, the formerly unhappy circumstances in our lives, we know they are healed. With a rigid, humorless approach to any aspect of our lives, we still have work to do. Bill's droll sense of humor pervaded his life and is the single characteristic I believe he would most want remembered.

While finishing the interviews for this book, Hugh Prather, best-selling author and one of Bill's confidants, and I reminisced by phone about the gift he was to us, especially about how witty and funny he could be. One of Bill's favorite early *Course* stories, told with kindhearted laughter, was about a gentleman who discovered his address in Manhattan and came knocking on his door. When Bill answered, the man earnestly announced that he was a new *ACIM* student and that the Holy Spirit told him to find Bill and ask him for $10,000. Without missing a beat, Bill responded that the Holy Spirit had already alerted him to this request and indicated he was not to give it to him. I can still see Bill's delighted smile as he recounted such entertaining tales about humankind in general and *Course*-related drama in particular. He often said he thought he should write a book entitled *A Course In Miracles Follies* about the craziness that occurred while bringing this material into the world, as well as some of the strange ideas and misperceptions that have been perpetuated in its name. To his credit, he found these occurrences amusing rather than alarming, and we would all benefit from emulating his lighthearted approach.

Why write a book about Bill now, years after publication of the *Course* in 1975 and his death in 1988? Helen was asked a similar question: Why had she heard her "Voice" from 1965 onward and not at some other time? Her answer applies both to *ACIM* and now to Bill's biography:

> I was given a sort of mental "explanation" . . . in the form of a series of related thoughts that crossed my mind in rapid succession and made a reasonably coherent whole. According to this "information," the world

situation was worsening at an alarming pace. People all over the world were being called on to help, and were making their individual contributions as part of an overall, prearranged plan. I had apparently agreed to take down a course in miracles as it would be given me. The Voice was fulfilling its part in the agreement, as I would fulfill mine. I would be using abilities I had developed very long ago, and which I was not really ready to use again. Because of the acute emergency, however, the usual slow, evolutionary process of spiritual development was being bypassed in what might be described as a "celestial speed-up." I could sense the urgency that lay behind this "explanation," whatever I might think about its content. The feeling was conveyed to me that time was running out.[2]

I remember that phrase, "celestial speed-up," from my earliest conversations with Bill; it seemed odd but accurate. Now, thirty years later, it is even more so. Our world appears to be increasingly less stable, more complex, the years moving by at an accelerated pace. William (Whit) Whitson, introduced later in this chronology, writes, "Unknowingly, Bill and Helen had forewarned and forearmed America for what Helen believed was the coming social and metaphysical crisis."[3] Now that crisis seems to be upon us. *A Course In Miracles* reminds us that we are completely confused about what is valuable and what is not. Our values are upside down and backwards, and we put precious and powerful attention on what doesn't matter, steadily ignoring what does. We believe our actions and their influence are of great importance, but thoughts are our own private business and, being invisible and silent, do not count for much. Hence we set great store on the externals of our lives—our careers, material possessions, the face we present to the world—while being oblivious to our internal processes. With this in mind, we begin Bill's story with highlights of his external life: early history, the jobs he held, his overriding interests—those areas that were compelling and fascinating for him. These will serve as the framework for becoming better acquainted with his interior life—his choices, struggles, gifts, and most of all, his loving presence. We shall observe the process as Bill steadily moves forward in releasing his ego—"the block to the awareness of Love's presence"—just as we must do if we want to be joyous, free, safe, and abundantly cared for.[4]

Lest one think Bill's life was easier or more charmed than others and that living the *Course* was inherently less challenging for him, his early years come alive via excerpts from an essay entitled "I Live Again," which he wrote as an English assignment when he was fifteen years old. Of his parents, John Randolph and Edna Mae Thetford, he wrote:

> Then began an early married life of hard work and sacrifice and of the rearing of three children. John, Jr., the first child, died in infancy after seven days' struggle for life. A curly haired, beautiful baby girl, Patricia Ann, next entered our busy household three years later. . . . On a bleak April morning [in Chicago, IL] in 1923, . . . the author of this chronicle first saw the light of day. . . . When I look back upon what a strong-tempered little vixen I was, always getting into scrapes, I realize how much extra trouble my behavior caused her [his mother].
>
> Patricia was the big dominating force of my early life—outside of Mother. The sun rose and set upon Patsy Ann. I was her constant shadow and continual worshipper. A fostering of an unmanly interest in dolls and tea parties and other effeminate things was the result of my close association with Patsy and her girl friends. In fact, my fascination for the opposite sex has never deserted me.
>
> In May of 1930, when I was seven years old, my beloved sister was stricken with a fatal infection of the throat. Three weeks later she passed away leaving our family dazed with grief, hardly believing that death could strike one so young and vibrantly alive. Even now, after eight years have elapsed, it scarcely seems possible that the playmate of my youth can be gone. . . .

The following December after having been quarantined for three weeks with scarlet fever, I arose one morning, only to find my body wracked with rheumatic pains and fever. This led within a few days, to a serious heart ailment. For three whole months I was unable to raise my head off the pillow. During these long months of fighting to live, Mother was my nurse, playmate and teacher. . . . Considering my illness as only a temporary thing, I soon began to plan as to how I would spend my days in the outdoors playing baseball and other games and sports, until I overheard a telephone conversation in which Mother, in whispers, remarked that I would not be able to get out of bed for at least another year and a half. [5]

Bill and sister Patricia

Bill told me he was devastated by that conversation and made a determined choice to live, despite the doctor's gloomy prognosis, rather than have his parents suffer the loss of all three of their children. Early on, he seemed aware that he had a choice in the matter—quite a challenge for a seven-year-old and revealing of his heightened awareness. In retrospect,

Bill recognized that his serious illness, commencing six months after his sister's passing, was not a coincidence. Those who work with grieving families observe that siblings of children who die often feel guilty that they remain after the brother or sister has gone. Or they worry over the effect of the death on their parents' stability, and thus on their own welfare, and/or try diligently to deny the loss in their young lives. *A Course In Miracles* is unequivocal about the role that guilt, fear, and anger play in projecting the dis-ease or dis-harmony within our minds onto the physical body and the role forgiveness plays in restoring both mind and body to health. Hundreds of pages address this topic in no uncertain terms. "Sickness is a decision. It is not a thing that happens to you, quite unsought, which makes you weak and brings you suffering. It is a choice you make, a plan you lay, when for an instant truth arises in your own deluded mind, and all your world appears to totter and prepare to fall. Now are you sick, that truth may go away and threaten your establishments no more."[6]

In his essay, Bill continues:

> The world all of a sudden caved in upon me. It was unbelievable that I must lie flat on my back, imprisoned by four walls, for that seeming eternity. Gradually, however, I became accustomed to the thought and soon it held no terror for me. Constant reading and the kindness of our family friends made the days fly but too quickly. . . . Despite relapses, when I hovered near death's door, I continued to progress, until after two and a half years of shut-in convalescence, I took my first step outside. My first glimpse of the brilliant blue of the sky, after months of seclusion, caused me to emit a gasp of wonderment. At the time I thought it was the most beautiful sight I had ever seen. I was very unsteady on my feet, and in fact, I had to learn anew how to walk. . . . My rediscovery of the world is the most thrilling and vivid of all my recollections. Being out of circulation had made me very shy and I found it extremely difficult to mix with people.[7]

From the beginning, Bill was innately at home in the world of the abstract, and for him this inner world was real, vivid, and as satisfying as if he were physically engaged. He credits "reading and family friends" as causing the time to fly, but that observation is incomplete. He doesn't mention his rich inner life, taking that for granted and very likely assuming, as we all do in our earlier years, that everyone processes life as we do and that our own approach to circumstances is the norm. That is hardly the case. He wrote this essay before he knew about personality types or had yet realized that not everyone has such readily available intuitive ability. His being socialized to be alone was actually in keeping with his basic tendencies. People today, particularly those with more outgoing temperaments, might find such confinement unimaginable considering there were no TVs, video games, or cell phones for distraction.

It also seems, from our vantage point, that Bill learned the art of surrender at an early age. His long, solitary stay in bed, with its enforced introspection, facilitated a capacity for acceptance that would have great transfer value to other dimensions of his unfolding life. Just as Helen noted that the urgency of the times required her to practice the art of "inner dictation" sooner than a more leisurely pace of spiritual evolution might allow, it seems that Bill's nascent spiritual development was also accelerated. His years of quiet seclusion were like being in a monastery, where he could examine such thoughts as "Who am I?" or "What is life's purpose?" Catherine Prescott, a friend he met many years later, remembers, "Bill described himself as being very slow in reaction time, . . . in his childhood there was always so much time that he would savor each moment; he didn't have to rush. So that if one little thing happened, he was always slowing time down to make the moment last. I think part of his wisdom was the ability to hesitate and ponder what was going on."[8]

After a three-year absence from school, during which his mother tutored him, Bill was placed in a school for children who were crippled or had cardiac problems. His continued poor health caused him to miss from six weeks to two months of classes each semester. Despite these prolonged absences, however, he completed grammar school (through the eighth grade) in three years.

Like every other child, Bill simply wanted to be normal. His early years had certainly been atypical, and once returned to school, he was moved into classes, then taken out and reinstalled elsewhere as his teachers tried to balance his extraordinary intellectual ability and, through lack of exposure, his underdeveloped social skills. With all the shifting around, he still ended up entering high school at age twelve. He did what he could to fit in, attempting to compensate for being sick and missing three years of school. He was innately gifted and intellectually far ahead of his age group from the constant reading during his recovery period.

Bill was also gifted in terms of music and theater. Classical music, especially Mozart, which he would discover during his college days, provided an important refuge and immense delight for him throughout his life. During his high school years, as his health returned, Bill took voice and piano lessons, for which he was a natural. In his school essay, he noted: "While I never expect to be a finished pianist, nor a second Nelson Eddy, I find music a soothing as well as stimulating recreation. Bill [his best friend at the time] and I have had a lot of fun appearing in amateur shows and neighborhood musicals. This summer I sang my first church solo at the Chicago Lawn Congregational Church, which church I attend regularly." Commenting on his current school, Lindblom High, he said:

> It is here I have really found myself, in its numerous activities. The
> A Cappella choir is my first love, even though Mr. Taylor makes me sing
> tenor when I have a naturally bass voice. Participating in boys' clubs,
> the Music Club, Camera Club and the Eagle have broadened my social

experiences and have helped me to overcome an innate timidity. . . . Realizing that I will never be able to do strenuous physical work, I wish to obtain a good educational foundation, with the possibility of becoming a teacher.[9]

He did become a teacher, although he rather famously proclaimed during his college years that the one thing he would never become was a professor, as he insisted he had nothing to profess. And wouldn't you know, almost every position he held thereafter involved a professorship as part of the job description. Never say "never"!

College years

After graduating from high school in 1940, where he was among the top ten students in a class of about one thousand, Bill entered DePauw University in Greencastle, Indiana, on a full scholarship. As part of his continuing quest for normalcy and for companionship in this first experience living away from home, Bill joined a fraternity. He had no idea what he was getting into, believing this would be a support system of some kind. Having known Bill well, I cannot imagine him amid the noise and uproar of a fraternity house after long periods of near isolation, but somehow he managed. He indicated it was a difficult challenge for him, with his strong need for privacy and his genuine interest in scholarship. It was hardly the support system he had naively envisioned.

During high school Bill had reconnected with a kindergarten friend, Jo, whom he had lost track of during the intervening years of his illness. Simply good friends in high school (she was "going steady" with someone else then), their relationship evolved into something more after graduation. She was his only acknowledged girl friend, according to all available information. Their parents knew each other and the two young people were definitely considered an "item." At Thanksgiving in 1943 he gave her his fraternity pin, in those days considered almost the same as an engagement ring. Jo remembers:

> I kept saying, "Bill, why? Why do you want me to take your fraternity pin?" thinking that he would say, "I love you. I want to marry you." But he didn't. He just said, "Because I want you to wear it more than anyone else in the world." He just kept insisting I take it.

> Yet I wasn't swept off my feet. He was also still my good kindergarten buddy. Anyway, I thought that if he wants me to wear it, I guess I'll wear it, although I felt kind of awkward. I went back to the sorority house where I was staying as their guest. That night the girls came and got me, and brought me out to the front of the house about midnight. The

Lambda Chi guys, with Bill right in the foreground, serenaded me. . . .
I felt a bit guilty about it all, because all the girls were congratulating
me and I just couldn't tell them that it didn't mean what they thought
it meant.[10]

They went together, as a long-distance romance (he was at DePauw until
his graduation in February 1944), for the next year, and in the fall of 1944,
Jo left for the University of California at Berkeley. As she prepared to board
the train, Bill gave her an orchid corsage and she questioned him about the
fraternity pin. He remained vague and would make no other commitment
than, "Please wear my fraternity pin." After a week at Berkeley, Jo was swept
off her feet by a young marine whom she ultimately married. She finally
wrote to Bill of her new love and returned his pin in the spring of 1945;
Jo heard no more from him until the late 1970s.

From our current perspective, we can only imagine Bill's situation. His
girlfriend was out of his life; he had been suspecting his latent homosexuality but being open about it was taboo at that time. A gay lifestyle
was so unsupported in American society that he could not accept it totally
within himself. It's possible, however, that living in a fraternity house
in close quarters with many young men, he allowed himself to be more
honest privately about his inclinations, an honesty that had been too
difficult before.

W orld War II started while Bill was in college, but on graduating, he was rejected for the draft because of his rheumatic heart condition. Thus, after receiving his undergraduate degree in psychology from DePauw in February 1944 and being unable to participate in the military, Bill submitted his application and was accepted into the University of Chicago Medical School for the upcoming fall term. In addition to taking courses necessary for his psychology degree, he had also completed all necessary pre-med classes. Hoping to earn money for his first year of medical school during the intervening six months, Bill applied for work at the University of Chicago. He was hired as one of ten administrative officers overseeing several buildings used as testing areas for some highly classified research. Later, he learned it was research on atomic energy—the Manhattan Project. Soon after being hired, he was promoted to the faculty payroll and given a private office and secretary. "One of my special assignments was to be in charge of a special crew of men," Bill later wrote, "who went through various radioactive areas and tried to decontaminate them. I was required to wear a Geiger counter from the time I arrived in the morning until I left at night."[1]

Atomic energy research was occurring in several locations around the country at that time, the University of Chicago being one of them, in a furious race with the Nazis to build a bomb during the final years of World War II. This research was the best-kept secret around. More than 100,000 people were involved with the project in various locations, but most were in the dark about its exact nature and specific purpose, including Vice President Truman, who was told the details of the project only on assuming the presidency after Roosevelt's death. Everyone did know, however, that the United States and its allies were joined in a life-or-death struggle with a formidable enemy.

Bill felt the excitement of this project he was part of but, like others, was unaware of its purpose or ramifications; he was told only that if these experiments were not successful in giving the United States the upper hand, it might mean the end of Western civilization as he knew it. One testing area for which he was responsible was beneath the stands of the University of Chicago football stadium, made available for research because the university's president had eliminated intercollegiate football as an interference to academic learning. The first chain reaction in the world took place there in December 1942. The irony was not lost on twenty-year-old Bill. Given the heightened tensions throughout the country and the sense of urgency related to his supposedly interim job, Bill chose to continue on for another year, foregoing medical school that fall. The bombs were dropped on Japan in August 1945, and he resigned shortly thereafter on seeing the horrific results of the project's success.

Although the university had given Bill the option to postpone entering medical school to continue with the Manhattan Project, he decided, after some consideration, not to enroll at all. Thus, in the fall of 1945, without much thought about where it would lead, he enrolled in the University of Chicago's graduate school in psychology where the already noted psychologist, Carl Rogers, was beginning to hold forth. Unaware of what people sensed about him, Bill was confused and surprised when Rogers offered him a teaching position almost immediately; he was younger than almost all the other students and did not yet have a master's degree. He was also the only member of Rogers's staff not imported from Ohio State University. Soon thereafter, Rogers invited him to participate in research on the merits of his signature "client-centered psychotherapy." This was an innovative new approach to psychotherapy that emphasized the importance of relationships. Specifically, the Rogerian approach was based on "unconditional positive regard," or perfect love, and its essential place in the success of client-centered therapy.

Bill actually worked as a part-time Rogerian therapist for about a year but did not feel called to it. Researching the science that provided the foundation for therapy was more to his liking. That inclination to examine therapeutic foundations through research into personality development would dominate his work for decades. Within this framework of emphasis on relationships, however, Bill received his Ph.D. in psychology in the spring of 1949; his research focused on the psycho-physiological changes in galvanic skin response, heart rate, and respiration in clients tested before and after Rogerian psychotherapy, as compared to a control group. Simply stated, his research showed that being loved, appreciated, and listened to positively affects both mind and body. Although now, sixty years later, that is old information, at the time it was revolutionary. Everyone who knew Bill remembers his saying how bizarre it was for him to be involved, even though unknowingly, first with a project that resulted in merciless devastation, and then with one that espoused the practice of "unconditional positive regard."

As part of a standard psychology curriculum, Bill would have been familiar with the work of Dr. Gardner Murphy, a pioneer in the field. In his book, *Personality–A Biosocial Approach to Origins and Structure*, published in 1947, Murphy gives an excellent and comprehensive overview of the world of personality research at the time Bill entered the field. In the foreword, he writes, "But lest the reader waste time upon what he does not want, it must be emphasized that this is not a book on diagnosis or therapy of personality problems, or upon any type of clinical approach. It is simply an attempt at evaluation of data on how personality grows."[2] It is fortunate for readers that he limited his topic to this single one as, 927 pages later, we have a recap of those major areas of research to which Bill would contribute significantly.

From today's viewpoint, the information Dr. Murphy provides, current at that time, seems limited. It lacks today's high level of technological sophistication that has made possible amazing advances in neuroscience. Much less was known then about brain function, genetics and epigenetics, and the body-mind connection, specifically as they relate to personality development. Nor was the interest in Eastern philosophies as wide-spread then as now. Because of such limitations, Bill was very attracted to any new and different approaches, particularly any related to the influence of positive relationships.

Murphy championed the idea that people are already highly formed at birth with fundamentally different and unique predispositions. First voiced by Hippocrates in 370 B.C., the idea was predominant for centuries. Only in the early twentieth century did researchers of the time, constrained by nineteenth-century models of both the universe and the individual, formulate behaviorism, the notion that people are born without predispositions and could have their behavior molded at will. By midcentury, when Bill was entering the field of psychology, that temporary reversal of psychological theory was coming to a close, and the earlier premise that we are born inherently unique with distinctive energy patterns was being rediscovered and newly researched.

Murphy also lamented Western researchers' failure to examine the Eastern approach to man's psychology, which included the spiritual dimensions of life.

In a future psychology of personality, there will surely be a place for directly grappling with the question of man's response to the cosmos, his sense of unity with it, the nature of his esthetic demands upon it, and his feelings of loneliness or of consummation in his contemplation of it. . . . It is quite likely that selfhood will be better understood when reference is made to the primordial non-self matrix from which it arises, and that the synthesis, the capacity of human nature to function at self and non-self levels at the same time, or to alternate when it so desires, may prove to be an enrichment of personality far greater than that which the cult of self-contained, self-defined individuality can grant.[3]

With this Murphy seems to anticipate both modern-day quantum physics and the foundational premise of *A Course In Miracles*.

In addition to what he was learning about psychology in general and client-centered psychotherapy in particular, Bill's exposure to music broadened and deepened during his years in graduate school, both interests dear to his heart. All who knew him in later life can attest to his deep and abiding love for music; his home was continuously filled with music playing in the background. He had listened to friends' classical music collections as much as possible during his years at the University of Chicago and fell in love with Mozart. In fact, he was so intimately acquainted with Mozart's music that after hearing a few bars of a recorded piece, he could accurately identify both the performers and the conductor of that particular recording. As he became more musically sophisticated during this time, his love of opera grew and he realized that a good way to become more familiar with it was to usher at the Chicago Opera House, home to several large opera companies. He was on a tight budget, but after saving enough to buy a tuxedo (required for the position), he did indeed become an usher there. Through attending every performance possible, he developed a deep appreciation for and knowledge of that particular art form.

After receiving his Ph.D., something he had doubted he would ever get,

Bill still wasn't sure what to do with it, although he knew it provided something akin to a union card in his field. He also realized that psychology really did appeal to him and that this field felt exciting, rewarding, and compatible with his most basic nature. In his autobiography he noted that, for the first time, he really started to feel good (healthwise), to find himself, and to form some good and lasting friendships.

Although feeling at home and invigorated in the intellectual world of psychology, Bill was also experiencing some disappointments. He had hoped his parents would be proud of him for earning a Ph.D., and at such a young age (twenty-five), but they seemed incapable of understanding his field, his basic interests, or his talents and accomplishments. To put his early years in context, theirs was a lower-middle-class family, the parents knowing no other than hard physical work. His father was one of ten children from a poor, coal-mining family in southern Illinois, though later he became a superintendent in the building and construction department of the telephone company. Survival was important; culture was not. Bill had become ill at age seven during the depths of the Great Depression when life was generally difficult. Having lost two children earlier, his father worried greatly about how he might have to support this ailing child who very likely would never be able to do strenuous physical work. How would he be able to support himself? His father often verbalized his fear that Bill would end up on the "dole," a welfare case. With their worldview, his parents could hardly appreciate his academic pursuits; they thought a Ph.D. was a worthless piece of paper to hang on the wall—useless in finding a real job.

Of course, Bill was aware of their lack of support for his accomplishments and took that as a personal affront, adding grievances to his growing store. We know he had been greatly affected by his sister's early death and can assume there was some upset about Jo's "Dear John" letter. These hurts and disappointments were internalized and carried forward for decades, creating a basis for later conflicts and frustrations.

As Bill was graduating, his parents retired to Florida because his mother was not well; she had been diagnosed with multiple sclerosis and advised to move to a better climate. Alone now in Chicago, though more content than ever, his next venture was at the Michael Reese Hospital, a major Jewish training hospital in Chicago and *the* place to be. A fellow graduate student mentioned to Bill that a position had unexpectedly become available with Dr. Samuel Beck, head of the psychology department and a leading authority on the Rorschach test (a method of psychological evaluation in which subjects' perceptions of inkblots are recorded and then analyzed using intuitive insight and/or complex scientifically derived algorithms. This test is used to examine personality characteristics and emotional function). Bill applied and Beck offered him a position to study schizophrenia and the Rorschach test, funded by the National Institute for Mental Health. After Bill explained that he knew nothing about the Rorschach test, Beck assured him he considered that to be an asset, as it would allow him to conduct research uncorrupted by someone else's teaching. He was also enthusiastic about Bill's Ph.D. dissertation, thinking it sounded most scientific, a plus. This first position as a doctor of psychology allowed Bill to become acquainted with, among other things, personality tests and measurements, which would prove useful as his career unfolded. Working there also provided the unusual experience of being the only non-Jewish member of the department. He wondered if he would be accepted, a question of possible reverse discrimination, but he certainly was; his fellow staffers even explained their Yiddish jokes to him. After two-and-a-half years, the grant ended and he chose to move on, but where? The University of Chicago and Michael Reese Hospital were the city's most interesting and challenging places to work, and he had now "been there, done that."

Like so many, Bill had moved forward from high school graduation without a clear-cut sense of destiny or even an idea about what he wanted to do next. He certainly didn't know what he was getting into when he took the administrative job at the University of Chicago related to the Manhattan Project. He also wasn't particularly sure, at the outset, what pursuing a degree in psychology was about, but by 1945 he had lost interest in medical school, something of a fantasy anyway given that he hadn't the funds to pay for it and his family couldn't help even if they had been inclined. Moving to Michael Reese Hospital had a certain aimless quality about it, from the world's point of view, but in hindsight his particular destiny was unfolding perfectly. As a harbinger of things to come, Bill said he would occasionally wonder why he was studying psychology in the first place, and an inner response would indicate that he would not know for many years—but when he finally did, it would make him indescribably happy.

What *was* the underlying impetus that led him to study psychology? The decision might have seemed a casual one, when other fields were also open to him, but many major decisions in life are made offhandedly, without exploring their ramifications, because we are unaware at the time that they *are* leading to major changes. We know that only after the fact. Even at a young age Bill had demonstrated his ability as an able, trustworthy administrator. He had more than a little talent for music and theater, and he certainly had the qualifications to succeed in medicine, which he once considered. He had also mused about a teaching career but was led inexorably to the field of psychology, following the intuition that led him throughout his life.

Because research into personality types became Bill's specialty, the centerpiece of his academic research, and to understand him better, I am including a brief look at personality types. Men of genius through the ages have recognized not only that human beings are born with specific characteristics but that humankind seems to fall naturally into four distinct categories of temperament, character, and intelligence or, in short, personality. Such categories were named according to the understanding available at the time. An abbreviated list of persons who recognized four basic types include:

> Plato (c340 B.C.), Aristotle (c325 B.C.), Galen (c190 A.D.), Paracelsus (1550), Adickes (1905), Spranger (1914), Kretschmer (1920), Fromm (1947), Myers (1958). . . .

> And so the idea that individuals are predisposed to develop into one of four different configurations of attitude and action has survived for well over two thousand years. Surely this idea would not have been employed for so long, by so many people, in so many countries, had there not been some sort of widely shared recognition of its usefulness.[4]

The last person on the list, Isabel Myers, with her mother Kathryn Briggs, developed the now well-known system for identifying personality types—the Myers-Briggs Type Indicator. To this we add its shorter, but equally valid cousin, the Keirsey Temperament Sorter. These tests, based on Carl Jung's discoveries, started being used as research tools in the early 1950s. Thus, Gardner Murphy did not mention them in his 1947 book, nor were they available during Bill's early work under Carl Rogers in Chicago.

Both these more recent tests use four sets of opposites to identify temperaments: I/E—introvert/extrovert; N/S—intuitive/sensory; T/F—thinking/feeling; and J/P—judging/perceiving. Through her research, Myers discovered, like her predecessors, that the sixteen possible combinations reduce to four major categories, SP, SJ, NF, and NT, with characteristics consistent with the four types deduced by the earlier researchers listed above. For a more in-depth explanation, I recommend David Keirsey's *Please Understand Me, II* as a guide to understanding personality traits, especially those unlike our own. One of those early observers of humankind was Plato.

> Plato was the quintessential Idealist [known as the NF, an abbreviation
> for the intuitive-feeling type in the Myers-Briggs personality lexicon],
> the inventor of a philosophy in which ideas are even more real than earth
> and its inhabitants. Plato's word for an idealist like himself was noetic,
> which, roughly translated, means "intuitive thought," that is, pure think-
> ing done without recourse to either logical or empirical investigation.[5]

Bill Thetford was the poster child for the NF, or intuitive-feeling type,
as was his mentor, Carl Rogers. Keirsey gives some insight into what
pulled Bill toward psychology and away from what seemed to be equally
viable options:

> Diplomacy is the ability to deal with people in a skillful, tactful man-
> ner . . . a metaphor for the interpersonal touch or sensitivity in which
> Idealists [or NFs] seem to be both interested and particularly talented.
> This sensitive way with people shows up *so early in NFs that it is tempt-
> ing to assume they are born with it* [emphasis added]—born to use their
> personal empathy and interpersonal skills to improve relations between
> people. . . . With their instinct for seeking common ground, with their
> ability to interpret each side's communications in a positive way, with
> their gift for putting themselves in the other's place, and with their
> metaphorical language easily and fluidly turning one thing into another,
> Idealists are well-equipped for the difficult task of influencing people's
> attitudes and actions, not only inspiring them to grow, but also set-
> tling differences among them, smoothing difficulties—ever looking to
> enlighten the people around them and to forge unity among them.[6]

Thus, we are drawn in certain directions even when, in our earlier days,
we might not have a vocabulary to explain that attraction. As natural and
automatic as the quest for self-realization is for the NFs, it is quite bewil-
dering to the other three types.

Idealists regard this search for identity as the most important enterprise in their lives and with their gift for language they can be powerful advocates for its being a necessary pilgrimage for all people. Very often the other types, the SJs, NTs, and SPs, are troubled by the thought that they ought to be pursuing this goal, even if the search for Self does not beckon them. The reluctance of over ninety percent of humanity to join the search for self-actualization is a great source of mystification to the Idealists.[7]

This brief description of the NF, though general, gives us much insight into Bill Thetford in particular. The vast amount of research on personality types available today, some of it done by Bill himself, provides the opportunity for anyone to understand basic, human motivating factors more fully than ever. Without such explanations, others' choices and inclinations seem uninformed at best, and defective at worst—hardly a prescription for tolerance or empathy.

One advantage of living several decades, whether we know our personality type or not, is that we can see patterns in our lives, and how seemingly accidental, unrelated experiences all contribute to our unfolding awareness, a prerequisite for healing the fearful ideas we hold about ourselves. *A Course In Miracles* promises that our lives are not random and that "those who are to meet, will meet." Although we each have an individualized curriculum in terms of where we go, who we meet, the jobs we hold, the abilities we develop, the places we live, and the lessons we encounter, the *Course* assures us that all encounters are designed for our maximal and mutual healing. This is a very reassuring idea, and embracing it allays anxiety about the correctness of our decisions. Keeping in mind *ACIM*'s major teaching of forgiveness, all circumstances become perfect venues for its practice.

We may never fully recognize all the reasons for acquiring our particular skills, but we can learn to trust that there are no accidents.

> What could you not accept, if you but knew that everything that happens, all events, past, present and to come, are gently planned by One Whose only purpose is your good? Perhaps you have misunderstood His plan, for He would never offer pain to you. But your defenses did not let you see His loving blessing shine in every step you ever took. While you made plans for death [or the strengthening of the ego], He led you gently to eternal life.[8]

In 1950, Bill did not know any of this and, at twenty-seven, did not have the advantage of age from which to view his seemingly arbitrary choices. Speaking of his inclination to study psychology, he often commented that he had observed many psychologists and their endless, competing theories, but that nothing really seemed to come of them. He saw no one integrating them in a way that actually changed the nature of one's life experience. One of his favorite sayings was that "the emperor has no clothes"—a prescient observation, as many years later he would read the section on unhealed healers in the *Course:* "Such evident inconsistencies account for why no one has really explained what happens in psychotherapy. Nothing really does. Nothing real has happened to the unhealed healer, and he must learn from his own teaching."[9]

About the time Bill felt his interesting work opportunities in Chicago were complete, he was recruited by the Central Intelligence Agency, the country's newly reorganized intelligence service. All of Bill's education and training up to that point had involved working with leading-edge scientists, innovators in science and medicine. Because his mentors and colleagues were well known, and publishing is always an integral and necessary aspect of academia, he had become widely recognized and respected throughout his field as a result of his own publications and others to which he contributed. Thus, he was also easy to track, even before the age of computers and modern-day surveillance. A friend of mine and Bill's, conversant with how the CIA operates, indicated they had levels of connections back then, far beyond what we might imagine, to identify potential recruits who could prove useful to the Agency. Clearly, Bill fell into the "useful" category.

Although working for the CIA would seem an implausible choice of work for him, it turned out to be essential for his path. The Manhattan Project, the job he had "wandered into" ostensibly to earn money for living expenses and medical school, had provided Bill with a high security clearance. His work with Carl Rogers, with its emphasis on relationships, fed the soul of this young NF, and he had gained some skill with early biofeedback techniques using scientific equipment then available. Next, he had become conversant with tests and measurement construction at the Michael Reese Hospital, and all of these combined to grant him entrée to the next important chapter of his life, work with the CIA. Outwardly, he was following a career path. In retrospect, we see he was led through the necessary steps, including all that emerged during his time with the CIA, toward his major spiritual fulfillment of co-authoring *A Course In Miracles.*

It all seems so obvious once our lives are over. If only we could trust the rightness of everything *while* it is happening. Watching Bill's destiny unfold after the fact, we can see that events and circumstances were always in good order, leading inexorably to his choice for peace of mind.

> Yet there is no step along the road that anyone takes but by chance. It has already been taken by him, although he has not yet embarked on it. For time but seems to go in one direction. We but undertake a journey that is over. Yet it seems to have a future still unknown to us.

> Time is a trick, a sleight of hand, a vast illusion in which figures come and go as if by magic. Yet there is a plan behind appearances that does not change. The script is written. When experience will come to end your doubting has been set. For we but see the journey from the point at which it ended, looking back on it, imagining we make it once again; reviewing mentally what has gone by.[1]

Patriotism was one of several factors in Bill's decision to join the CIA, though not the primary one. Someone asked Jack Luckett, one of Bill's closest friends in his later years, if he found Bill to be patriotic toward the end of his life. Jack replied, "Not in the normal sense. He saw himself as a citizen of the universe. He was secretly proud of his CIA connection, and because of my 'spook' background, chatted with me about it. It was more pride in adventure than dedication to eliminating enemies."[2]

The CIA's predecessor, the Office of Strategic Services (OSS), which was responsible for US intelligence operations during World War II, was disbanded shortly after the war ended. At that time, however, the cold war with the Soviet Union was intensifying and the United States recognized the imperative need for strategic intelligence. After some reshuffling of functions into various other agencies, the National Security Act established the CIA in 1947. It was unorganized, had no official headquarters, and was generally a mess, bearing little resemblance to the present-day organization. From "William Newton Thetford and the Central Intelligence Agency":

> As the global total cold war gathered momentum, it became clear that the young CIA desperately needed help. An extraordinary network of civilian universities and government agencies had provided OSS with a steady stream of raw intelligence to guide the total war against Nazi Germany and Japan. In contrast, the young CIA in 1947 was treated like a stepchild, its experienced leadership in short supply, its actual and legal authority still unclear. The new CIA needed more than old files from the OSS. Their greatest need was for personnel. During hearings on the National Security Act of 1947, the new director of central intelligence, Allen Dulles, said, "The new intelligence entity would be directed by a relatively small but elite corps of men with a passion for anonymity and a willingness to stick at that particular job. The agency must have a corps of the most competent men, which this country can produce, to evaluate and correlate the intelligence obtained."[3]

The challenge was how to recruit and evaluate this badly needed group of people. At that time, various schools of psychology had been around for about one hundred years; they seemed to hold the keys to human behavior—a must-have for evaluating foreign leaders and how they might respond under different circumstances—and to methods for recruiting those essential intelligence officers. In 1950, the year before Bill was hired, the CIA had offered John Gittinger the position of director of its assessment and evaluation staff. Bill, hired in 1951 as one of about ten senior psychologists at that time, worked for Gittinger in that department and would continue to work indirectly with him throughout much of his academic career. John made a tremendous impression on Bill and became a pivotal player in his life.

Bill's duties included administering a series of tests to applicants seeking to become intelligence officers and/or spies, then interviewing and recommending them or not. There was a sense of danger in the air and great urgency about staffing up as the cold war with the Soviet Union escalated and the Korean War progressed. Obviously, in screening potential hires, the psychologists needed insight, intuition, and the ability to read people accurately, all of which were Bill's strong suits. Because of the sensitive nature of this work—interviewing those who would be working for the Agency in various intelligence capacities—Bill soon attained a top secret security clearance, something that usually took a while to earn. It would serve him later as his worldly saga unfolded.

Working with the CIA offered Bill, in addition to his position on the assessment and evaluation team, the added opportunity to learn more about Gittinger's new project to assess people's capabilities under various conditions, stressful and otherwise. These innovations and their potential importance greatly impressed Bill, providing the next chapter of his series of psychological explorations. Gittinger had developed a process, originally to describe the dynamics and adjustments of mental dysfunction, but later widely used as a technique for general psychological assessment. He reportedly was very charismatic and loved to talk for hours about his theories. An early colleague of Bill's reported, "You couldn't ignore John; he was there, he filled up a room. He was a pied-piper, guru-type, interesting individual who developed a theory in terms of how people progressed through life. I know Bill was intrigued and would often sit and listen to John expound his theories."[4]

During his first year with the CIA, Gittinger continued work on his model of personality development, newly named the Personality Assessment System, or PAS. For more than two decades, John and others, including Bill, continued to refine what eventually Bill considered the most powerful and efficient descriptive and predictive personality assessment system in the world, deserving to be ranked with Freud and Jung's discoveries. Leaders in intelligence circles wholeheartedly agreed with this assessment.

At that time [1961] CIA psychologists began to substitute such direct evidence as body language and overt behavior for the one-hour test to assess personality. However, the PAS remained the conceptual structure that guided any such assessment from direct observation. Using the PAS to analyze and make accurate predictions about key world leaders, Gittinger advised several presidents until his retirement in 1978. As early as the Cuban missile crisis in October 1962, he conferred with President Kennedy about the likely behavior of Nikolai Khrushchev under stress. The astonishing accuracy of the PAS eventually won for Gittinger promotion to the role of Chief Psychologist of CIA for World Wide Operations.[5]

Early in our friendship, Bill told me more than once about his helping to develop a test that could ferret out potential double agents. It seemed to have some special appeal to him, as he became more animated when he spoke of it. I knew nothing about the CIA's early history at that point and couldn't fully appreciate the scope of the work and Bill's major contributions to refining that assessment tool, but I did recognize his enthusiasm. Even as a young man, when it came to understanding human behavior, Bill was already in the vanguard and Gittinger recognized that talent. As David Goodrich, a colleague of Bill's, reported:

John was not a doctor of psychology; he had a master's degree in counseling. That's not a big deal but I think it was to John, so someone with Bill's credentials was very attractive to him. And, obviously, he held a most favorable opinion of him. Everyone who ever worked with Bill realized he was an extremely bright guy. John considered Bill one of his real protégés. Basically, John was a very human guy, always somewhat overweight, and as part of his theory, he believed that people were born with or soon acquired something that either made them attractive or unattractive to people. He believed the world treated the cute baby or the attractive little child very differently, allowing them to develop a totally different perspective than people like John believed himself to be. A great deal of John's thinking was that those unattractive people had to compensate. That was his own self-account. John was motivated by a sincere desire to be helpful to the Agency and he was. He also had a huge investment in this theory and had at least as much ego as the rest of us, if not more.[6]

The purpose of the PAS is to predict a person's future behavior so that the responding behavior can be appropriate in relation to it. Where you cannot give the test directly—as for instance, to a foreign leader—it is important to have ways to determine the personality that underlies observable behavior, thus making it possible to predict that person's future actions. Obviously, greater comprehension of human behavior is very important in many other areas, as well—all types of counseling and psychotherapy, personnel work, classroom assessments, crime detection and prevention, to name a few—and, of course, foreign relations.

According to the Personality Assessment System Foundation web site, the PAS contributes to the prediction of behavior in several ways:

- It indicates the kinds of internal and external cues the individual is most likely to respond to overtly;

- It suggests the types of stimuli most likely to produce behavior change;

- It provides an understanding of the quality of environments in which the individual is most likely to behave efficiently;

- It offers insight into situations that are stressful for the individual;

- It permits prediction of the probable nature of maladjusted behavior, should maladjusted behavior occur.

The PAS thus contributes to individual assessment by providing practical insights into a highly personalized pattern of strengths and weaknesses. At the same time, the system allows objective comparisons among the personality features of different individuals, thereby offering a suitable framework for behavioral research and definitive investigations of personality structure and function.[7]

In other words, the PAS is an elaborate system for describing how personality is built from infancy through adolescence and all the compensations required when we reject our innate characteristics and inclinations, when we are not self-accepting. This applies to every person born. *A Course In Miracles* also speaks with revealing eloquence on the subject, though with a decidedly different slant:

The building of a concept of the self is what the learning of the world is for. This is its purpose; that you come without a self, and make one as you go along. And by the time you reach "maturity" you have perfected it, to meet the world on equal terms, at one with its demands. . . .

A concept of the self is made by you. It bears no likeness to yourself at all. It is an idol, made to take the place of your reality as Son of God. . . . [8]

You will make many concepts of the self as learning goes along. Each one will show the changes in your own relationships, as your perception of yourself is changed. There will be some confusion every time there is a shift, but be you thankful that the learning of the world is loosening its grasp upon your mind. And be you sure and happy in the confidence that it will go at last, and leave your mind at peace.[9]

Working with John Gittinger, Bill was becoming enamored with the PAS, this very sophisticated process of describing how a personality is built and under what conditions. The Myers-Briggs test, excellent and helpful though it is, does not have this level of sophistication. *ACIM* had not yet been written, although it would have much to say about personality development in years to come. We can already look ahead and compare the foundations on which the PAS is built to those of the *Course*, and the life-altering decision that lay ahead for Bill.

Referencing personality development, "William Newton Thetford and the Central Intelligence Agency" includes a firsthand description of twenty-seven-year-old Bill by one of his colleagues in 1950. Realizing that no observation is objective but colored by the mind-set of the observer, I think the correlations between the theory of Bill's personality (see Appendix One) and this firsthand account are worth noting:

> An independent but socially involved person, Bill had a high sense of mission. He was typically well organized, systematic, self-disciplined and socially effective, if often aloof. Although he could be intensely individualistic and unconventional, he was rarely revolutionary, preferring to dedicate his practical, pragmatic nature to improving, not dismantling, organizations and procedures. He was very conscious of his own needs, which he usually kept under effective control. He was equally perceptive of the needs of others but was not likely to be dominated by them. As a manager, he was thus concerned but relatively dispassionate, sometimes appearing detached or even unsupportive if others failed to meet his high standards. He was typically ahead of or on top of events, confident of his ability to cope with most situations and able to prepare for those that promised to be challenging. He rarely got caught off guard or over his head.[10]

In researching this book, I spoke with three of Bill's colleagues, then also senior psychologists with the CIA, who indicated that in the early 1950s they recruited only the "brightest and best," originally graduates from Yale and Harvard but later from other institutions as well. They said it was a very interesting and exciting time, with much innovative work in the assessment area and a great sense of esprit de corps. Feeling part of the inner group, these bright young people entrusted with sensitive, high-priority tasks were always very supportive of one another. Friends conversant with the CIA from its earliest days confirmed the collegial culture there and indicated that many who worked together stayed in touch long after leaving their official employment with the Agency, continuing to support each other and their interests whenever possible. Apparently, one never really retires from the CIA.

One of his new friends at the Agency described Bill, on first meeting, as very young in appearance (he was twenty-eight), bright-eyed, intelligent, very enthusiastic about his interests, fun to be around, friendly and gregarious, but somewhat restless, as if he had not quite found himself. For all his outward charm, Bill was reticent about revealing himself; he did not discuss his private life or how he felt.

Despite his youthful enthusiasm, it seemed that Bill was not going to make Washington and the Agency a permanent stop. He spent as many weekends as possible in New York attending the theater, his passion even then, and feeling very much at home in the city. Music and theater were already part of his very soul. Friends remembered him wearing his tight-fitting khaki pants and boots, conveying more the essence of the theatrical world than a government job. One colleague said they often had lunch with a woman, Gertrude, who was also especially interested in the theater; Bill was close to her although she was ten years his senior. With this early draw to New York and its culture, he was not finding or establishing roots in Washington, D.C., despite being dedicated to his work there.

Bill preferred the company of women to the military or "macho" men who were in the majority at the CIA. That was understandable because by then he had recognized and accepted his homosexuality, which would seem an impossible situation since homosexuals were not allowed in the CIA. Applicants were required to take a polygraph test that should have revealed as much. Bill indicated many years later, however, that his familiarity with biofeedback and various scientific instruments used during his time with Carl Rogers and the completing of his Ph.D. taught him how to make the polygraph machine read "inconclusive," and he was hired. He made certain his apartment was clear of anything that could give him away, and when it was covertly checked—he had ways to determine if it was—no evidence was there to find.

David Goodrich described him as a remarkably competent guy, very perceptive, a delightful friend and companion with a great sense of humor—a trait everyone in his life admired and found noteworthy. More than thirty years later they met again, this former colleague having discovered Bill's involvement with *ACIM* and now a student of it himself. He had wondered if he would see Bill differently, as an "ascended master" of some kind, but he did not. However, he found the same characteristics Bill had displayed in the 1950s—being very present, very casual, easy to relate to, and intensely sincere—were still in place.

In 2007 I met with Goodrich and again we discussed their last meeting about a year before Bill's passing. He pondered over why he had still seen him as a wonderful person but was not struck forcefully, like so many others, by the power of his quiet presence. The *Course* speaks to this issue, stating that we bring all past associations with us when we observe anything, whether a person, object, or situation. In this man's case, he was seeing Bill again but not with a clean lens, so to speak, inadvertently bringing his old perceptions of him, positive though they were, to the encounter. *ACIM* exhorts us to practice viewing everything with new eyes, allowing ourselves to see without the usual interpretations, judgments, biases, and ever-present question, "How can I use this for my benefit?" It promises a sense of well-being and peace when we view anything without our past history laid on it, without the obstacle of accumulated thought. People who met Bill for the first time in his later years, with no expectations, were the ones who found the experience extraordinary and comforting.

Although the CIA's promise of discovering exciting new psychological processes was certainly alluring and served the purpose of relocating him to Washington, D.C., the Washington School of Psychiatry (WSP) founded by Dr. Harry Stack Sullivan, was the major draw and the real reason Bill agreed to take the CIA position. He couldn't know in the beginning how important his association with John Gittinger and the PAS would turn out to be long term, but he did know he was fascinated by Sullivan's philosophy, with its focus on interpersonal relations. This pattern of emphasis on relationships anticipates the central role they will play later on in *A Course In Miracles*. Sullivan was also intrigued by personality development in children, another interest Bill shared with him. Incidentally, more than half the professional papers Bill published before he moved to Washington focused on children.

Once again, that inevitable pull toward self-discovery, yearning for an undefined something just out of reach, was at work. At the WSP he was able to study with some of the brightest lights in psychology and psychiatry at the time, usually in the evening so not to interfere with his work at the CIA, taking every class offered. The philosophy of the school was consistent with the work he had done earlier with Carl Rogers and was very helpful with his work at the Agency.

We can also imagine he felt at home at the WSP and was likely surrounded by fellow seekers, at that time mostly M.D.s but some Ph.D.s like Bill. According to the NF profile:

Idealists heavily populate the social sciences, particularly the fields of mental healing and personal or religious counseling—professions directed toward human metamorphosis, or the unfolding of the mind and heart toward greater self-understanding and spiritual peace. NFs find great satisfaction in the mental health services, where they tend to take the most humanistic of approaches, those advocating growth models of counseling and psychotherapy rather than the more confronting or controlling models.[11]

No wonder he took every class; from the profile given above, we can infer that the place was swarming with fellow NFs like moths drawn to the same flame. His WSP experience made a lasting impression on Bill for he spoke of it often, as if it were an honor to have been there.

David Goodrich first met Bill when both were enrolled in a postdoctoral certification program at the Washington School of Psychiatry. He remembered,

Bill and I were in a class on psychological testing and I thought I was pretty good but, by golly, I had this one case and it was something, it was terrific, and Bill just ran circles not only around me but everybody else. It was amazing what he could come up with. Subsequently, I learned that he did this on the basis of his work with John Gittinger, who later funded his research up in New York. He had developed an approach to personality assessment that was quite unique. The only problem was that it certainly didn't work all the time or even necessarily most of the time, but when it did, it was fantastic. This was one of those times when it worked. Now in fairness both to Bill and to John, though esoteric, it is an approach still carried on by its followers and used very extensively by the Agency around the world.[12]

Over the years, it became apparent to many that, in addition to his excellent training and education, Bill had a specific, innate aptitude for interpreting tests; psychometrics was his strong suit. Bill did base much of his case work on John Gittinger's research but, of course, also brought his own intuitive talent to bear. Another passage from *Please Understand Me, II* illustrates this:

> Idealists are naturally inductive in their thought and speech, which is to say that they move quickly from part to whole, from a few particulars to sweeping generalizations, from the smallest sign of something to its entirety. With their focus on unseen potentials, on the not visible and the not yet, Idealists show an extraordinary sensitivity to hints of things, mere suggestions, inklings, intimations, symbols. To be sure, such inductive inferences, requiring what is called the "intuitive leap," can be astonishing to others, especially in cases of mind reading and extrasensory perception. At the very least, Idealists are the best suited of all the types to read between the lines, to have a sixth sense about people, and they do indeed follow their hunches, heed their feelings, and insist they "just know" what people are really up to or what they really mean. Even with complicated issues, NFs need hear only the first words of an explanation to feel they understand the subject fully, jumping from telling details to larger meanings.[13]

A third CIA colleague referred to Bill as very congenial, well liked, and conscientious in his work; he was trusted with all kinds of secrets—early evidence of his ability to compartmentalize various areas of his life and play his cards close to the chest. He said that at one point, as Bill was assigned potential employees to evaluate, the Agency apparently decided that some interviews, certainly those involving foreign agents (spies), should occur somewhere other than the CIA offices. Thus, Bill conducted some of these at a local hotel and, for a while, actually lived there on the Agency's behalf, subletting his own apartment to this friend and colleague because the CIA thought it might appear strange if he were at the hotel consistently in the daytime, but left no trace of sleeping there.

It's difficult to convey just how out of character Bill's later affiliation with

ACIM seemed to those who knew him as a dedicated and accomplished psychologist with the Agency. One woman saw the article in Psychology Today (September 1980) about the *Course* and Bill's involvement in it and thought it so strange because it was atypical of his interests when she knew him. In fact, before the *Course* became central to his life, Bill and many of his associates thought religion lacked intellectual respectability. Although deeply involved with the psychological aspects of his fellow human beings, Bill was not at all interested in organized religion or spirituality. In his youth, his parents followed the Christian Science teachings, but after the death of their first two children and Bill's severe illness, they lost faith in religion and never returned to it. Thus, they never encouraged him in this area, although as noted earlier, he did sing at the Chicago Lawn Congregational Church as a teenager. I would guess this was motivated by his great love of music and an opportunity to sing rather than by any interest in theology.

Bill was more traditional by today's standards but quite on the leading edge of psychology for that time. Goodrich spoke with John Gittinger before his death expressly to discuss Bill's role with *A Course In Miracles*. In that conversation, he told John that Bill had mentioned his fear of losing the research grants funded indirectly by Gittinger if he had learned of his involvement with *A Course In Miracles*. John replied, "Oh, heavens, no! I wondered what he was doing and would have been skeptical, but tolerant."[14] He added that, since Bill was doing such great work for him, he would not in any way have withheld support.

The intricacies of how Bill received support from Gittinger is beyond the scope of this book, but through him and his continuing covert CIA connections, Bill was awarded ongoing, substantial grants to continue refining the PAS. Those grants followed him to Columbia University; both he and Helen Schucman were conducting PAS research there, among other projects, when the *Course* entered their lives. That research continued in parallel throughout the scribing of *ACIM*, as Bill regarded the PAS system as the most sophisticated personality test available at the time. Of course, research on assessing personality traits and their consequent behaviors extended far beyond usefulness to the CIA; it was well within the civilian domain of research psychology and took place at other institutions besides Columbia. (For a list of Bill's publications related to that research, please see Appendix Two.)

It is important to correct and clarify some false and misleading information currently on the Internet concerning Bill's years with the CIA. After Bill's death, John Gittinger himself stressed that although Bill worked tirelessly on refining the PAS, he was *never* involved with the operational side of the CIA, including any behavior manipulation, drug experiments, mind control, or anything that could possibly be considered coloring outside the lines of propriety. In fact, persons on the operational side were somewhat scornful of the psychological approach to information gathering and preferred more dramatic exploration and practices. Also, the paymaster in charge of sending grant-related funds to Bill, a personal friend of Whit Whitson, has stated unequivocally that none of Bill's funding every came through MKUltra, a controversial experimental project. Some Internet articles falsely state that Bill was funded through that project.

Bill had seemed restless even as he began his work at the CIA, perhaps realizing this was only a point along his career path but not a long-term commitment. In 1953, after gaining experience with the Agency and having completed his work at the Washington School of Psychiatry, he felt it was time to move on and gave notice to that effect. One colleague said she believed that, although he was fascinated by Gittinger's work, Bill recognized that a great deal of it was based on intuition and seemed somewhat unscientific. She speculated he may have left the Agency for other institutions in order to search for a hard scientific basis for the derived assessments, as that type of research was not part of his primary job there—testing and evaluating potential intelligence officers. She was at least partly right.

After receiving his resignation, the Agency asked Bill to reconsider his decision, and as part of an inducement package, sent him to the Middle East for several months as a special consultant to the Foreign Service Institute at the American University in Beirut, Lebanon. This assignment was topped off by several weeks of vacation in Europe and the Middle East. He said, in retrospect, that his Middle East trip was the most marvelous of his life. After returning, he was generously promised a range of positions with the Agency, not necessarily in Washington, and felt some obligation to stay on for a while. He continued with the CIA until the summer of 1954, then was impelled to move on.

Since he had been drawn to New York for some years, Bill thought the next obvious step was actually to apply for work there, which he did at the New York Unemployment Service Psychological Placement Bureau. Although he indicated he wanted to live in the city, the head of the service said, "They want you in Hartford [CT]. That's where you have to go, the Institute of Living."[15] He sent Bill immediately to the institute, an adjunct of the Hartford Hospital, one of the first mental health centers in the country and then the largest psychiatric hospital in the United States. There is now reason to believe that, unknown to Bill at the time, the CIA had a covert hand in steering him in that direction, and at the ripe old age of thirty-one, he was hired as director of clinical psychology. Although many well-known people were doing interesting things at the institute, he felt it was not quite his place; it was not New York. He did leave his imprint there, however, and according to the 1956 annual report, the Division of Clinical Psychology under Bill's direction expanded its research to include "better diagnosis of organic pathology through psychological tests, the use of projective techniques in predicting aggressive behavior, and appraising changes resulting from psychotherapy."[16] This research was indeed a continuation of his work with the PAS, and John Gittinger was involved with its funding.

During Bill's short tenure at the institute, Dr. Harold Wolff, a world-famous neurologist, one of the founders of psychosomatic medicine, and chairman of the Neurology Department at Cornell University Medical Center in New York, invited Bill to join him. Bill used to joke that if his qualification for employment at Michael Reese Hospital had been to know nothing about the Rorschach test, his qualifications for the Cornell position were singular. Not only was his work in Washington germane to the Cornell program, he was the only clinical psychologist around with top secret security clearance and trained in neurophysiology. Dr. Wolff had been offered the opportunity to do cross-cultural studies funded by the CIA and he hired Bill as head of the psychological research program. Part of Bill's job was to revise the PAS for use with foreign cultures, particularly the Chinese. In addition to his research work there, which was primary, he also became first an instructor and soon thereafter an assistant professor of psychology in the Department of Psychiatry.

Regarding his time there, Bill wrote of his "lunch time" experiences with the famous and driven Dr. Wolff:

> At first I thought he really meant for us to have lunch, but that was ridiculous. I could never eat anything because Wolff would start interrogating me the minute I sat down. "What have you learned this morning in terms of highest integrative functions? Are you going to change this and get our next publication out by tomorrow?" He used to go on and on like that, so I would never eat lunch. I was used to working under high pressure, but I wasn't used to that sort of thing. I did turn things out

pretty fast, though, and I could type quickly. When he wanted something he would say, "I'm leaving in a few minutes; would you please prepare an abstract for the International Biological Psychiatry Congress. I'll have to have it in fifteen minutes." I would go to my typewriter and dash off what he wanted. I would tap into some inner source and put it into some sort of English. I learned to make it sound super scientific.[17]

Once again his comments reveal that Bill recognized—and trusted—his intuition, or as he called it, inner source. That intuition or guidance is always present for all of us, but we normally pay little if any attention to it, relying instead on our intellects and personal desires to direct us until that proves futile and we start honoring our inner wisdom. This is a particular conflict for those who pride themselves on being rigorously scientific, as Bill did, but who also are very aware of "just knowing." He indicated that in his early days he acknowledged this gift and took it for granted, but felt he couldn't talk about it, fearing he would be misunderstood.

As part of the research at Cornell, Bill worked with a number of Chinese stranded in the U.S. after the Communists established the People's Republic of China in 1949. Some could not and others chose not to return. While conducting research with them and their particular reactions to stress, he was abruptly asked to go to China on a secret mission to escort Harriet Mills on her return to the United States. She was a Fulbright Scholar and Ph.D. candidate at Columbia University. While doing field research there for her dissertation, Mills had come under suspicion and was subsequently jailed by the Communist government. The daughter of Presbyterian missionaries, Mills was born in Japan but reared in China, was fluent in the language, and familiar with Chinese customs—all of which had raised a red flag for them. After four and a half years, she was finally tried, released, and ordered to leave the country.

This assignment, initiated indirectly from the CIA, both frightened and fascinated thirty-two-year-old Bill—a real, live, James Bond-type secret mission where he knew only as much as was provided at any given time. He was booked passage on a freighter, the last available vessel out of Hong Kong, where Mills had been taken after being put on trial and expelled from China. Bill said in his biography, "All arrangements were made secretly and undercover. I was not told where I was first going, which was Manila [Philippines], before proceeding to Hong Kong to board the ship."[18] The freighter was Mills' choice of transportation after her years in a Beijing prison. As there were only a handful of passengers, Bill and Harriet met almost immediately and became friends. She later told her sister, with whom I spoke in 2007, that after a few days she realized Bill was "put on board to grill her." She was right. He took notes on thin paper and kept them hidden in his pockets. He didn't want to leave anything lying around indiscriminately, as he didn't know who else might be on the ship watching them. They arrived safely in Vancouver, Canada, just before Christmas of 1955, and his extensive notes were ultimately included as part of Harold Wolff's testimony before the House Committee on brainwashing in 1975. According to her sister, Mills still won't talk about what happened during her confinement, so we don't know what she may have disclosed to Bill, who elicited deep trust from virtually everyone. He particularly enjoyed telling this story and was highly amused by the drama of the intrigue, especially since the mission had a satisfactory ending.

After two and a half years in the relentlessly high-pressured job at Cornell, Bill was approached by an old friend from Chicago about a possible appointment at Columbia University. The job offered—designing a doctoral program, writing grants, and assuming an assistant professorship—didn't particularly appeal to him, but out of courtesy he agreed to meet with the head of the psychiatry department. Bill told him, thinking he could bring this episode to closure before it began, that he might be interested if they offered him a higher professional rank, which he was certain they would not consider as medical school hierarchies are quite rigid. To his surprise, they accepted his condition, added a prestigious title, and in the fall of 1957 appointed him to the faculty as an associate professor of medical psychology in the College of Physicians and Surgeons at Columbia University Medical School. As with his clandestine trip to Hong Kong, he always laughed as he told these stories, as if the way everything had turned out, the improbable series of events, was all a delightful comedy.

Although I cannot prove beyond doubt—either through interviews with key players (now deceased) or through the Freedom of Information Act (I also tried this route)—it seems obvious that the CIA and John Gittinger were again maneuvering behind the scenes to place Bill in this important post, as well as the earlier ones. Jack Luckett's conversations with Bill also supported this hypothesis; Bill believed the Agency had a hand in arranging his various career opportunities. It especially makes sense given the Agency's propensity to develop a person's strengths, to push them along, so to speak. Gittinger told Dr. Marshall Heyman, another former CIA colleague of Bill's, that Bill and later Helen were the only two "outsiders" (non-CIA employees—Bill was an ex-employee and Helen never worked for the CIA, nor did she know it was the source of some of their funding) at that time whom he authorized to talk publicly about, hold seminars on, and generally endorse the PAS and their research related to it. Other institutions and individuals were doing PAS research, but Bill and Helen became Gittinger's surrogates of sorts, since he could not publicly comment on his internal classified research. In later years, Gittinger, by then head of the CIA's psychological services worldwide, visited Bill and Helen in New York and sometimes attended their seminars anonymously. He very much enjoyed the company of the academics there and being involved with someone of Bill's reputation and stature.

Although Bill was, in fact, a bit uncomfortable accepting money indirectly from the CIA, his intense intellectual curiosity regarding the formation and maintenance of the personality/ego and his conviction that this was meaningful research tipped the scale in favor of his continuing to receive funding. The archivist at Columbia University, with whom I spoke in 2008, found records for six of the grants listed on Bill's curriculum vitae obtained from 1961–1964, totaling $120,410. He received additional grant money but the records could not be found. Publication of PAS-related research continued until the early 1970s. Psychological Assessment Associates, Gittinger's non-CIA business that promoted the PAS, had a file card on record at Columbia, but there was no attendant folder or paperwork related to it.

It is amusing at this point, as we see the CIA almost assuredly working behind the scenes to move Bill forward in his "outer" career, to realize that the Holy Spirit, to use *ACIM* terminology, is "using" the CIA just as the CIA is "using" Bill, to place him on a collision course with Helen and the consequent birth of the *Course*. As I write, I sense Bill's presence, laughing at the notion that we think we, at the ego level, are in charge—life is in charge!

In addition to the duties described to Bill when the job was offered at Columbia, more were added when he arrived in February 1958. Not yet thirty-five, he was additionally appointed as director of the Division of Psychology at Presbyterian Hospital, an adjunct to Columbia University and the largest private medical center in the country employing thousands of people. He was responsible for all clinical psychology practiced there. Attempting to bring order and cohesion to an essentially unorganized department was wearing and complicated, given the disparate organizations involved and the turf battles and jealousies that plague so much of academia. In addition, he was required to include the New York State Psychiatric

Institute in his attempt at administrative reorganization. Ultimately, therefore, he had responsibilities at the hospital, the university, and the institute, which he found incredibly complicated. And the majority of his work history was in research and writing, not administration, so the challenges were immense.

We had 475 faculty members in the Department of Psychiatry alone. Now, most of them were part-time and in affiliated hospitals and things of that kind, but it was an enormous complex maze. I also found out that there was divided authority and responsibility, and you had to report to the president of the hospital as well as the chairman of the department, but there was a vice president in charge of professional affairs that you really had to see first, but you couldn't see him unless you check through the business manager, and there were three business managers because there were three institutions that were part of this—not only the university but the Presbyterian Hospital and the New York Psychiatric Institute, which were all part of this complex.

There were power struggles going on and people seemed quite happy to injure their colleague's reputation or career if they could get another office. And to get a secretary, oh that was fantastic. You'd do anything—kill your grandmother, I guess. It was the most competitive and power-driven setting that I had ever been in, although I had seen a few.[19]

U p to this point, the events, training, and circumstances in Bill's life had conspired to develop his many innate skills and to acquire general life experience. Now the plot thickens. Shortly after his appointment to Columbia, Bill was asked to hire a psychologist with skills in creating instruments to test infants and young children; the position would fulfill the requirements of a grant offered to the university. Although he was certainly knowledgeable in the general field of tests and measurements and had a great deal of experience working with children, he had not designed tests for them and needed a specialist in this area. He checked with a colleague, well known in the field, who promised to help if he could. Shortly thereafter, Bill received a phone call from a woman who introduced herself thus: "My name is Dr. Helen Schucman. I was told to tell you that I am the person you are looking for."

Of course, she was the person Bill was looking for in more ways than one, and he hired her, but not for a job she particularly liked. Bill's colleague, also a friend of Helen's, had called her on hearing Bill's request and told her to forget looking anywhere else and to call Dr. Thetford immediately. On hearing his emphatic tone, Helen decided to forego her other options and called Bill.

> I did not particularly want to work in a medical setting, and the little my
> friend had told me about the job was not very appealing. Nevertheless,

in view of his sense of urgency, I did make Dr. Thetford my first call. When I walked into his office a few days later, I made the first of a series of silent remarks, which I did not understand myself. "And there he is," I said to myself. "He's the one I'm supposed to help."[1]

After Helen and Bill had become better acquainted, a second odd moment of recollection occurred:

> For a brief interval, I seemed to be somewhere else, saying as if in answer to a silent but urgent call. "Of course, I'll go, Father. He's stuck and needs help. Besides, it will be only for such a little while!" The situation had something of the quality of a long-forgotten memory, and I was somehow aware of being in a very happy place. I had no idea to whom I was speaking, but I was sure that I was making some sort of definite commitment that I would not break. Nevertheless, the actual remark I made meant as little to me as did the previous one in Bill's office at the time of our first meeting.[2]

Over the next few years, Helen worked in a research position, only later shifting into more teaching, training, and clinical work, for which she had a natural aptitude. In fact, years later, many who knew her personally described in glowing terms just how talented she was when working with clients, how kind, thoughtful, and loving she could be, and how quickly she could assess a person's actual situation and offer the most appropriate guidance. Bill found her psychodynamic insights profound, and ultimately, promoted her to the position of chief psychologist at the Neurological Institute within the medical center, making her his assistant, which allowed them to spend more time together and, of course, to prepare for what neither knew was about to unfold.

Bill later described his circumstances at Columbia at the time as absolutely frightful. Co-workers were suspicious and hostile, the atmosphere was chaotic, and the workload overwhelming. He divided his time among administrative duties, teaching, conducting research, writing research grants, editing journals, and publishing—moving through a mountain of work without any sustained sense of satisfaction or well-being. In retrospect, colleagues at the time noted that Bill produced a prodigious amount of "regular" work, all expertly handled, while his secret life with the *Course* was ongoing. For one thing, Bill could multitask in a very unusual way; he could, for instance, type the notes for one research project while discussing the details of something entirely unrelated. To many this was disconcerting, as if he were not paying attention to them, but it was, instead, evidence of Bill's peculiar ability to compartmentalize, the trait that routinely appeared in other areas of his life as well.

With Helen, some of their work together proceeded purposefully and effectively, but in other areas they had a terrible time getting along. Even though they had major personality differences and each handled their upsets differently, it never occurred to either to stop working together. Both felt an unexplained compulsion to be there together, and they very much wanted to work out their difficulties, but they seemed to have no idea how to do that. Helen wrote of their early years together:

When I reached the hospital about a year afterward [after Bill arrived at Columbia] there was little doubt that Bill did need help. He looked haggard and badly needed someone to talk to. Gradually, he told me about the many problems with which he had been confronted since coming to the hospital. There had been no real psychology department before he arrived. A number of psychologists were working independently throughout the hospital, some of whom had never even met. In fact, a major though not previously specified part of Bill's job had been to organize and administer a cohesive departmental unit. It was a hard assignment. When I arrived the newly established department was split into factions, and beset by political rivalries and bitter resentments. Besides the obvious hostilities there was also a curious apathy toward the department. Bill seemed to be the only person there who really cared about it. As he told me one day, "I would do anything for the department," and it was evident that he meant it. That was the first note of real devotion I had heard since I came, and it called forth an immediate response. Bill and I entered into an agreement to work out the departmental problems together.

Our attempts were heart-breaking at first, although neither of us seriously thought of withdrawing our commitment. My initial efforts were spent in frantically writing up grant proposals against dead-lines, in a desperate attempt to bring in badly-needed funds. It was exhausting work for both Bill and me, and a dead end as well. We were given encouragement and promises of support, but nothing actually materialized. Besides repeated discouragements of this kind, there was another source of strain which we both found even more difficult to handle. Bill and I were an unlikely team, and in spite of our shared goal, we grated on each other's already jangled nerves a good part of the time.[3]

Despite their considerable challenges, for the several years before the *Course* began, they worked together very closely, having lunch together every day and, among other things, sharing their fascination for personality theory. Bill was always interested in the entire topic of personal identity. At some point, he had brought Helen into the ongoing PAS research, to which she made many valuable contributions, and they jointly published many papers on their continuing refinements to it. Both considered experts in their field, they were often called in jointly to consult on "high-powered private patients" at Columbia; other psychological associations in New York City also invited them to share their expertise. Dorothy Ulmann, a colleague at Cornell University in New York City, remembered, "Once in a while I'd go up there [Columbia] with Helen and Bill and their colleagues. I remember there were all these big-shot psychologists and psychiatrists, who were frequently mentioned in the New York Times' columns. . . .

But these were Helen and Bill's colleagues at lunch."[4]

Obviously, from Bill's recounting of what the university was like in general and his relationships with Helen and others in particular, he was projecting his own "shadow side," his long-held fears and grievances, into his situation there. Every beginning *ACIM* student learns that the subjective experience of one's outer circumstances faithfully reflects an inner state of mind. Stated more bluntly, the more guilt one carries, even though unconsciously, the more one feels punished by outer conditions. Bill certainly contributed to the problems in his environment as he projected his own judgments, fears, unconscious conditioning, and unexamined assumptions about how life should be into the situation, as do we all. He knew about projection theoretically—the process of seeing in others what we fear to own in ourselves—but clearly knew little about dealing with that process personally. Despite his talents, training, and potential, he was as sound asleep as the rest of us. Early in *ACIM*'s text, one finds, "Yet the Bible says that a deep sleep fell upon Adam, and nowhere is there reference to his waking up. The world has not yet experienced any comprehensive reawakening or rebirth. Such a rebirth is impossible as long as you continue to project or mis-create."[5] After the *Course* arrived and Bill became more familiar with its uncompromising tenets on how we cause our own distress, he ultimately became willing to begin changing his mind, and that willingness led to success—to his actual waking up.

Regarding their relationship, on one hand Bill felt Helen was genuinely, and perhaps uniquely, interested in furthering his academic career and, on the other, Helen desperately wanted Bill to play out her romantic fantasies about him. Her childhood had been singularly barren in terms of affection and warmth from her family, and as the *Course* points out, we try to find in our current relationships what was missing in former ones, to require of present companions what past ones seemed to withhold.

I also played multiple roles for Helen. I was her boss, her fantasy love object, her savior in terms of this material, and I was expected to do everything that had to be done at all times. I was a substitute for her husband, her brother, and her father. I was supposed to make up for her feelings about her father, and what he didn't do in her life. I don't know why I accepted this. It was a very complicated relationship.[6]

If he played multiple roles for her, he was also expecting something from her in return. No one can be disappointed with someone unless roles have first been appointed. He, too, had dysfunction in his family with a critical father and an over-protective mother and couldn't help but search for acknowledgment not received earlier. We endure a great deal in search of validation.

Bill's comment in the video, *The Story of A Course In Miracles*, that "Helen felt a closer personal relationship with me than I felt I could reciprocate," was a massive understatement.[7] Helen wanted to possess Bill and did everything she could to be involved in and to control all areas of his life.

As an example, Judith Skutch Whitson, who later entered the *Course's* chronology, commented that after *ACIM* was scribed and she had become one of the principal players, Bill, Helen, and Kenneth Wapnick, also yet to be introduced in this narrative, often met at the Skutch home in the late afternoons. Helen and Ken would leave and Bill often stayed for dinner, enjoying some lighthearted time with the Skutches. Helen would call later, upset because he was still there, and insist he finish his dinner and leave.

A more bizarre example of her possessiveness involves Bill's social life. His most private life was with his male friends, and it was private. Charles Lehman, who was Bill's partner for three years from 1954–1957, comments on his uncompromising secrecy:

Perhaps one difference between Bill and me was on the business of being gay. Bill was very reluctant to come out publicly as being gay. I can understand that because up until the early 1970s, the American Psychiatric Association was really defining gay people as psychoneurotic or as having character disorders, like being sociopaths. And being so directly involved in that field, I can understand that he would want to stay in the closet. Even after he moved to California, I think he had perhaps an underlying feeling that if he came out publicly, it might somehow impair his credibility and the credibility of *A Course In Miracles*.[8]

I have not included more specific information about Bill's gay life because none is available. His two major partners from the New York era are both deceased and no one I interviewed knows about any others or how to contact them. I also have no way to determine who he may have known in his last years in La Jolla, although there is a consensus that he had twelve or fifteen good friends within that community. He lived alone there except for the time he shared a home with the Lucketts. Many persons I spoke with said he never commented on his private life, so that aspect of Bill's history, however important it was to him, remains a closed book.

Fire Island July 1959

Nonetheless, Helen wanted to be involved. At one point, Bill and a number of his close friends rented a house for weekend use on Fire Island, an area known for its gay community. Helen insisted they rent a place with a room for her and her husband Louis as well, which they did; thus, on many occasions the improbable combination of Helen, Louis, Bill, and various friends of his shared a house. During part of those New York years, Bill and another friend owned a small house in Watermill on Long Island, and Helen actually paid for a room and bath to be added to the house for her and her husband. She insisted on being included in *all* aspects of his life, inside the university and out. Everyone noticed this infringement on Bill's time and space. Cal Hatcher, an administrator at the hospital and a good friend of Bill's, commented, "I think sometimes I'd go out of my skin if I were Bill. This was because Helen would call him up anytime, day or night."[9] Ken Wapnick later confirmed that to call Helen possessive was definitely the mildest of understatements. And to thoroughly confound everyone, Helen was genuinely devoted to her husband despite her obsession with Bill. Bill's friends also commented that even if he had been "in love" with Helen, he would never have acted on it because he was so ethical he would not have strayed into an illicit relationship.

A selection from the *Course* text entitled "Shadows of the Past" says it all about the drama in Helen's and Bill's lives and the reason anyone is drawn into ego-based relationships. The "shadows" in this excerpt refer to what we project onto, and then see in one another, when we look through the ego's unloving perspective.

> They [shadow figures] offer you the "reasons" why you should enter into unholy alliances to support the ego's goals, and make your relationships the witness to its power.
>
> It is these shadow figures that would make the ego holy in your sight, and teach you what you do to keep it safe is really love. The shadow

figures always speak for vengeance, and all relationships into which they enter are totally insane. Without exception, these relationships have as their purpose the exclusion of the truth about the other, and of yourself. This is why you see in both what is not there, and make of both the slaves of vengeance. And why whatever reminds you of your past grievances attracts you, and seems to go by the name of love, no matter how distorted the associations by which you arrive at the connection may be. And finally, why all such relationships become attempts at union through the body, for only bodies can be seen as means for vengeance.[10]

Years after Helen and Bill began working together, another of the men who provided their research grants, the lifeblood of academia, visited them in New York. He sized up the situation after being with them a while and rather indelicately commented that Helen had the "hots" for Bill even though she knew he was gay, a term not used at that time, and was "mad as hell" about his lack of cooperation in her romantic fantasies.

How could their relationship be anything but tortuous under these extreme circumstances, with both "mad as hell"? The early 1960s were a really low point for Bill. His parents had passed away in the mid 1950s, and he was alone in the world so far as family was concerned. As pressure mounted, related to various facets of his work—seemingly always in crisis mode—and the continual turmoil with Helen, Bill finally reached his limit. He had not yet realized we bring this seemingly "loveless" condition on ourselves. He felt surrounded by hostility and paranoia and was disappointed and unhappy despite his fame and prestige. He had mastered his field, and yet something was still missing. It can be shattering to work so diligently and for so long toward your goal, bringing everything one has to bear and finally achieving it, only to find happiness and fulfillment are still absent.

The ego is certain that love is dangerous, and this is always its central teaching. It never puts it this way; on the contrary, everyone who believes that the ego is salvation seems to be intensely engaged in the search for love [or recognition, value, etc.]. Yet the ego, though encouraging the search for love very actively, makes one proviso; do not find it. Its dictates, then, can be summed up simply as: "Seek and do not find." This is the one promise the ego holds out to you, and the one promise it will keep. For the ego pursues its goal with fanatic insistence, and its judgment, though severely impaired, is completely consistent.[11]

A real spiritual crisis was in the making. Bill was afflicted with the "divine discontent" all of us experience sooner or later. This world simply is not satisfying no matter how much we may be getting our way, and the insistence that it be inherently meaningful drives us insane. As the *Course* says, "Tolerance for pain may be high, but it is not without limit. Eventually everyone begins to recognize, however dimly, that there must be a better way."[12] Bill's elegant comprehension of how we form and maintain egos was not serving him here and could not relieve him of his pain—a great example of seeking to find satisfaction "out there" rather than through means that actually do bring peace. Helen's observations corroborate Bill's:

Along the way, Bill and I had become consultants to a research project at a nearby medical center, where we spent an hour a week. We hated it. The various disciplines working on the project quarreled constantly and became increasingly angry and competitive. Our weekly meetings there were hardly a relief from our own all-too-similar professional setting. Meanwhile the relationship between Bill and me deteriorated steadily. While we had grown interdependent, we had also developed considerable anger towards each other, and our genuine attempts to cooperate were offset by our growing resentments.[13]

Bill was now forty-two, the well-known "midlife crisis" time. He was in such pain, *something* had to give. He was at a breaking point and in June

1965, just before yet another power struggle-type meeting, poured out his heart in his now famous declaration, "There must be a better way and I'm determined to find it." Helen remembers the specifics of that conversation:

> Bill proposed, quite specifically, to try out a new approach that day at the research meeting. He was not going to get angry and he was not going to attack. He was going to look for a constructive side in what the people there said and did, and was not going to focus on mistakes and point up errors. He was going to cooperate rather than compete. It was time to take a new direction. We had obviously been headed the wrong way. It was a long speech for Bill, and he spoke with unaccustomed emphasis as he delivered it. When it was over he waited for my response in obvious discomfort. Whatever reaction he may have expected, it was not the one he got. I jumped up, told Bill with genuine conviction that he was right, and said I would try the new approach with him.[14]

Thus Helen, impressed and moved by his passion, agreed and their joint venture began. Bill always emphasized how touching and amazing he found her response—her promise to help—as it was so out of character under the circumstances. This interaction between Bill and Helen, this sincere and urgent heartfelt request for relief from pain, signaled the time for *ACIM*'s arrival into the world. The scribes were ready to listen.

Neither Bill nor Helen thought they had been very successful at that fateful June meeting, the anticipation of which had brought on Bill's determination to try a different way, but it was their beginning. Helen remembered:

> Many unexpected things have happened since. At the factual level, the whole climate of the department gradually changed. Bill worked particularly hard on the departmental problems, determined to turn hostilities into friendships. This took considerable effort on his part at first, but he did succeed eventually. Tensions lessened and antagonisms dropped

away. The wrong people left, though on friendly terms, and the right ones came along almost immediately. A secure and interesting position opened up for me. Although our efforts were inconsistent and often half-hearted, there is little doubt that they showed results. The department became smooth-functioning, relaxed, and efficient.[15]

Both also felt they needed to work on mending rifts in their respective social lives as well, and both were happy with those results, although their personal relationship still suffered. Helen had the vague sense that these reparative steps in healing assorted relationships were part of a mandatory preparation for something, but what that was remained unknown.

As another sign that shifts in consciousness were occurring, almost immediately after Bill's crisis in the spring of 1965, Helen began having waking visions and strange dreams; she acutely feared losing her vision and, indeed, her mind. Those dreams and waking visions, in retrospect, pointed to the coming of *ACIM,* but at the time seemed obscure and unintelligible. For instance, one vision involved Helen's seeing herself in a small boat being carried along a lovely canal. She mused about the possibility of buried treasure in the area and noticed a long pole with a hook in the bottom of the boat. She dropped the hook into the water and pulled up an ancient treasure chest; on opening it, she was disappointed to find nothing but a large black book, specifically a black thesis binder, exactly like those that would be used years later to store the typed notes of *A Course In Miracles* for safekeeping. Down the spine was written one word in gold, *Aesculapius.* Neither Bill nor Helen knew what it meant, although it had a familiar ring to it. A few nights later, she dreamed of that black book again, now with pearls draped around it. Aesculapius was the Greek god of healing and historians believe the legends surrounding his medical work were based on the life of an historical person. A well-known physician of the second century, Galen, did much research at the Aesculapion in Pergamon, Turkey (then part of the Roman Empire), and embodied the Aesculapion traditions for treating not just the physically but the mentally ill, as well. Helen's dream surely was an accurate premonition of the healing treasure to come.

Other visions involved Helen's experiences as a priestess in many times and places, and they almost always included Bill. Sometimes the two were married, sometimes they collaborated in healing work, and sometimes they were deadly enemies. Often the visions had a profound emotional impact, eliciting either sublime joy or abject terror. In one major vision, she was ready to kill him with a spear poised between his eyes over the theft of a ruby from her priestess crown. She backed off at the last moment and died shortly thereafter. Helen's response to telling Bill about this particular vision gives some clue about her ongoing intense anger toward him:

> The emotional effect of this last episode was intense and long-lasting. I still felt the anger after the images faded, and it later blazed into open fury as I told Bill the story the next day, particularly when I spoke of the theft of the ruby. It is as if it were happening all over again. A picture of the ruby, beautiful and blazing red, rose before my eyes and for a brief period the scene became reality for me. Again I berated myself for dying for a rebellious slave who was nothing but a common thief. I could barely contain my fury at Bill, who was understandably upset. So was I. The intensity of my anger was quite surprising to both of us. It was a while before the next episodes in the series appeared. It was almost as though I had to recover a little before going on. Fortunately, the next installment was different, although it, too, did not turn out too well for me.[1]

Speaking of Helens's temper, her anger wasn't directly solely at Bill but at anyone who threatened her ego. *ACIM* asserts that anger is a response to feeling powerless and Tammy Cohen's (Judith Skutch Whitson's daughter) commentary reveals something of Helen's split mind, apparently known to all who knew her:

> My mother catered to Helen's every whim and it didn't take too long for me to realize that everyone else did as well. Helen had a presence about her which demanded attention and care-taking. Yet I noticed that on

the one hand she played the frail, fragile little old lady to get her way. But on the other, when she wasn't getting what she wanted, her presence grew to the size of a Sumo wrestler. With merely a glance or a quick slice from her sharp tongue, she could make the largest of men shrink to the size of a pea. As soon as she got what she wanted, though, she instantly returned to her proper lady-like persona, like a genie returns to its lamp after a wish is fulfilled.[2]

During midsummer, another particularly meaningful vision occurred at the conclusion of what Helen termed the second (out of three) series of visions, this time with a more positive outcome:

The series ended on a note of final achievement and even glory. I was standing in a room that seemed to be on the top floor of a church building. Bill, seated at a large, old-fashioned church organ, was play-ing Handel's *Hallelujah Chorus* with his face lit with joy. We had finally reached our goal. I was standing in front of a simple brown wooden altar, on which two words were written one underneath the other. I cannot imagine a less appropriate pair. The top word was "Elohim," which I did not recognize at the time, and only later discovered is one of the Hebrew names for God. The other word, "Evoe," I did identify as the cry of the Greek Bacchantes [a priestess or female votary of Bacchus; a female participant in a drunken or orgiastic revel] in celebrating the rites of Bacchus [the god of grape-growing and of wine]. As I watched, a streak of lightning from the back of the church struck the altar and obliterated the second word entirely. Only "Elohim" remained, written in bright gold letters. The *Hallelujah Chorus* rose to a crescendo, and a figure outlined in brilliant light which I recognized immediately as Jesus stepped from behind the altar and came toward me. I started to kneel in front of him, but he came around to my side and knelt at the altar with me. Bill rose and knelt at his other side. And then a Voice, with which I was to become increasingly familiar, said in silent but perfectly clear words, "That altar is within you." The emotional impact of the conclusion was so powerful that I burst into tears.[3]

Helen kept a running account of those episodes and shared them with Bill, who was extremely interested in all aspects of her unusual experiences. He had recently discovered the famous "sleeping prophet," Edgar Cayce, and was becoming increasingly intrigued with his work. He urged Helen to read some of his books, but she found them disturbing even though she tried to keep an open mind. Her visions and waking dreams were followed by a growing capacity for other types of psychic phenomena—remote viewing, and sending and receiving messages at a distance. She was both fascinated and worried about her "magic phase," as she called it, which abruptly concluded with an episode that verified she had made a clear and irrevocable choice:

> I saw myself entering a cave cut into a rock formation on a bleak, wind-swept seacoast. All I found in the cave was a large and very old parchment scroll. Its ends were attached to heavy gold-tipped poles, and the scroll was wrapped around them so that they met in the middle of the scroll and were tied tightly together. With some difficulty I managed to untie the ends and open the scroll just enough to reveal the center panel, on which two words were written: "God is." Then I unrolled the scroll all the way. As I did so, tiny letters began to appear on both sides of the panel. The silent Voice, which I had "heard" before explained the situation mentally to me:
>
>> "If you look at the left side you will be able to read the past." said the Voice. "If you look at the right side you will be able to read the future."
>
> The little letters on the sides of the panel were becoming clearer, but I hesitated only a moment before rolling up the scroll sufficiently to conceal everything except the center panel.
>
>> "I'm not interested in reading the past or the future," I said with finality. "I'll just stop with this."

The Voice sounded both reassured and reassuring.

"You made it that time," it said. "Thank you."

And that, it seemed, was that.[4]

As they moved through the summer, both Helen's psychic capacity and Bill's interest in the entire subject expanded. She told him she had a growing sense that something unexpected and unusual was about to take place and had written him a letter during that time stating, "Dear Bill, I'm not sure I want to write this, but I have an idea I'm obeying an order. These orders are rather stern and the main feeling I get is that I wouldn't dare disobey them."[5] He urged her to keep a notebook with her at all times so that if the "something unexpected" occurred, she could immediately write about it.

As a parenthetical note, in the early 1960s, before the *Course* transmission began, Bill was appointed to a space-planning committee for a new research building for the Department of Psychiatry. In that capacity, he was able to create two very private, secluded offices for himself and Helen in one wing of the new building, with their own private entrance; even their secretaries were quartered in a building across the street. Bill said he felt strongly at the time that there was a purpose for having a secluded space, but he had no idea what that might be. The new research building was completed in the fall of 1965, and shortly after settling in, the "something unexpected" began.

One October evening, as Helen was writing some notes to herself, the Voice, by now familiar to her, said, "This is a course in miracles. Please take notes." Very frightened, she called Bill who asked if it was the same familiar Voice; she replied that it was. After a short exchange, they agreed she would take the notes but not read them. She would bring them to work the next morning, and if they were nonsense, they could throw them away and no one would know. The first notes she received were the introduction to the text, and both were understandably stunned on reading it.

The abbreviated version of *ACIM*'s genesis is that over a seven-year period beginning in October 1965, Helen received an inner "dictation," as it seemed to her, which she wrote down in shorthand. (She was exceptionally fast at shorthand, having devised her own hybrid method.) She could feel the writing coming on, usually several times a day, but it never conflicted with work or social activities. She recalled:

> The writing was highly interruptible. At the office I could lay the notebook down to answer the telephone, talk to a patient, supervise a junior staff member, or attend to one of our numerous emergencies, and return to the writing without even checking back to see where I left off. At home, I could talk with my husband, chat with a friend, take a nap, going back to the notebook afterwards without disturbing the flow of words in the slightest. It did not matter whether I had stopped at the end of a paragraph or in the middle of a sentence. It was as if the Voice merely waited until I came back and then started in again. I wrote with equal ease at home, in the office, on a park bench, or in a taxi, bus, or subway. The presence of other people did not interfere at all. When the time for writing came, external circumstances appeared to be irrelevant.[6]

Almost every day she would take her most recent notes to Bill's conveniently private office, where they would lock the door, pull down the shades as an extra precaution against being discovered, and she would read while Bill typed. By her own admission, she was almost always in a state of panic, and the reading required tremendous effort on her part. She would yawn, cough, cry, stutter, or sometimes lose her voice completely and, in every conceivable manner, attempt to avoid speaking the words she had received. She wrote:

> For the most part, I was bleakly unbelieving, suspicious, and afraid. Yet distressing as the writing generally was, reading the material to Bill afterwards was infinitely more so. We had agreed that I would read my notes to him at the end of the day, and he would type them. I hated to hear what I had written. I was sure it would be incoherent, foolish, and meaningless. On the other hand, I was likely to be unexpectedly and deeply moved and suddenly burst into tears.[7]

Bill with the ACIM typewriter

After each typing session, they would jointly go over the typed version and carefully check each word against her shorthand notes for accuracy, of major import to Helen in particular. She told Bill, most irrationally, "You're responsible for what it says," and declared her part was to assure grammatical correctness and purity. She announced that she would simply refuse to continue if the dictation contained grammatical errors. Fortunately, Helen did commit to this assignment absolutely, despite the torment to her. A good thing, too, because she couldn't permanently turn it off. Periodically, she would rebel and refuse to take notes for a while, whereupon she became unable to sleep and generally dysfunctional, soon returning to the dictation.

Bill assessed the situation, noting that Helen was never in a trance or altered state when the scribing occurred:

> So when Helen started hearing an inner voice, I knew it wasn't something that she was making up. In her attempts to gain attention, Helen had a strong self-dramatizing tendency, but I knew this wasn't that. It didn't fit that category at all. This was something that was quite authentic. She was frightened of it, but acknowledged it as having the kind of authenticity that was not characteristic of her own ideas. Yet she was also actually indifferent about it, despite its very compelling quality. And contrary to what some might think, Helen said she did not hear an external voice. What she heard really was a part of her mind which was clearly separated from her ordinary ego consciousness or awareness.[8]

In Helen's process, she didn't hear voices in the way a schizophrenic does; in her own words she described it not so much a matter of audition as a sense of knowing. She said the material came very rapidly and smoothly, and she never knew how a sentence would end. Had she not been proficient in shorthand, she couldn't have kept up with it. Sometimes she asked the Voice to repeat an unclear message; in response, the material then showed up on a sort of interior "blackboard" where she could read it. She said all the writing was voluntary, never "automatic writing," which she could start and stop at will, and she was pleased with its coherence even though the material was antithetical to everything she believed. That, she said, confused her no end. She ended her commentary by saying that the process of scribing is simply impossible to explain in words: "I do not understand the events that led up to the writing, I do not understand the process, and I certainly do not understand the authorship. It would be pointless for me to attempt an explanation."[9]

Bill, too, found it impossible to describe a phenomena beyond the intellect's comprehension: "If one talked about the Holy Spirit or Jesus or Christ or Higher Authority, whatever the term might be, it seemed to me that we were talking at a level which was beyond conceptualization. And I couldn't really pinpoint or identify that, except that I knew it went way beyond our egos. It had nothing to do with our ordinary state of consciousness and awareness. So I think I was perhaps more hesitant to talk in very specific Biblical terms."[10]

Bill almost never referred to Jesus, not out of denial but because he personally felt it confused people and fostered the already prevalent idea about the historic Jesus being the author. Although the material is sometimes written in the first person as if a specific person dictated the *Course*, it was not a personal Jesus speaking through Helen as if she were a telephone line unrelated to the transmitted message. "The name of Jesus Christ as such is but a symbol. But it stands for love that is not of this world."[11] When specifically asked about *ACIM*'s authorship, Bill tended to skirt the question, not wanting to trivialize it or give a simplistic answer. Thus, in deference to Bill's protocol, I use the words "Author" or "Source" of *ACIM* throughout this work, rather than the name Jesus.

From the *ACIM* teacher's manual:

> The name of Jesus is the name of one who was a man but saw the face of Christ in all his brothers and remembered God. So he became identified with Christ, a man no longer, but at one with God. The man was an illusion, for he seemed to be a separate being, walking by himself, within a body that appeared to hold his self from Self, as all illusions do. . . .

And Christ needed his form that He might appear to men and save them from their own illusions.[12]

Ken Wapnick wrote:

> Again, Jesus [the Christ] does not speak in words. To say it differently and succinctly here, his is the content, our minds (and brains) supply the form. Therefore, Helen's decision-making mind identified itself with the non-ego presence that is in everyone. This non-judgmental thought system of love was represented for her by Jesus, as it is for so many of us. Her mind took that non-specific love and translated it into words, in much the same way as our brains translate the upside-down image cast on the retina into right-side-up perceptions. And so, as I have said many times, the form of the *Course* is from Helen. . . . The content of *A Course in Miracles*, however, is clearly not Helen's, at least not the Helen the world knew or the person she consciously identified with. This explains why she felt at liberty to change the form, though never the content. Helen knew what the published *Course* ought to be. One could make recommendations, and Bill and I did from time to time, but Helen had the finished form already in her head.[13]

Finally, *ACIM*'s origin will remain unfathomable to our intellects, but closer to us than our own breath. Since our goal is ultimately to experience the Source, we are better served by focusing on forgiveness rather than on what our human minds can never fully grasp.

Though they couldn't comprehend its source, they were convinced of *ACIM*'s legitimacy and Bill's support was unwavering and reassuring. He said that many times he typed with one hand and held Helen's with the other to try to mitigate her extreme anxiety about the material she was relaying, which was so at odds with her own ego-based beliefs. Bill, for his part, was also somewhat panicked, often making typographical errors, rare for him, both because of the material's implications and the possible repercussions if anyone found out what they were up to. They would likely have lost their jobs and fine reputations, so long in the making. And, of course, the entire process of scribing *ACIM* was woven throughout their already impossibly busy schedules. They made quite a pair.

And thus was born the three-volume work consisting of a text, workbook, and manual for teachers called *A Course In Miracles*—a title, by the way, neither of them found acceptable in the beginning, thinking it sounded embarrassing, awkward, and unscientific. They even wanted the Author to change it, which did not happen. Once they developed a greater understanding of the meaning of miracle (the love that sustains the universe; a shift in perception that removes the barriers to the awareness of love's presence in our lives), they concluded it was, indeed, the only possible title.

Early on in the process, Bill and Helen both sensed they had started a mission they had promised to fulfill at an earlier, unknown time and place and were recommencing where they had left off. Despite their "wildly contradictory feelings," as Helen described them, neither considered abandoning the project. Two psychic readings given by talented, intuitive individuals, well known in their fields, had much to say about Helen, Bill, their joint undertaking, and their relationships in other lifetimes. The material given in the readings was remarkably similar to the visions and dreams Helen had experienced before "dictation" began. Incidentally, the issue of reincarnation, of ever increasing interest to Bill, is addressed in the teacher's manual under the chapter, "Is Reincarnation So?"

> In the ultimate sense, reincarnation is impossible. There is no past or future, and the idea of birth into a body has no meaning either once or many times. Reincarnation cannot, then, be true in any real sense. Our only question should be, "Is the concept helpful?" And that depends, of course, on what it is used for. If it is used to strengthen the recognition of

the eternal nature of life, it is helpful, indeed. . . .

Does this mean that the teacher of God should not believe in reincarnation himself, or discuss it with others who do? The answer is, certainly not! If he does believe in reincarnation, it would be a mistake for him to renounce the belief unless his internal Teacher so advised. And this is most unlikely. . . .

The emphasis of this course always remains the same;—it is at this moment that complete salvation is offered you, and it is at this moment that you can accept it. This is still your one responsibility.[14]

When these readings took place, neither psychic knew Bill, nor were they familiar with the *Course* itself. In addition, both were in a trance state and unaware of what was said until the sessions were over. The first excerpts are from a reading given for Bill in the spring of 1976 by Paul Solomon shortly after *ACIM* was finished but not yet published. While a guest in the Skutch home, Paul had offered to do a reading for Judy and she asked that he read for Bill instead. The second, in 1980, came at my request through LeRoy Zemke, a long-time family friend, four years after the *Course*'s initial publication. Bill was receptive to both these opportunities.

Bill, curious about his next function, had queried Paul, who responded that Bill did not yet understand his relationship to the *Course*. He stated that he should consider his contribution in terms of a father/mother concept— a polarity—and that his presence was as necessary as Helen's in bringing the work to fruition. He stated, "Begin to understand some of the laws of polarity and of the priesthood, for in this sense you acted as a priest, a priest in the sense of the go-between, the mediator, an energy that allowed the birth of the material . . . participating as one encouraging, as a comrade, counselor."[15]

Paul then referred to another life experience in which Bill and Helen, as priest and priestess, had joined together in the highest and noblest sense to evoke the oracle, to experience completion. He indicated Bill would be unable to take his next step related to the *Course* until he understood and owned his full participation in its conception and birth. Once he did this, Paul said,

> There is another step, as might well be described—a step of application, a step of completion, a step of commentary, as it will be seen concerning this *Course*—as you will be the listener, the recorder, not the scribe necessarily, but the listener. And this step will describe two purposes . . . the demonstration of the laws spoken of in the *Course* itself, the application. It is the demonstration of the completion of application and the recording of that effect that has been prophesied.[16]

Paul stated further that the vast potential for bringing *ACIM* forward existed in Helen, but Bill provided the energetic stimulus or key that allowed the flow to begin. He suggested,

> Now see yourself in that role in relation to that which has been born and be responsible concerning that birth and growth and maturity, for your responsibility ends not with the introduction of this to the world, but with its maturity and application, the responsibility of learning from it, using it, not controlling how it shall be used but rather experiencing that which is given to experience. Go out to the people on your own and express, assist, share ideas, be a part of the Source of the material, and demonstrate its growth.

> As to the past and its relationship to the present, understand here there are so many times you've experienced this plane of existence, and every time is directly involved with this in some way. Many times you have known those who are close in this time, not only the channel for this material, but others that are as a part of the family even in this time. You have returned together for a purpose, as men are inclined to do, and each earlier time has played its part, its role, in the preparation.[17]

Paul suggested, as do many other intuitives, that in various life experiences we play different roles with those we are close to in the current lifetime, and this provides a compelling force for returning together. He stated that Bill and Helen had been husband and wife before, but just as important, they had been in a teacher/student relationship, with Bill as the paternal teacher, instructing her how to listen as a channel. Further highlighting Bill's challenges, Paul said:

> And your tendency has been, in that time and others, to isolate the self, to set the self apart, to become a monk, a separated one. And in the most recent life [before this one], disappointment, disillusionment in marriage turned to a depth of spiritual quality that made you feel that separation, isolation, being alone is best for soul growth, for development, and yet that decision toward loneliness in that time has, in this time, produced a regret, a feeling of loneliness, isolation. Then you see how these things work together, that one time tempers another and you are the product of all the times that you lived and all the experiences, one tempering the other to produce that which is perfect for this moment to express that which must be expressed through it.
>
> Now you still continue with the illusion that each moment must have its purpose in productivity. Something must be produced. There must be a reason for this moment. You must have a goal. There will not be that clarity of specific purpose, goal, or job until there is the acceptance that living has purpose now. When being what you are is sufficient unto itself, then the means of listening and the next step will appear.
>
> Understand that the concerns for the physical are largely related to that just given. The energy needed will be found in finding purpose. When there is a specific project, there is sufficient energy there too. When there is a feeling of not having direct purpose, there is a feeling of loss of energy, debilitation, lack of direction. Let the moment, let living, let relationships—the relationship with God—be sufficient to that motivation and build the energy for it.[18]

Before I knew about this reading with Paul, I was conversing with Jaison Kayn, a friend from Denver Bill would meet later. "Bill would defer to Helen because she did the actual scribing," he observed, as have many others close to Bill, "but not a chance in hell it would have happened without him. She required not only support but the confidence that he gave simply from the power of his presence. . . . His respect, admiration, and appreciation for her helped her go on. They were a team and he knew that."[19] All who knew him commented on the obvious—Bill was an equal, essential part of the *Course*'s coming forth; he held the key to its transmission and was ultimately responsible for its coming to pass. Without him, this work would never have happened. Of course, this is not to minimize Helen's part, but to correct any misperception that the *Course* was "her work" and Bill was the "helper."

In 1980, LeRoy Zemke made many comments in a lengthy reading for Bill about his and Helen's relationship and its ancient origins. Referring to Helen, LeRoy told him:

> There is here another challenge for you and that involves the channel through whom the energy [of *ACIM*] itself was directed. The initial connection with this woman was a very, very powerful one. It is still very powerful on the highest level of your being. There is within you a deep, abiding love, a love which goes back centuries into the past, and it is the expression of a love, a connection initially made in the ancient land of Egypt. You were both in the male form and your work involved the founding of a school that became a kind of guideline for the training of the priesthood that would form the foundations of the consciousness of healing in the Egyptian religion of its time. The school itself was thwarted, aborted. And the commitment to establish this energy as a teaching has now been brought into this present time. It will be done without the form of the traditional school, but is still the teaching that is here before you. . . . There is perhaps one additional idea. When this

effort in ancient Saqqara [Egypt] was initiated, this entity, Helen, was in the male form. You were both in the male form at that time, as you know, and the energy there was intensely powerful. She felt a tremendous commitment and made a very powerful promise at some junction to come forward with that which would be beneficial for those ready to enter a force field that would permit the unfolding of the new Christ, the Cosmic Christ.

Additional important information is that, from that period until this, there have been other embodiments involved with commitments to experiences of like essence and, in this life, the wrestling with the powers of the spirit has been very intense. As a result of that commitment made in ancient Egypt and the experiences in other dimensions of being, there is a reluctance within her consciousness to let go, and it is only through this deliberate shift created by the personality to allow . . . this promise to be made whole through you [Bill].

Bill then questioned LeRoy, who was still in a trance state:

I think I have been a very reluctant teacher in this life, and I'm aware of feeling that teaching is part of my function, but there has always been a sense of drag about this. . . . Somehow I have a great deal of fear—a totally irrational, neurotic fear—about getting up before groups, particularly large groups of people. Is there anything that would be helpful in that regard?

Zemke answered:

There are several indications here that are significant. In the past, much of your in-depth work, in terms of the way in which you have related to people, has been in a one-to-one setting. You have often been involved in the Catholic Church as a priest and have lived the scholastic life, a very secluded, scholarly life. And much of your work has thus been involved in communicating with only one person or a very small and/or select group. That energy from those life experiences is very much a part of your consciousness. It's a very powerful memory that acts as a resistance to your present setting since you are no longer in the priesthood but have been in an academic environment where that same secluded atmosphere has been prevalent. . . . Part of this fear comes from the past. In the priesthood role, your teaching was, as it were, protected. It came out of a very sacred dimension that might be challenged by the outer world, but never fully challenged because the priesthood acts as a shield to protect it. Therefore, whatever the priests have taught, be it true or false, has had the aura of the Church to give it sanction. However, in this life, that is no longer available to you. Now you are drawing much closer to the Source and having to stand alone without the shield as you make the statements that need to be made. . . . You have no difficulty communicating your ideas, as such, but there is that fear that you are, in some way, going to dishonor the body of information and the power of the God-force within in attempting to represent it accurately. That holds you back.[20]

What our energy fields reveal about any of us is fascinating. We simply can't hide what is going on in our so-called private space. Judith Skutch Whitson's first impression of Bill was that of a trapped monk. She noted his darting eyes and very straight back poised as if he were always getting ready to leave. About five months into their friendship she mentioned that first impression, at which point he smiled and said, "I knew you knew." What she noted was not Bill's usual demeanor, but the fear LeRoy identified occasionally revealed itself.

It's apparent by now that Bill and Helen's relationship was unique, to say the least. To illustrate, Whit Whitson recounts an early experience with Judy and the *Course:*

In the spring of 1979, Judy visited Washington and we got together. While she was there, I hoped to explore the relationship, if any, between the PAS "ego" [personality] and the "ego" as defined by the *Course.* To do that, I decided to introduce Mike [a colleague knowledgeable about the PAS] to Judy. Judy and Mike hit it off immediately at the lunch I had arranged for us. Soon Mike asked her to tell him about *A Course In Miracles*. I knew he would be somewhat skeptical about the fundamental precepts of the *Course* and whoever had "dreamed up" such a system of thought.

At the time, Bill and Helen had pledged Judy to silence about their roles in scribing the *Course*, insisting on remaining anonymous. So Judy refused to give Mike their names or even the locale of their university. But as she continued to describe them—their personalities and relationship with one another—Mike suddenly asked, "Are you talking about Bill Thetford and Helen Schucman?"

Judy was dumbfounded. She wondered what she had said to reveal Helen and Bill's secret. In turn, Mike stared at Judy in disbelief, telling her that he knew them, but that he never knew they had produced *A Course In Miracles*. Mike explained that he couldn't think of anyone else who fit Judy's descriptions; he would now have to reassess his prior judgments of Bill and Helen. He also told Judy that he had worked with them and knew them as a truly remarkable team. [Mike's association with them related to funding many of their projects.] He remembered Bill as being the stable, imperturbable academic—calm and easy-going—which contrasted with Helen's assertive vitality. He thought of Helen as a tough-minded New York intellectual with a no-nonsense, intensive, questioning mind. Yet as a team professionally, he found them incredibly productive.[21]

So much for trying to hide!

Bill and Helen's relationship was most unusual in other ways as well. Ken Wapnick noted that, although they could fight endlessly, when either really needed help or support, the other was there without condition and for as long as needed. Also, when involved in *Course* work, they were loving and kind to one another, all enmity put aside. On returning to their academic work, however, the sniping would resume. Bill would write,

Helen would ferociously edit, he would take that personally, and they were off and running. It's as if they continually flipped a switch, operating at extremes—a real love-hate relationship, but both were resolute in their commitment to the *Course* and to avoiding endangering its transmission in any way.

Their battles were not limited to normal work hours. I asked Ken if he was included in the "after-hours war" once he joined the project, and he answered emphatically,

> Oh, God, yes—always! In general, we'd be together all day and they would argue all the time, I'd go home with Helen to have dinner with her and Louis. After dinner, Helen would call Bill or he would call her, I'd go to another room, and they'd continue where they left off for up to another hour. For a long time we'd have lunch together on Saturday, then go to Bill's apartment or take a walk in the park if it was nice, and then go to Bill's apartment and continue. At some point, we stopped doing it because it was just awful, the arguing was enough already.[22]

They both seemed determined to make themselves miserable. Bill used to say he thought he and Helen needed the *Course* because they intensely resisted each other's egos. To say they were astonished as the message unfolded would be a gross understatement. Bill quickly recognized he would need to examine and release virtually everything he believed and seriously questioned his ability to do that. In fact, he described being in shock for a while, wondering how such an abrupt shift could be possible. How important were all his academic achievements and recognition? What was really valuable? Everything would have to be reevaluated. To live that schizophrenic kind of life, pursuing a career in traditional psychology on one hand and trying to deal with the dynamics of the *Course* and its ramifications on the other, was a huge feat for both of them. From what Bill told me, the endless, wrenching nature of this dichotomy was incredibly difficult for him.

Relentlessly, day after day, the *Course* pointed out the mirroring nature of our world—relationships, situations, circumstances—and the inescapable fact that we are fully responsible for our subjective experience.

> The world you see depicts exactly what you thought you did. Except that now you think that what you did is being done to you. . . .

> The world but demonstrates an ancient truth; you will believe that others do to you exactly what you think you did to them. But once deluded into blaming them, you will not see the cause of what they do, because you want the guilt to rest on them. . . .

> The secret to salvation is but this: That you are doing this unto yourself. No matter what the form of the attack, this still is true. Whoever takes the role of enemy and of attacker, still is this the truth. Whatever seems to be the cause of any pain and suffering you feel, this is still true.[23]

As Bill and Helen worked together to produce a typescript of the *Course,* they felt genuine excitement as the project unfolded, providing a truly meaningful function as they joined in common purpose, and it was rewarding in ways their regular work at Columbia was not. Bill said later that it felt amazingly familiar, a feeling not unique to them. I have spoken with many people who have described how much at home they felt with the material, how it resonated at a profound level like a long-lost truth. Once when Bill and I were discussing the *Course,* I told him I felt like it was mine, almost like I had written it. He answered, "I'm sure you did." He did not mean that I literally had something to do with scribing it in its current form but that we are all part of the unified Self from which it derives. At some level, we have all collectively written it in anticipation of our comprehensive waking up.

Bill and Helen sometimes asked the Author, the Voice Helen "heard," why they were chosen to bring this material forward, because they often felt unfit for the job. The Voice indicated that the confidence in them was not misplaced, as their commitment and agreement to do this work was already known. Eventually, they realized the inevitability of their commitment, and neither seriously considered giving it up. The answer Bill gave, in the few interviews he granted, to the question of "Why us?" was "Because you're doing it." That was a correct but insufficient answer. In the Urtext, defined as "a reconstructed proto-text set up as the basis of variants in extant later texts,"[24] and in this case, Bill's original, unedited typed notes of *ACIM*, the Author gave them a more complete and direct answer:

> You have been chosen to teach the Atonement precisely because you have been extreme examples of allegiance to your thought systems and, therefore, have developed the capacity for allegiance. It has, indeed, been misplaced. Bill has become an outstanding example of allegiance to apathy, and you [Helen] have become a startling example of fidelity to variability. But this is a form of faith, which you yourselves had grown willing to redirect. You cannot doubt the strength of your devotion when you consider how faithfully you observed it. It was quite evident that you had already developed the ability to follow a better model, if you could accept it.[25]

Because Helen was so easily upset and challenged by the subject matter of the *Course*, it was difficult for them to discuss the content once they assured its accuracy. Therefore, Bill, sworn to secrecy, had no one with whom to explore the ideas, to discover what they actually said and how to apply them in his life. In the beginning, absolutely no one knew about the *ACIM* project, which they carefully fit in around the edges of their official jobs.

Several months before the dilemma of having no one to talk with became acute, Bill's friend at the hospital, Cal Hatcher, had approached him about his desire to discuss religious or spiritual matters. Bill assured him he was talking to the wrong guy, because he had no knowledge or interest in such subjects at that time. Therefore, when *ACIM* turned his values, his assumptions, and his very life upside down, Bill instinctively knew Cal was the person he could trust with their secret. Although this thought system was entirely different from anything he had learned or that psychology taught, it seemed imminently practical and thus very appealing. He was anxious to try it out. Predictably, Helen was more than upset when he told her that Cal would now be his confidant. Bill wrote:

> Afterward [after making the arrangement with Cal], when I would type up the three copies, I would give Helen the original, keep one copy and give Cal the other each morning. For several years we met in my office early in the morning, before 8am, because we had to meet before scheduled activities. I would go over the material that I had typed the preceding day and try to explain it to Cal. This was my attempt to learn what it meant by trying to teach it to him, and it was enormously helpful. Cal knew much more than I did about the Bible, which was all very new to me. He had a critical, inquiring mind, and wanted to know what this meant, what the implications might be. This gave me my first opportunity to try to find out what I thought about it. Our talks were extremely helpful and made it possible for Helen and me to continue even when I felt we were not learning it together. It was much more difficult to go over the material with Helen.[26]

Although Cal proved to be a much needed partner in studying the material, Bill was deeply disturbed that he and Helen seemed unable to decide harmoniously *how* to use *ACIM* to work on their relationship, much less actually put it into practice. In fact, he felt their situation worsened as the *Course* continued to unfold. Helen became increasingly hostile as she projected onto Bill the sense of threat engendered by the material, and from his perspective, she actively attempted to undermine him. He took the *Course* statements seriously and literally when it referred to "you, Helen and Bill," which they later translated throughout the books into "the two of you" or "you and your brother." He agonized over the observable lack of progress with her; he used to say it was impossible to express how much this seeming failure with Helen upset him. And his ongoing angst with her was just a subplot in the pressure cooker that was the highly competitive medical center. As he commented later, "Much of the time what I felt was a constant temptation to walk the plank."[27]

Because increased upset is such a common experience for new students of *ACIM*, I believe it should be addressed. I have worked with many people who found that at some point in their early practice of the *Course*, life seemed to get worse rather than better. In fact, in my classes I warn students this is likely to happen and that it's reasonable to ask why they should embark on a practice that might stir up more upset. The answer, of course, is that sooner or later it's our only choice. Addressing our fears is ultimately required of everyone, not to inflict punishment but because this is how to release them. Bill found—as everyone eventually finds—that tolerance for pain is only so high. The introduction to the text speaks of removing the blocks to the awareness of love's presence. When we ask for help, we become aware of those blocks or fears so that we can address them directly and make happier, more sane and peaceful choices.

Since Bill and Helen were devoting extensive time to the *Course* project, but seemed to be getting nowhere with healing their relationship, Bill decided to test its premises with other, less volatile relationships that needed attention. If it could produce changes with a difficult colleague, he thought, it ought to work anywhere. Judy Skutch Whitson recalls Bill's telling her more than a few times, with unusual (for him) seriousness, about one of his first dedicated attempts to practice *ACIM* as the lessons were being dictated.

Art was co-director of the department of psychology with Bill. [In fact, he had been instrumental in Bill's coming to Columbia in the first place.] They were friends, had had a long walk together professionally, and I think accepted and liked each other. Then Bill hired Helen and all hell broke loose. Art didn't like Helen, really didn't like her, and had great antipathy toward her. Bill told me that Art thought she certainly did excellent research work but that she was too much trouble, a high-maintenance lady and distracting at meetings. He found her sharp; in other words, they didn't get along. At times, he asked Bill to fire Helen and Bill dug in, unequivocally refusing to do that.

Of course, Art had no idea what was going on in their office as far as the *Course* was concerned. As dictation on the workbook began, Bill recognized it provided a process one could pragmatically use to change relationships or re-envision them. Wondering if it would really work, he chose Art, who was currently not talking to him, for his experiment. Art now had as much antipathy toward Bill as Helen and was including him as a target of his anger. This fractured relationship with Art over Helen's presence was a major contributing factor to the chaos that made birthing the *Course* so difficult.

Art wouldn't even look him in the eye, so Bill decided to go to his office in the morning before work, knowing Art always went in early to read the paper. On his first attempt, Bill knocked on the door and asked if he could come in; Art didn't look up from his newspaper. Bill entered and sat quietly on a chair right across from Art's desk. Art never put down his newspaper, so after a while Bill left. Every day for about a month Bill went in and Art never put down his paper or acknowledged him. By then he felt much more comfortable and knew that he was guided to persevere. One day he said, "Good morning, Art," who grunted from behind his newspaper. For Bill, this was a very big sign. After several months of this routine, Bill had an early morning appointment elsewhere and came to his office later than usual. Around lunchtime, Bill saw Art, who said,

"Where were you this morning? You didn't come in." Bill told him of his appointment and that was the beginning of their talking again.

Not long after that, all the upper staff members were invited to a conference where Bill and Art represented their department at the university. Checking into the hotel, although not together, each found the hotel had overbooked and there was a shortage of rooms. The hotel staff asked those who knew each other to double up. Art approached Bill and asked if he would like to share a room, stating, "There is no one here I would rather be with." Bill said he would be delighted, and after unpacking their things, they went down to the bar before dinner. As they sat there talking and waiting for dinner to be announced, Art took three almonds from a little bowl on their table, passed them to Bill, and said, "Edgar Cayce says they're very good for you." Bill said he nearly dropped his front teeth. "Edgar Cayce, Art?" Art replied, "Yes, he's this very famous psychic. During the war I was stationed in Virginia Beach and I used to go to his house for lunch on Sundays. He was really a very great guy." Bill said at that moment he knew it was over. The situation with Art was the first time he had deliberately practiced *ACIM*, and of course, their changed relationship improved the department's functioning. This quiet way was typical of Bill. He didn't go to Art saying, "Look, I know how you're feeling about the situation and I don't blame you, but you're making me really uncomfortable and here are the reasons for my decisions," etc. Instead, he sat there in the chair quietly.[28]

The mention of Edgar Cayce was so meaningful to Bill because shortly before Bill's urgent speech to Helen that precipitated the onset of *ACIM*, he had read a book by Hugh Lynn Cayce, Edgar's son. Although the claims regarding Cayce's abilities seemed preposterous by his own scientific standards, Bill sensed inwardly that the stories about him were legitimate. On that basis, he planned a trip for Helen and himself to Virginia Beach to meet Hugh Lynn. Helen resisted going as she didn't want to be considered a "psychic" or be associated with them, although she was privately impressed with her growing psychic abilities. She was often ambivalent about rejecting or embracing aspects of herself. Their visit took place in the fall of 1965 after her several months of "heightened visual imagery," just before the *Course* began in October. Bill always thought that trip gave her "permission" to open up to her immense intuitive abilities and also provided some rudimentary preparation for him. He began to think "outside the box" and looked with growing, though quiet, appreciation of his own intuitive abilities.

The healing with Art was only one of a number of relationships that seemed smoother as Bill attempted to follow his own guidance and the *Course* instructions. Those around him began to notice that the department seemed less harried, and his secretary, having no idea of the real meaning behind what she was saying, would periodically proclaim, "Oh, Dr. Thetford has just performed another miracle."[29] Or a close colleague, the chairman of the psychology department at the University of Chicago, would say, "There's Bill, walking on water again."[30] Bill himself felt that by the time he left the medical center, he had reached his goal—healing all his relationships there—all, of course, except the primary one with Helen.

Although neither Bill nor Helen had been consciously interested in religious or spiritual matters before *ACIM* dictation began, Bill quickly recognized the universal nature of the material and began a serious inquiry into the world's major religious traditions and teachings. In his search for corroboration, he discovered the nondualistic teaching of Advaita Vedanta from India and immediately saw its parallels to the *Course*. Thus he dubbed *ACIM* the "Christian Vedanta" because of its use of Christian language to present these truths. He became more impressed with the *Course* as his study deepened, finding it integrated and synthesized the best of the teachings he investigated—and it was practical. He read extensively in his newly discovered field of interest and became extremely well versed in this formerly uninteresting subject. Many of Bill's friends and colleagues said he had an astounding capacity to absorb vast quantities of written material quickly, a valuable trait given that he had five thousand years of mystical traditions to explore. Years later, he noted with some disappointment that the PAS, on which he had lavished so much time and attention, did not explain or even address the spiritual dimension of our life experience. How unexpectedly our lives can change and even reverse course.

As Bill was deepening his research into metaphysics, he became intrigued with a chapter about mysticism and schizophrenia in the book, *Higher States of Consciousness,* by John White. It was written by Kenneth Wapnick, a young psychologist, and Bill shared it with one of his graduate students, Father Benedict, a Capuchin friar. Benedict, one of the three or four people entrusted with their "guilty secret," as Bill jokingly called it, subsequently became friendly with Ken and later introduced him to Bill and Helen. Shortly after they met in late 1972, Ken left New York for Israel to live in a monastery, presumably to be his permanent home, having converted from Judaism to Catholicism. Once there, however, he couldn't get that meeting out of his mind; he dreamt of it, aware of a very strong connection with both of them, especially Helen. His guidance prevailed and in the spring of 1973, as if on cue, he returned to New York (the last place he thought he wanted to be) to meet with them again and to find out more about the manuscript his new friends had mentioned to him earlier. One look and that intriguing book "knocked him off his feet," to use his words—his fate was sealed. He notified his Israeli friends of his change of plans and re-established himself in New York to be close to "*ACIM* Central." Thus, as the dictation was concluding, Kenneth Wapnick officially entered the picture, commencing three more years of editing, rereading, checking for errors, and improving section and chapter titles.

As if there were not enough turmoil and high drama around Bill and Helen's busy professional lives, punctuated with general angst and their unrelenting distress with each other, Ken's arrival stirred the pot even more. Despite serious difficulties, they were extremely codependent and genuinely and deeply cared for one another; introducing a third party into the mix was more than a little unsettling for Bill. Ken's services were badly needed and truly appreciated, but they came at a price from his perspective. Helen and Ken's apparent mutual adoration, which developed right away, was the perfect setup to trigger within Bill a deep sense of rejection and betrayal. Notice the word is *trigger* and not *cause*, as that feeling of rejection was already in place. This new situation brought those painful feelings into conscious awareness, exactly what the *Course* and life under its guidance is designed to do in order to be free of them.

The harshness and sarcasm evident in some of the following stories and quotes is not an indictment of Ken, Helen, or Bill himself. Helen and Ken were, and are, brilliant, dedicated, and of incalculable value in the *ACIM* saga, executing their special functions on schedule and as promised. Bill's upset was clearly his own responsibility, which he ultimately recognized, but at this point, he responded like most of humanity, not realizing that the difficult characters in his "drama" were merely reflecting back to him the unloving projections of his own ego and the fears he had thus far refused to own. Bill remembers in his autobiography:

> Helen and I were working desperately on a chapter for the *Comprehensive Textbook of Psychiatry*. We were on a deadline and we had to turn out a lot of material. We had decided to cover one personality theorist a week, which was the only way we could get it all done. I was doing all the reference work and Helen was writing the material. It was a big job, and it had to be done well.
>
> Ken surfaced in the midst of all this. Helen and I were both edgy, partly because we were trying to get our work done. I also had a lot of other things I had to do. We were sharp with each other. Ken was appalled at our relationship. Here we had this holy book—this wonderful spiritual material—and we didn't know how to relate to each other. The two of us were bickering and carrying on in a terrible way. We were obviously not being loving and holy. Ken decided he was going to demonstrate how relationships could be healed, to demonstrate perfect love and that sort of thing, how to do it properly. He would take Helen on as the demonstration and show me the power of love—or holiness—in action. I was apparently to learn from watching.[1]

Ken observed:

> That first summer I spent a lot of time with them. They were writing

this chapter for a very prestigious publication on personality theories. They would argue and fight—it was awful. We were just getting to know one another so we spent a lot of time together. When we talked about the *Course* and the path that led me to them, there was no acrimony, none whatsoever. We would finish, they'd go back to the chapter [for the textbook] and start going at each other. It was almost like Bill and Helen had a pact that they would not screw up the *Course*. They would screw everything else up, but they would be faithful to this.[2]

Bill continued:

Helen was susceptible to all this attention and massive devotion from Ken. It was amazing; she now had the word of Jesus and the whole thing—this was it. Ken thought Helen was sort of the Mother of God, the Virgin Mary. Helen thought Ken was one of the world's greatest saints of all time. She would say things like, "I can't think of any saint in history who was as beatific as Ken." So I would have lunch with the Virgin Mary and the world's greatest saint. Of course, I was the world's greatest sinner; I was the terrible guilty party. I'm not sure why I was guilty; that was more obscure. But someone had to be guilty, so I was it. Probably one thing was that I was not being loving enough with Helen. I wasn't impressed by the fact that she was the Mother of God. This sort of thing went on for quite a while and I was both relieved and annoyed by it all.[3]

Clearly, Bill felt both replaced by Ken and, by his own acknowledgment, some panic that he was not following the injunction to heal his relationship with Helen. What would happen over that perceived failure? He also acknowledged that Ken tried to be inclusive, but the situation remained difficult.

Ken offers a revealing, and very different, perspective. When I asked if he had felt as troubled by Bill as Bill had been by him, he answered that he had not. He said Bill would so thoroughly hide his true feelings that he often didn't know Bill was upset with him until he heard about it from someone else. He would then approach Bill to address the problem. In his experience, there was very little tension between them and none at all when the *Course* dominated their discussions. He acknowledged that Bill and Helen's relationship was terrible in many respects and that, indeed, it did get worse after he arrived. His role was often that of a sounding board as they complained about each other. I asked Ken what they could still find to argue about after all those years and he answered,

> They would recycle. It was always the same—you said that, and you did this, and didn't do that. I was there and I don't even remember. It didn't matter; they had a strong love-hate relationship, they didn't like each other. Their personalities were so different. I'm sure they argued about me, but not in front of me. Helen would tell me about it later.

> Helen thought Bill never fully understood the *Course*, so that would come up occasionally. They would argue a lot about Bill's choice of partners; that was a big one. Then there was Harold, who lived with Bill for a year or so. Helen didn't like Harold at all and let him know that in no uncertain terms. Helen got very angry when Bill asked if I would see Harold [professionally], which I did. Conversely, if one of them was in trouble or needed help, the other one would be right there. They were very supportive of each other, very faithful to each other in that way. It was very strange, very unusual, I was *very* struck by it.[4]

Because Ken and Helen were so close, he offers an entry point into a third perspective—Helen's.

> One of the ways you could see their ̶ ̶ rences was that Helen was overtly aggressive and Bill was passive agg ̶ ̶ ̶ e; you always knew where you stood with Helen. Also, Helen was m ̶ ̶ ̶ ore aware of her anger than Bill was. Helen was clear and she real ̶ ̶ ̶ tried to justify it; I knew her very, very well and it was kind of a ̶ ̶ ̶ She did not forgive Bill, did not want to forgive Bill, would not fo ̶ ̶ ̶ ̶ , and she wasn't say-

ing this was a spiritual position. Bill, on the other hand, was not aware. I can give you one example that typified the whole issue. They had three offices, an outer office and their two private offices, very secluded. You have to picture this. We were sitting in Helen's office; there was Helen and her desk, I sat against the wall adjacent to her desk, and Bill would be standing in the doorway, which he would do since every once in a while he would go to his office and smoke. I was literally in the middle. Bill, who did this more often than Helen, tried to put me in the middle [of their battle]. I don't remember what it was about, but they were at each other's throats. They were sniping at each other, the tension was building, and Bill turned to me, asking me to support him against Helen, saying something like, "Wouldn't you agree, Kenneth?" It was obvious they were both contributing, but Bill, I know, was not conscious of what he was doing. He was being very snide; he was wonderful with words, a master. I finessed it by saying, "Well, you're both doing it," which was true. Bill stormed out, really angry; Helen looked at me and said, "Now you see what I'm up against." She meant Bill's being passive aggressive and not knowing it; that was very, very common. He was just not aware of his own anger and how he was expressing it. Helen was just as much at fault, but she was right in your face, she knew what she was doing. Helen was clear, Bill was not, and that was often the problem. Since he was so good with words, he could make a comment and not even know he was doing it. That particular morning typified, I think, what their relationship was like.

Basically, Bill blamed Helen for problem^n the relationship. Even after Helen died, I noticed there was a lot o^ ^terness. That's what Helen had trouble understanding. When she s^ ^ll didn't understand the *Course*, that is part of what she meant. ^ ^now, he thought the relationship was not healed because Helen v^ ^t change her mind. He was always blaming her and feeling that^ ^Helen would change, he would be healed. A lot of Bill's and ^ ^ssions and our work together had to do with that. That was a ^ ^for Bill, making it impossible for him because Helen was not going to change her mind. On the other hand, she did not blame Bill for the relationship, she blamed him for just being Bill. She was very clear about her own choices, how they kept the acrimony going. She was brilliant, very insightful and basically said, "I'm not going to do it [forgive him]." She would be very clear with people, "Do what I write, not what I do." We spent many, many hours—as an understatement—talking about Bill and what she was doing. What really impressed me about Bill was that, despite what he felt, there was a deep sense of commitment and trust to whatever this was with Helen.[5]

Helen and Bill—the good times

During the year 1965–1966, as an exception to their established norm, Helen and Bill's relationship did improve. They diligently practiced the *Course* lessons and, as promised, their hostility lessened considerably but they didn't keep it up. Ken said, "They tried very, very hard to look at their projections, accept them, and just be responsible for them. I have some of their letters in my book [*Absence From Felicity*], plus they both told me about this.[6] Then it got to be too much and they couldn't sustain it. It got worse and worse, and when I met them, their relationship was at an all-time low."[7]

To do them justice and to balance out the picture, however, Ken said the three of them had many wonderful and funny times together. They laughed a lot, kidded each other, and shared a common sense of humor and total devotion to the *Course*. As contradictory and nearly impossible as it sounds, they actually shared great love and trust in one another that carried them through some very difficult times. Others around Bill and Helen also commented on their real love for one another, though it was often eclipsed by their antagonism.

When Ken returned to New York from Israel in April 1973, exactly how he was going to be included in this monumental project was a bit unclear. Since Ken was now frequently in their offices, Bill found him a part-time job to justify his spending so much time there, observing normal protocol as much as possible to avoid arousing suspicion about their hidden work. As Ken looked over the previously edited material, now referred to as the Hugh Lynn Cayce version (so named because Helen and Bill had made a copy for Hugh Lynn and presented it to him as a gift in gratitude for his considerable support and encouragement), he felt additional work was needed and he was correct.[8] Helen and Bill had already gone through the text more than once, and though they had removed much personal material as well as references to Freud, Jung, Cayce, and several friends and colleagues, the capitalization was inconsistent, some section headings were not clear, and some personal information remained. Bill was burned out by the initial editing process, but he recognized the need for more and had been urging Helen, although with ambivalence, for several months to join him in renewing the process; she refused. Now, however, with growing admiration for Ken—tireless, enthusiastic, and ready to serve her completely—she was persuaded to start another round of editing.

When *ACIM* dictation first began, Bill and Helen had no idea what was unfolding; they presumed it was a long and comprehensive answer to their request for a better way to live. Therefore, Helen wrote everything as it appeared in her mind without discrimination. Why not? After all, it was for them. Bill often had a list of questions for Helen to ask the Voice, and answering them seemed helpful in facilitating her ability to receive. As the material continued to appear, it became clear that some of it was not intended to be part of the *Course* itself, but was personal advice, answers to specific questions, something of a three-way conversation. Now it is obvious that the nonpersonal *Course* is for anyone who chooses to practice it, but that did not dawn on them until the Voice settled into a monologue format, rather than the dialogue that seemed predominant in the early text.

As various versions of the *Course* have become available since the original publication in 1976, controversy has surfaced over who did what kind of editing. Judith Skutch Whitson remarked that although she was not yet involved during the time of the editing, she was included in subsequent decisions that characterized Bill and Helen's interactions:

> Helen was totally in charge. Bill made suggestions gently, Ken sat by quietly and unobtrusively, and Helen would "rule the roost." For those who promote the idea that Ken made all the final decisions and had final editorial approval, quite the opposite was the case. I remember during the proofreading of the "blues" [final copy before printing], when challenges to inappropriate capitalizations were made, Ken would just shrug and Helen would always get her way. The same was true even when it came to the color of the book's cover. Bill and I wanted blue; Ken also felt that would be an appropriate color, but Helen was adamant about black and would not change her mind. Finally Ken quietly queried if we should ask the book's Author for a decision. Helen made a sour face but agreed that we should be silent, ask the question, and listen for the answer. When

we opened our eyes, she muttered, "Okay, he says blue, but a *very dark blue!*" And so, for the cloth-covered first edition, it was a very dark blue indeed.[9]

Ken confirmed Helen's position as "ruler of the roost" and said absolutely no one, not even the Author of the *Course*, could persuade her to take another position once her mind was made up.

"Ken was difficult to know at first," Bill writes of this editing time. "He was always nice and he was going to work on Helen, not on me. It was a difficult triangle when the three of us were together. After some exposure to all this, I told him I couldn't stand it and I thought there was a lot of spiritual grandiosity going on. I didn't think that was the spirit of the *Course* and I was fed up with it!"[10] Though he didn't express it directly, Bill's early and biased perception of this "difficult triangle" was that Ken talked down to him and interceded between himself and Helen.

Ken returned to Israel in June 1973, but not before extracting a promise from Helen that she would come over for a visit. That August, Helen, Louis, and Bill joined him for what Bill described as a very meaningful, magical trip—one that brought an unexplainable closure as they revisited some of the places he had enjoyed on his 1953 trip. He particularly identified with the Holy Land, as well as Egypt and Greece, which comes as no surprise; his various psychic and trance readings placed him in those locales at major turning points in the evolution of his consciousness.

Bill acknowledged that Ken's help and knowledge of the country made possible a much more meaningful adventure than they might have had, and he was grateful for his contribution. A highlight for all of them was an extraordinary experience they shared while visiting Qumran, the site where the Dead Sea scrolls were discovered. Helen suddenly shifted consciousness, as if flipping back in time:

As they approached the actual area where the scrolls had been found, Helen abruptly stopped, visibly shaken. She stared at the opening of the cave and suddenly burst into tears. Although Bill and Louis tried desperately to comfort her, she was unable to speak for almost five minutes. When she finally regained her composure, she spoke so quietly that the others had to strain to hear her.[11]

"This is the cave," she said in a tremulous voice; "this is the cave where I saw the scroll that said, "GOD IS.""[12] None of the others said a word; there was nothing to say.

A short while later, while they were breathing in the historical atmosphere of the Dead Sea surroundings, Helen began musing half to herself. "You know," she said, "something's wrong with the water level. It's too low; it used to be much higher." Bill, who took none of Helen's thoughts lightly, opened a guide book he had bought when they had arrived in Israel and began thumbing through it. "Very interesting, Helen," he remarked. "It says here that at the time of the Essenes, the water level of the Dead Sea was a good deal higher." Everyone was quiet and finally Helen, visibly moved, remarked quietly, "This is the holiest place on earth."[13]

L ife was very hard for Bill on returning home. He felt depressed and lonely after the breakup of a long-term personal relationship with Charles Parrish and shut out of the "special relationship" that he perceived Helen and Ken were pursuing without him. Bill was also increasingly dissatisfied with the absence of spiritual focus in his job. He even considered leaving the medical center entirely, wanting only to hurry up, complete the last clerical details of the *Course*, and call the whole thing finished. Both Helen and Bill were clear that marketing and distribution were not theirs to do once the final editing was complete in 1975, and not knowing how else to proceed, Bill made twelve copies of the entire work, put them in thesis binders, and locked them in the bottom drawer of his file cabinet.

Obviously, this monumental work was not destined to remain in the bottom drawer. In the spring of 1975, through a serendipitous series of events, Bill and Helen placed *ACIM* into the capable hands of Judith Skutch (Whitson), who became the undisputed matriarch of *A Course In Miracles* and ultimately provided for its publication and widespread distribution. Bill had become intrigued with a new acquaintance, Douglas Dean—a scientist interested in paranormal healing—and had made plans to have lunch with him. Dean rescheduled their meeting so he could bring his friend, Judith Skutch, for he felt strongly that she should accompany him. Judy was known as a "cosmic catalyst and den mother to parapsychology," a leader in the field of consciousness exploration and the paranormal. On

May 29, 1975, Judy, Douglas, Helen, Bill, and Ken had lunch in the faculty dining room at Columbia. During lunch, as their conversation evolved, Judy found herself unexpectedly saying to Helen, "You're hearing a voice, aren't you?" Everyone was stunned. Therefore, after lunch in the privacy of Bill's office, the three collaborators showed Judy and Douglas the *Course*, still a secret known only to a handful of people.

> We gave a copy to Judy to take home and read. Apparently, that evening when she began reading the *Course*, she couldn't put it down and read it the night through. She was overwhelmed with the *Course*'s material. Helen and I liked Judy immediately, and we all—she, Ken, and I—became fast friends. Judy's arrival on the scene was both fortuitous and miraculous. She had a very specific role, although we didn't know it in the beginning.[1]

Almost immediately, Judy became an integral part of the *ACIM* enterprise, and Ken, Helen, and Bill spent more and more time at the Skutch home in Manhattan. Shortly after their meeting, they began to discuss the possibility of publishing the material. Bill and Helen would not have tackled this on their own, but Judy had the necessary skill and enthusiasm, and it became a serious consideration. They showed the work to several friends possibly interested in publishing it, but all wanted to change it in some way. As with every decision related to the *Course*, they jointly consulted their guidance and were told to leave it intact and publish it themselves. They questioned this advice from a financial perspective but were told to commit and trust. They did. The day after committing to its publication, Judy received a call from Reed Erickson, a satisfied and inspired student (of a xeroxed copy), who said he felt *ACIM* needed to be published officially and that he was sending a check for $60,000 to fund the first five thousand sets. (Originally, the text, workbook, and teacher's manual were bound as separate books and later combined into one volume.)

Several years before their meeting, Judy and her husband at the time, Robert Skutch, had founded a nonprofit organization, the Foundation for Parasensory Investigation, to help fund research for parapsychology. Deciding that name did not convey the purpose of *ACIM*, they all agreed to retitle it the Foundation for Inner Peace, and in 1975 Helen entrusted to it the copyright to *A Course In Miracles*. As of October 2003, the original copyright entered into the public domain. However, the Foundation for Inner Peace, the parent organization, and its sister organization, the Foundation for A Course In Miracles, are the repositories of all original archival materials.

With Judy now on the scene, the trio had evolved into a quartet and the dynamics changed quite dramatically. The anger between Bill and Helen was not healed, but it was diffused and deflected. An alliance was formed with Bill clearly allying himself with Judy and against Helen. (This does not imply Judy was against Helen, quite the contrary.) Ken recalls:

Bill became a big supporter of Judy's; they were very, very close. Since I was identified with Helen, it's as if sides had been chosen as far as they were concerned, and Helen would get annoyed if I spent time with Bill. She withdrew more and more. She and Bill argued less because he wasn't around as much. He spent more and more time with Judy and I spent more time with Helen and Louis. We would meet at Judy's apartment, then Helen and I would go home and Bill would stay. From his point of view, Judy was a breath of fresh air; he was very comfortable with her, enjoying a relationship that didn't include Helen. Helen had her own relationship with Judy, who was now sometimes the recipient of her anger, but still they were close. When both Bill and Judy moved to the West Coast in 1978, that was the end as far as Helen was concerned. She was very bitter about that, but I think Bill felt a sense of freedom. That's when everything changed for him, like he was let out of prison. But again, to Helen's credit, she was always well aware of what she was doing and that made dealing with her easier in a way. She was very possessive of me and other people. She was furious at Bill, but in fact she knew that I knew, and I knew that she knew, and we really didn't talk much about it because what's the point? That's how she was, how she wanted to be.

I think when Judy came along they were very happy to step back. They both felt comfortable turning the reins over to her and gave a big sigh of relief, "Okay we're done." They both made the decision and it was not right or wrong, it's just what they did. Bill felt a clear sense of mission and purpose for this *Course*; Helen felt that, too, and they were very faithful to it. However, they did not see that they had to be faithful to each other in the sense of healing the relationship and they did not feel their role included anything else. I think it was unfortunate that they abdicated all responsibility for the *Course*. They gave it to Judy to take to the world and basically withdrew from any kind of leadership or authority. If they hadn't, the *Course* would have gone a different way. Although nothing is better nor worse, there are alternate scripts and I think there was clearly a script for Helen, Bill, and myself to have more of a sense of responsibility for shepherding the *Course*. It was also very clear to me that Helen could have written down more things, but she refused. Bill, as you know, . . . had such conflict over being an authority, being a teacher, that he went the other way—he became a nonauthority. It was always bizarre when we had those meetings and Bill said nothing as the most outrageous things were being said. Not that he had to say something, but it was clear he chose not to. I think it was a real fear of being an authority, which he was. Until that meeting in Hawaii in 1985 [a one-time workshop featuring the early *Course* "family" sponsored by the Unity Church in Honolulu], I had never heard him speak publicly with a prepared talk, rather than simply answering questions, and he was masterful, very funny, very good, a wonderful voice. But seeing his fear of standing up and professing, that never left me. He had a wonderful presence, was a wonderful speaker, but he chose not to do it, and Helen, who was not afraid of teaching—she was an excellent teacher—nonetheless, did not want any more of this *Course*.[2]

Bill was innately a private person, an introvert, so he chose not to draw attention to himself or seek publicity, although privately he was happy with his accomplishments. He avoided everything that would bring him notoriety related to *ACIM*; he gave very few interviews for print media about the *Course* and did not make TV appearances or write books under his own name, although he substantively assisted others with theirs. Until the end of their lives, neither Bill nor Helen had any desire to be in the spotlight; they consistently withdrew from public attention.

By the mid 1970s, the *Course* was finished and its next phase was unfolding with Judy at the helm. The four principals—Judy, Bill, Helen, and Ken—had established a pattern of meeting regularly at the Skutch apartment in the late afternoons. Judy confirms Ken's observations that when Bill and Helen were working on their scholastic endeavors—about 90 percent of their time—hostility was the norm. However, when they were involved with *Course* dictation and transcription, or what needed to be done with it, they were of one mind, merging as "Bilen," a contraction of Bill and Helen denoting their beautiful sense of communion and shared purpose. So there were times during those late afternoon meetings when all was tranquil and others when it most certainly was not.

On more than one occasion at the Skutches, as tension between them would mount, Bill could keep his composure sufficiently to make light of the situation, diffusing it before it became a problem with yet another application of his quick wit and grand sense of humor. Judy recalls:

> Bill was taking a break from some intense stuff, and then we decided there should be a musical of *ACIM* and Bill started to make up songs based on different shows. Bill announced that as a take-off on *Call Me Madam*, they would present one called *Call Me Mad*, whereupon he gave Helen, who had a beautiful operatic-type singing voice, her lines:

I hear voices but there's no one there, I hear voices but the room is bare.

Then Bill would enter with his little soft-shoe dance number, singing:

You sure need analyzing and it's not so surprisin'

> and they would sing their parts contrapuntally. Bill's impromptu musical
> numbers provided those rare occasions when Helen could not contain her
> laughter. Though perhaps unwilling to give credit, they each recognized
> the other's beautiful singing voice, but only under those circumstances
> did they ever sing together. Both of them adored Gilbert and Sullivan
> musicals and both were very articulate. Bill could kid around at my
> house, though never at the office, and periodically, to everyone's delight,
> he would add characters to the *ACIM* "musical."[3]

What a loss that the words were never recorded for posterity!

On other occasions, not even Bill's sense of humor was enough to end
a dispute. When he reached the end of his rope, he would simply walk
out of the room in a wave of passive aggression, an act of stinging rejection. During those moments, he must have been driven to uncontrollable
distress, because virtually everyone I've spoken with has commented on
Bill's extreme patience with Helen as she acted out her more preposterous
ego positions. At other times, their personal war would escalate even
further. Judy remembers the following example in vivid detail:

> Bill, Helen, Ken, and I were in our New York apartment late one after-
> noon, a sparkling, unusually clear October day. It was so impressive that
> everyone had considered going for a walk, but it never materialized. We
> were talking and Helen and Bill got into a scrap. They were sitting next
> to each other on a loveseat opposite where Ken and I were sitting, and
> it was like watching two cats suddenly rear up their backs and spit at
> each other. Characteristically, Helen would attack and Bill would defend.
> Finally, the words were flying and Ken knew enough to get up, kindly
> take Bill by the arm, and guide him out on our back landing for a smoke.
> Bill was smoking up a storm in those days. Helen stood up—she was very

erect for a tiny person as she deliberately practiced her posture—and she was seething! Her fists were clinched and her shoulders heaved with rage. She went to the window and looked out at Central Park, a happy, busy, peaceful scene—people riding bikes, mothers and children, nannies, dogs. She was looking but seeing nothing, just looking out the window and shaking. I made the mistake of putting my arm around her shoulder and said, "Mama (she liked for me to call her Mama), why can't you be a little nicer to him?" which was really a dumb thing to do.

Of course, I was so uncomfortable as I had just witnessed the "parents" fighting. Helen turned on me and lifted her hands like a cat, almost to rake her very long, well-kept, manicured nails—this day painted red— down my cheek, saying, "You stupid, stupid child! Don't you know I would have followed him to the ends of the earth? I would have left everything, my work, my life, everything to be with him wherever he said, and he didn't want me![4]

A perfect example of the incisive observation: "Hell hath no fury like a woman scorned!"[5]

Judy continued, rhetorically, with a smile:

So what would the Holy Spirit do with something like that? It's as if He said, "You know you can't have him; I can't do that for you. However, I can keep him tied to you the rest of your life. How would you like to write A Course In Miracles? I'm going to give you a little bit every day and he's going to be so intrigued, believe me, he'll never leave you." There was all this furious, romantic rage and fantasy life, a lot of fantasy life, in her mind with Bill. This was not the only time. I once saw this same rage come out with Ken, where she literally scratched him, drawing blood, over his leaving for a counseling appointment when she wanted him to remain.[6]

Years later, when the Skutches and Bill, after much consideration, moved to California, Helen was so angry she wouldn't talk. As they walked out the door, she said jealously to Judy, "I always knew you would take him away from me!"

Helen and Bill's particular function of bringing the *Course* into the world did not give them a free pass to enlightenment. To benefit from the life-altering change of perspective taught through the *Course*, they would have to practice like everyone else. At this point, both their lives were certifiably a mess despite their brilliance and accomplishments. And all who feel hopeless, take note: Their egos were just like ours. Revealing their "dark sides" encourages us to do the same to facilitate our healing. It is fascinating and reassuring to know that from such intractable egocentricity, the *Course*, one of the most beautiful and profound teachings on earth, sprang forth easily and without compromise. Helen and Bill, despite fearing they were not healing as they should, steadfastly set aside their egos to produce it. Even in the midst of her frequent panic, Helen could completely suspend her ego and allow herself to enter into her right mind where the material existed already complete. Carefully and with great integrity, she listened and scribed. It seems she could move back and forth between her ego and spirit, her wrong and right mind, with more skill than almost anyone on the planet. For her, the veil was very thin.

Bill tried to define this most conflicted relationship. He always commented on his open and easy relationship with Louis, with nothing clouding their friendship, but lamented the difficulty he encountered with Helen despite his fascination with her "inner life" and his deep trust and respect for her. He also actually loved her very much. It sounds similar to LeRoy Zemke's comment about their enduring love for one another.

> On the other hand, my relationship with Helen was so complicated. I think I learned from it that love would persist despite everything that seemed to block it and interfere with it. I was aware of feeling close to Helen at some level that transcended rationality and relationship barriers.

It seemed to go against any form of logic. I wasn't that fond of Helen, but there was a deep love that continued in spite of everything. It had nothing to do with anything. It seemed to represent our joining in love and cooperation. We tried to do something that transcended our egos. That was the thing that seemed real, the only thing that seemed really to persist. Once having done that, there was no breaking away from it. It was a commitment that went on forever. If love is eternal, when you make that kind of commitment, you have made it. It doesn't have anything to do with the usual things about commitments.[7]

In retrospect, every position, encounter, and opportunity was essential for Bill's evolution, enabling him to tackle the huge assignment they had accepted, one they both recognized as a prior agreement. We can view our lives the same way, recognizing that each encounter and situation is not an accident, but part of our individualized curriculum for awakening. Helen was not the villain, nor was the absent father or any of the "learning partners" who paraded through Bill's life.

Early conditioning promotes the belief that our particular strong suits—those areas of vocation and avocation that come so naturally—our possessions, friends or family, and everything else exist for our own self-aggrandizement. The *Course*'s aim is to undo that perspective. It encourages us always to ask, "What is this for? How are we using these gifts?" Bill developed talents and acquired experience, as do we all, and was motivated by *ACIM*'s teachings to move from a sense of specialness—the desire to appropriate his particular portfolio of talents for personal gain—to his own unique special function, using those same gifts for a higher purpose. This shift in purpose provides the ideal opportunity for the unfolding of our own service and, thus, for maximal healing.

Such is the Holy Spirit's kind perception of specialness; His use of what you made, to heal instead of harm. To each He gives a special function in salvation he alone can fill; a part for only him. Nor is the plan complete until he finds his special function, and fulfills the part assigned to him, to make himself complete within a world where incompletion rules. . . .

Yet while in time, there is still much to do. And each must do what is allotted him, for on his part does all the plan depend. He has a special part in time for so he chose, and choosing it, he made it for himself. His wish was not denied but changed in form, to let it serve his brother and himself, and thus become a means to save instead of lose.[8]

One might reasonably ask, "What kind of healing? I'm not sick." *A Course In Miracles* reminds us that, indeed, our minds are sick; we engage daily in judgmental, unloving, defensive thoughts and behaviors that specifically interfere with our happiness. We need take only a cursory, unbiased look at the condition of the world to know that something is terribly wrong. It appears to be the domain of pain and suffering, and for most, that is the case. *ACIM* teaches, however, this need not be. Our beliefs, attitudes, self-absorption, and attachment to having our way, our unconscious programming, our endless attack, all can and must be changed if we are to be free of insecurity and lack. And it shows us how.

Bill was determined to heal his attitudes and practice shifting his purpose from specialness to special function, changing his mind from fear to love and from holding resentments to doing no harm. Like everyone, he began with a divided or compromised dedication, but the *Course* promises that only a little willingness is required to move from our fixed, unhelpful perspectives to those that bring peace of mind. It would have been understandable for Bill to retire once *ACIM* was finished, to rest on his academic laurels, congratulating himself for a job well done, and such a path would certainly have been deserved. But that was not to be his choice. So, fortified with a little willingness, Bill began to move away from his role of esteemed professor and to redefine his primary goal as the practice of forgiveness.

As with all chapters, Bill's time in New York was coming to a close. *ACIM* was finished and Helen, fourteen years his senior, had finally retired. He had managed to keep her employed past the usual retirement age of sixty-five to finish the last *Course* details. Before they had contemplated its publication, Bill had applied for and been granted a six-month sabbatical to begin in July 1976. Through no intentional planning, the first edition of *ACIM* made its debut the month before, in June 1976. With the next stage of the *Course*'s history unfolding, coupled with the fact that it was a difficult time at the university in general, it was a great time to leave. Bill felt he simply could not stay at Columbia now that their "guilty secret," as they called it, was out in the open, a potentially awkward situation for everyone else concerned, as well. (He did not specifically attempt to conceal or reveal his association with *ACIM*. Some colleagues found out about it through conversation or the few articles ultimately written about the work. Others may never have found out.) He had been through a ten-year, life-altering, spiritual overhaul, and to resume his work with traditional psychology as though nothing had happened, no matter how proficient he was, would have been an impossible backward step.

Bill had labored diligently on the PAS for approximately twenty years—teaching, mentoring, researching, writing papers, and teasing out every available bit of insight into how human beings predictably operate. Nevertheless, he closed that door, too. He gave up his research on the ego, which he considered his major academic contribution, as he and Helen became immersed in scribing and attempting to practice *ACIM*. The *Course* had dealt a devastating blow to his favorite topic:

> If you believe you understand something of the "dynamics" of the ego, let me assure you that you understand nothing of it. For of yourself you could not understand it. The study of the ego is not the study of your mind. In fact, the ego enjoys studying itself, and thoroughly approves the undertakings of students who would "analyze" it, thus approving its importance.[1]

After years of statements like this, Bill could feel the foundations of his academic life collapsing. Finally, he found it too bizarre and contradictory to research the intricacies of how egos form and operate on one hand and to actively practice undoing them on the other. He abandoned his search. As Whit Whitson stated at Bill's memorial service, "At the same time he was mapping the ego, he was channeling the process by which we could escape—like mapping an earthquake and then making a plan for how to get out of it."[2]

As his sabbatical was ending in early 1977, Bill took a leave of absence, then applied for another, but the second one was denied. He now had to make a final decision to stay or leave. He chose to leave. Because he had started at Columbia in February 1958, he was eligible for early retirement beginning in 1978. Thus, after beginning his sabbatical in mid 1976, he never returned to his academic or administrative duties. During that period of being employed but not actively working, he made several trips to California, at Judy's invitation, to meet with groups about the *Course*. (Helen also participated in a few of them, although under protest because she strongly disliked traveling.) These trips planted the seed in Bill and introduced the possibility of leaving not only Columbia, but New York itself. The Skutches were entertaining the idea of moving to Tiburon because Judy planned to work on her Ph.D. in San Francisco and, additionally, she knew many people in the Bay area. Also, Jerry Jampolsky, a close friend of Judy's, was a long-time resident of Tiburon. During those visits, Bill realized that both Jerry and Judy needed help with their personal lives and that living close to them would be ideal for offering his assistance. This provided a pivotal rationale for moving.

As he weighed his options, Bill also had to confront his fear about leaving his secure, tenured position, one not easily attained. In addition to his fine reputation and the prestige of being associated with Columbia, he was financially secure. Now he wavered as he looked at giving it all up, like standing with one foot on each side of an ever-widening chasm. It was that branching of the road we all come to eventually and he chose the California path.

Besides leaving academia behind, Bill also cut ties with most of his friends and, obviously, the New York lifestyle. He notes his propensity for leaving finished eras behind. "I talked about it [the *Course*] when it was necessary and then I would leave. Probably a lot of my life has been that way. I do whatever I think is necessary at the time and then I withdraw from it all."[3] In characteristic fashion, he abandoned his life, his career, the person he had been, like a suit of clothes left hanging in the closet. That time was over.

ACIM states: "Fear not that you will be abruptly lifted up and hurled into reality. Time is kind, and if you use it on behalf of reality, it will keep gentle pace with you in your transition. The urgency is only in dislodging your mind from its fixed position here."[4] I think Bill often felt that, indeed, he had been picked up and hurled into California by some volition not his own. Leaving New York was wrenching, even though he was following his excellent guidance in making the choice, the right and inevitable one for him. New York had been the center of Bill's world even during his early days in Washington, D.C., when he frequently traveled there on weekends.

As a sophisticated easterner, he did not fit the casual California stereotype, but he traded his daily coat and tie for jeans and a sweater and prepared to enter this new phase of his life, even if somewhat reluctantly at first. As with the end of any life chapter, there was a sense of loss and some grief at the prospect of leaving New York, but predictably, he found cause for warm good humor regarding his new home, often joking about the California lifestyle.

During the time of Bill's sabbatical and leave-taking, Jim Bolen—a friend of Judy's, devoted *Course* student, and editor of a popular magazine, *Psychic*—wanted to publish an article about *ACIM*. Bill and Helen felt it would be misleading to have it appear in a publication with that name, so at Bill's suggestion it was renamed *New Realities*. The article appeared in April 1977, and the response was overwhelming and widespread. What remained of the first five thousand sets of the *Course*, printed a year earlier with Reed Erickson's generous donation, quickly sold out, requiring an immediate second printing. Thousands of letters and inquiries flooded in, indicating *ACIM*'s immense impact on those first readers. With the word out far and wide, Bill, for better or worse, would never again enjoy anonymity regarding his role in birthing the *Course*.

In the spring of 1978, a friend gave our family a subscription to *New Realities* magazine and the inaugural issue featuring *A Course In Miracles* arrived soon after. As for many, it was my introduction to the *Course*. For many years, I had been looking for answers to only vaguely defined questions, reading endlessly, gradually getting in touch with feelings, looking more honestly at my motivations. I was fascinated with this article, and when I read the Introduction to the text, something in me responded. I could feel the power, the truth, and *life* coming through the words. I ordered the books, and when I finally held the newly delivered, unopened package, I knew without question that this was my way home. I had no clue about the enormity of the shift that was bound to take place; I only knew that my search was over.

I often tell students that "one's life has a life of its own" and Bill's was no exception, nor was mine. During the year Bill was closing the doors on New York, I was devouring the *Course* as the most amazing work I had ever encountered. It was literally irresistible. Second in importance only to raising my children, it became the most all-encompassing element in my life. In May 1978, on the last of Bill's several cross-country trips to finalize his move from New York to Tiburon, our paths crossed in Denver, Colorado, my home at that time. My life would never be the same again.

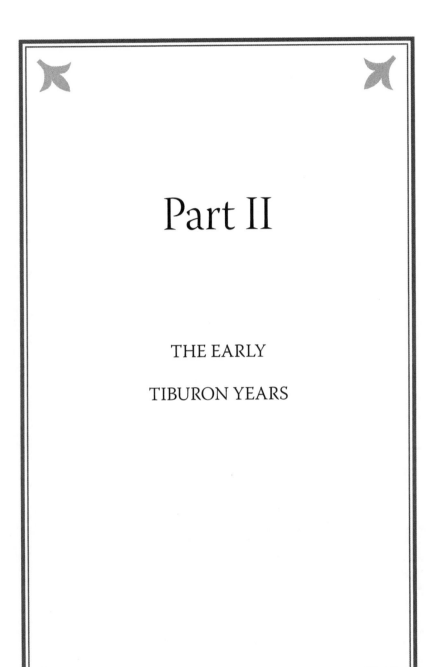

Part II

THE EARLY

TIBURON YEARS

This section includes some of my own personal experiences with Bill, along with those of others, since we met at the point of his transition from New York to California. After twenty-three years in New York, this was a major disruption for him, and our time together seemed to be about helping him anchor into his new home, accept his role with *ACIM*, and begin his final healing.

In the early spring of 1978, I received a brochure from the Association of Humanistic Psychology (as I was not a member, I had never before received a mailing from them, nor did I ever again) about their regional conference to be held in Denver, featuring the publisher of *A Course In Miracles*, Judith Skutch (Whitson). Most captivating of all, it stated that Bill Thetford would also be there, though not as a presenter. I was thrilled. By that time, I had been a devoted *Course* student for nine months. I loved it and would have gone to any lengths to meet anyone involved with *ACIM*, especially Bill or Helen. On the appointed evening, my husband Bob and I arrived at Regis College, the conference location, and were surprised to find folding chairs and a temporary stage set up outside, an ill-considered decision as May evenings in Colorado can be very cold; there had been no mention of an outdoor event in the brochure. We greatly enjoyed Judy's spirited presentation, which confirmed that *ACIM* was, indeed, a world-class enterprise, despite no sign of Bill. Since it was growing colder by the minute and I had brought only a lightweight sweater, I left shortly before the end of the presentation and headed for the nearest building.

On entering, I saw a tall, attractive man standing alone to one side of a large reception area and instantly knew it was Bill. And in that same instant, looking into those indescribable eyes, I felt an immediate and ancient recognition, a connection unlike any I had ever experienced before. The sense of familiarity I had felt with the *Course* was amplified severalfold on seeing him. I introduced myself, thanking him for all he had done to bring this marvelous work forward. In those delicious ten minutes before everyone else succumbed to the cold and came indoors, I had the opportunity to visit with him but, more important, to be in his powerful yet totally unassuming presence. Words fail here. He seemed to be a man with no mask, no pretense, nothing to hide, and no agenda to pursue, and he made no attempt to be impressive, or anything else, for that matter. He was simply present—a graceful, authentic human being, a rarity in my experience. As we spoke for those few minutes before the crowd discovered him, I was enchanted by his beautiful voice, although I cannot remember a word he said. Anyone fortunate enough to have heard Bill speak, especially in person, knows the healing quality of his lovely bass voice. After we shared a brief good-bye, I rode home in silence, spellbound and intensely moved by this instant heart-to-heart connection with a seeming "stranger."

Tiburon, California—a progressive, upscale community with gorgeous views of the Bay area, located across the Golden Gate Bridge from San Francisco—was about to become Bill's new home. Now fifty-five, he was only a few weeks away from beginning the California chapter of his life. Inwardly, he recognized there was really no choice about this move, although his ego mind was still ambivalent. Only later did I discover that his stop in Denver was on the last of several trips to California to finalize his moving plans.

On one of his earlier visits to Tiburon, while out for his usual morning walk, Bill had unexpectedly met a recent acquaintance. He asked him if he knew of any apartments for rent, and the man told him one was available next door to him and that it had been vacant for a while, most unusual for the area. Bill looked at it, declared it perfect on all accounts, and made arrangements to move in. His new home was on, aptly named, Paradise Drive right across from Angel Island, paralleling the water's edge with a stunning view of San Francisco Bay, and only a two-minute walk to Jerry Jampolsky's home. Dr. Gerald Jampolsky, one of the first and most influential *Course* advocates, had founded the Center for Attitudinal Healing in Tiburon based on *ACIM* principles in 1975. Judy and Bob Skutch, also newly transplanted from New York, were a few houses on the other side of Jerry, so all were neighbors and only a short walk to charming downtown Tiburon.

Bill's ease of finding a place to live was hardly the first serendipitous experience for him. In New York, the same inner direction had led him to the apartment of his dreams, where he lived for eighteen of his twenty-three years there. Of an earlier "perfect house find," Bill wrote:

> At the time, I didn't pay much attention to the fact that I had experienced this inner prompting because that would be unscientific; I couldn't acknowledge that. However, I did make note of it and thought it might be intuition so I could talk about it a little, but not too much. Yet I didn't know what to do with it and I certainly couldn't account for it. This was not the first time this sort of thing had happened to me, but was a major example and I couldn't ignore it.[1]

So here he was in June 1978 with a tabula rasa—a blank slate for a new chapter. Jules Finegold, a retired architect and one of Bill's early California acquaintances who became a close friend and companion, was instrumental in getting him settled into his apartment, decorating it with the few possessions Bill had sent from New York. When Bill left for his West Coast adventure, he had relinquished most of what he owned, including a great many books and most of his music except his entire Mozart collection, which was very dear to him. And what he left behind was not a huge amount, as he was not particularly into accumulating worldly possessions. For the ten years I knew him, he seemed more an advocate of voluntary simplicity than consumerism. In addition to leaving possessions behind, he abruptly cut almost all ties with friends and acquaintances of many years, both professional and social, as if clearing the decks for the final challenge of his life: to fully and completely practice forgiveness. Jules provided a service of paramount importance, helping him become familiar with the day-to-day requirements of living in Tiburon, because the practical matters of life were definitely Bill's short suit, especially in a strange setting.

New home in Tiburon

Right away their friendship deepened and they discovered common interests. Jules and Bill settled into a pattern of helping to edit some of Jerry Jampolsky's earlier books, a process that worked very well for all concerned. They also collaborated in editing a book of Helen's poetry, but their prize project was extracting some of their favorite excerpts from *ACIM*, the most beautiful and poetic, to create the book, *Choose Once Again*.[2] This extensive editing occurred over a period of several years and, interwoven with his other interests and projects, gave Bill an important focus during this regrouping phase of his life.

Bill often commented on the feeling of discontinuity between the various major chapters of his life. Many people feel that way when they take new jobs, end or begin marriages, or relocate to another city or country. It often seems, on settling into the new situation, that the old one was a faraway dream unrelated to the present. Happily, every moment is discontinuous from the one preceding it, always allowing us to make new choices about how to respond to current circumstances. Releasing past thoughts and concerns, and with it our stress, is essential, since indiscriminately allowing past programming to dictate our present approach to life is unsatisfactory at best and maddening at worst.

During the summer of 1978, as Bill adjusted to his new environment, a tiny *ACIM* community was evolving in Denver. I was still in my "evangelical" period, enthusiastically studying the *Course* and attempting to persuade everyone I knew to check it out. Many would open the book but immediately decide it was too long, too "religious" in language, or too complicated. Eventually, fourteen people coalesced who were sufficiently interested in the material to meet regularly, so in August, a close friend and colleague, Jaison Kayn, and I began facilitating our first study group.

Later that summer an acquaintance called to say that Bill and the Skutches had moved to Tiburon, California, a town I had never heard of. I mentally filed that away, and within a month Jaison unexpectedly announced he was going to Tiburon, of all places, for five weeks to study Aston Patterning, an integration of deep tissue work, massage, and movement education. He had been Rolfing for five years and was feeling a deep call to study this new work.[3] Little did he know the other reason he needed to go to

Tiburon. With that new information, I could practically hear Bill's voice in my mind calling, "Come out, come out," encouraging a visit to Tiburon—a most peculiar experience to say the least. I could not imagine that he even remembered our short conversation, much less that it would ever continue. In fact, it seemed the most arrogant and preposterous thought I could possibly entertain, but it strongly persisted. I had always recognized my intuitive faculty, very helpful when I listened, but I didn't always follow it; early conditioning prevailed. Yet this "call from Bill" was so strong I simply couldn't ignore it. The internal turmoil was escalating. As a first step and not knowing where it would lead, I wrote a letter of introduction to Bill on Jaison's behalf, hoping to arrange a meeting for them, and thanking him again for *ACIM*. Having no idea how to contact him, I sent the letter in care of the Foundation for Inner Peace and hoped for the best.

Two weeks later, October 31, while I was getting my little boys ready for Halloween, the phone rang and to my astonishment, there was Bill. He had received my letter and said he would be delighted to meet with Jaison, and asked if would I be coming out also. It seemed he, too, had recognized something familiar, a common bond. Ken Wapnick has noted that, for Bill, leaving New York was like leaving a prison and it apparently took him no time at all to start exploring other relationship options. At first, as an habitual response, I declined the invitation; the next morning, however, after considerable reflection, I accepted the incredible gift being offered. Of course, I would go to Tiburon; I must surely have lost my mind to consider doing otherwise. Everyone but me was saying yes. Bob was supportive of the plan and Jaison *insisted* I go. Bob was not particularly interested in studying metaphysics, including *ACIM*, but he never interfered with my pursuits. Thus, in mid November 1978, watching the Rocky Mountains pass far below, I marveled that I was really flying to California with no agenda, simply following my own instincts and challenging old, entrenched ideas about what I could or could not do. It was a crucial lesson for me—coming to terms with buried self-doubt as well as old habits of taking care of the needs of others but not acknowledging my own. I was not always my own best advocate. Now I was actually acting on an intuitive urge, assuming I had a place to fill, rather than repressing it in favor of "playing it safe" or being polite. It seemed a big risk at the time, but everything had worked so well, and the logistics were so uncomplicated, that the trip had every hallmark of "destiny," and it did turn out to be life-changing in many respects.

Jaison picked me up in Tiburon on a Thursday afternoon and took me to his friend's home where I stayed. Happily, it was within walking distance of the "*ACIM* neighborhood" on Paradise Drive. We contacted Bill right away and he invited us to come to his apartment the next morning. We arrived at the appointed hour and I will never forget that encounter. His home felt like a sanctuary, the peaceful quarters of an old monk. Bill was tall, smiling, and in his uniform—a favorite blue crewneck sweater and levis; I'm quite short so as we embraced in a big hug, my head was on his chest. I could hear his heart, which seemed very loud and large—it was an indescribably rich and wonderful moment. I was thrilled to have a chance to spend more time in his wonderful presence—a word that will appear often in this book because no other fits.

Jaison recalled his first impressions:

> I remember walking in and thinking he looked like a college professor. He was immediately warm and friendly, giving me a big hug, and the first thing he said to me was, "Oh, a healer." [At that time, Bill knew nothing about Jaison or his profession.] And it was like "Whoa!" He was just so conscious and so tuned into everything and had the appearance of not being. From that first meeting, we had a relationship. There was no building a relationship; it just started. I felt accepted immediately, without hesitation, and we were instant friends. That experience of his warm welcome will always be a profound and totally precious memory.[4]

From that first moment of reconnection, Bill and I both recognized we were old friends from some ancient time and place. We seemed to take up where we had left off, with a heartwarming degree of openness and lack of formality or pretense. He seemed very willing to include Jaison and me in his daily life, and a wonderful new chapter began to unfold for all three of us. We spent the rest of the morning at his apartment, then ambled down to Main Street for a four-hour lunch. When it was time to leave, Bill asked if we knew Jerry Jampolsky. We told him we did not and he said, "Well, you must meet Jerry," so off we went to his office a short distance away. Jerry was still a practicing psychiatrist, and his next patient was fortuitously late, so the four of us gathered in his office for a half-hour visit. Again, I experienced that intense, rich feeling, sensing the "family" was reconvening after a long absence; this feeling was accentuated by a strong pressure in my heart area, another first in my experience. It is difficult to describe that day except to say it was quite breathtaking.

Bill and I were together most of the time over the next several days, with Jaison joining us as his schedule permitted. The adventure simply got better and better. Jerry kindly invited Jaison and me to join what I came to call the "first family" of the *Course* at their daily study/prayer group, almost always held at his home but occasionally at the Skutches'. At nine o'clock every morning, Jerry, Bill, Bob and Judy Skutch, Frances Vaughn, and Roger Walsh, the man she later married, would meet for about an hour to read a lesson, sit quietly to see how it might apply personally, and visit in an open and sharing way. (Frances and Roger are both distinguished in their respective fields of psychology and psychiatry and pioneers in the area of transpersonal psychology.) Of paramount importance was the feeling in the room, the feeling of people deeply caring about one another. Jaison and I were most grateful to be included, and for the next several years, every time either of us were there, we were invited to the meeting. That courtesy was also extended to Jules Finegold, Pat Hopkins, and a few others who did not live in Tiburon, when they were in town. (Pat became a regular participant later when she moved to Tiburon.)

As an added bonus, Jaison and I spent a delightful evening with Bob and Judy Skutch. Judy is an effervescent, lively woman; Bob, her husband at the time and a man of fewer words, is engaging and supportive in a more subdued manner and still manages the business side of the Foundation for Inner Peace. As we became better acquainted that evening, Judy suddenly exclaimed, "I know why you're here. After all his years in academia, Bill needs to be socialized; I bequeath you Bill!" What exactly that would entail, I wasn't sure, but without doubt I was delighted with the assignment.

Right from the beginning, Judy seemed consistently to play the role of Bill's "big sister," offering comfort, stability, and a large dose of loving acceptance and good will. She said,

> I knew, the way knowing is encapsulated in your mind, that I was to take care of him [Bill] the rest of his life, just as Helen knew when she first saw Bill he was the one she was supposed to help. I can see the two of us, [she and I] played such a similar role. Layle [Luckett, who appears later in Bill's life] got a little rhapsodic and commented on what a great older sister I was, and I said, "Whoa, he was eight years older than I." She wrote back with a little smile sign and said, "It doesn't matter, you were his older sister." I never thought of it like that but I knew he was my assignment. It didn't mean I was to control his life, only that I would be his safety net.[5]

As if carried on a tide of good fortune, I found myself the junior partner in this "big sister" enterprise and, as with Judy, Bill did seem lighter and more reassured when we were together. Judy and I never confided our sisterly conspiracy to him, nor do we know what he might have thought about our prescription for his "re-socialization," but he did flourish during our times together. During his early days in California, Judy was still traveling, speaking extensively on behalf of *ACIM*, and was not in Tiburon on a regular basis. Thus, she welcomed anyone who could play a surrogate role and provide a stabilizing influence for Bill. He had spent decades operating at a frantic pace with his multifaceted work, including the time-consuming addition of the *Course* from 1965–1976. Considering all the upsets and opportunities for psychological growth that had occurred simultaneously with his workload at Columbia, Bill seriously did need to decompress, and if ever there was a project I could wholeheartedly embrace, it was this one. To say I felt richly blessed at the prospect of spending more time with Bill would be a major understatement.

As our friendship deepened, Bill confided that when my original letter arrived, he was not opening mail sent to him via the Foundation for Inner Peace (his own address and phone were unlisted). He was as surprised as I was that he not only felt compelled to read it but to respond. He chose not to open his letters then because he didn't want to deal with the inquiries or comments they may have contained; he was earnestly trying to dissociate himself from the *Course*. After I had spent some time with him, I realized how extraordinarily out of character it was for him to call me—and certainly to invite us to come out. Jaison and I were strangers and he was an intensely private man. I grew up in a socially active household with all sorts of activities—gatherings, houseguests, group meetings, celebratory meals—and it was entirely normal to invite persons we didn't know well, along with friends, to join us. My adulthood in Denver mimicked my growing-up years, so his warm invitation didn't seem odd, simply generous and altogether unexpected. Only later did I appreciate the leap of faith it took for him to call, just as it had been for me to respond. We were both being led into unfamiliar territory.

What *was* in character for Bill at the time, however, was being reclusive and pledging everyone to secrecy about his role with the *Course*. Hugh

Prather recalls when he and his wife Gayle planned their first meeting with Jerry Jampolsky:

> The first time I talked to Jerry, as we were setting up a lunch, he told me there was someone he wanted me to meet but he wouldn't tell me who it was. He was very mysterious about this. I think he referred to him as Dr. B or something like that. He really wanted to tell me but had promised he wouldn't. I think we pretty well figured out who it was with Jerry's "non-telling." In the beginning, Bill was very uncomfortable having people know that he was the person associated with the *Course*. He didn't even use his last name. When we met him, he was Dr. Bill. [6]

Having left Columbia only recently, Bill was reticent about openly acknowledging his connection to *A Course In Miracles*—the title itself sounded so peculiar and unscientific. He needed the security of a few close friends. Just as he had not come out as a homosexual, and never did officially, he had not yet come out of the *ACIM* "closet." Certainly, other psychologists have been involved with "channeling" or have received material from unusual and unknown sources, but few had careers as auspicious as his. In addition to his reticence about associating with the *Course*, the radical shift from academic to ordinary citizen was a shock, and he was grieving over the end of the New York era. He wrote, "I thought it was amazing that I could see so clearly and yet the same thing [old ego patterns] kept coming up. I had to leave the whole New York ambiance and go to a totally different setting to begin to let go. It was very difficult for me to do that. I was so dedicated to working things out there [with Helen]." [7]

Consistent with his ambivalence about his *ACIM* association, Bill procrastinated about giving Bob Skutch permission to publish his book on the *Course*'s origins, *Journey Without Distance*. [8] He had vetoed the earlier version because he was not yet ready for more unwanted publicity. Also, he was honoring Helen's request not to publish the chronicle of the *ACIM* scribing or their personal histories until after her death, which occurred in February 1981. Ultimately, of course, Bill saw the wisdom of a complete account of how the *Course* was written and worked with Bob to ensure its accuracy.

Bill attributed his reticence about publicity partly to his clear remembrance of a former life as Origen, one of the greatest theologians and biblical scholars of the early church. Martyred around 254AD for his heretical posture on many basic church doctrines, he was the most influential theologian of the church before St. Augustine. *ACIM* students will find the mystical nature of Origen's teachings strikingly familiar. Given the barbaric torture Origen endured for his beliefs, which probably hastened his death, Bill's reluctance to expressing his views publicly may have been rooted in a bleed-through awareness of that traumatic time. Incidentally, Helen also tuned into this former experience of Bill's. Once she suddenly interrupted discussion of an unrelated topic to disclose this former life to him, a confirmation he found both fascinating and illuminating. It was another of his favorite stories and he told it with his signature smile of amusement.

Early on in California, a coterie of people began to collect around Bill, all part of a grounding network vital to his continued unfolding, while mutually facilitating the healing for all concerned. The initial support group, consisting of Judy and Bob Skutch and Jerry Jampolsky, was already in place when Bill left New York. With the morning prayer group, Frances and Roger joined the circle and, along with Jules, became central to his anchoring into the area. With careers in psychology and psychiatry, they functioned as colleagues but also became his protégés. Additional members of Bill's support group, from different places and walks of life, showed up throughout his last ten years in precisely the proper order. Those closest to him were all *ACIM* students and formed a family of sorts; each provided different yet essential elements for his releasing, healing, comforting, and grounding. The foundation was being laid. Bill had made a commitment to practice the *Course's* version of forgiveness and help to do so was coalescing. Of course, he had many wonderful friends, colleagues, and partners during his first fifty-five years, but his goals then had been more worldly and divided; he had not yet fully dedicated himself to a spiritual practice. Additionally, many other friends and acquaintances were part of his California life, important in various ways, and who undoubtedly contributed to his well-being. The *Course* clearly states that there are no accidents—even the briefest encounter is meaningful and holds the possibility of great healing if we so choose. Nevertheless, Bill, like everyone, was destined to spend more time with some than others.

In the channeled reading he gave Bill in 1980, LeRoy Zemke predicted that key people would be drawn into his life to provide energy for his transformation and that being open to allowing them in would bring healing. At the time of this reading, Bill had met some, but not all, of those persons with whom he would spend significant time during his last ten years.

> Each of the persons you have mentioned [Bill had given him seven names] are parts of the pattern, are like keys in a pattern that will help you. There are many who will help you. What you must be willing to do is to allow them space in your life to assume some of the weight, some of the responsibility that is emerging. You, as you know, have an infinitely careful, painstaking quality about yourself. Whatever you attend to, you can very easily accomplish. . . . Now as these people appear, they have volunteered out of the love they bear for you and/or the larger essence of what has emerged, to dedicate a portion of their being to implementing that dimension. As you give them opportunity to assume the work, they will do it. And thus, what you can do involves a giving, both in the form of guidance and ideas that need to be set into motion, and secondly, the energy from your own being expressed as love.[1]

As Bill spent focused time with some, and then moved on to the next person or group, release was occurring.

> Once you accept His plan as the one function that you would fulfill, there will be nothing else the Holy Spirit will not arrange for you without your effort. He will go before you making straight your path, and leaving in your way no stones to trip on, and no obstacles to bar your way. Nothing you need will be denied you. Not one seeming difficulty but will melt away before you reach it. You need take thought for nothing, careless of everything except the only purpose that you would fulfill. As that was given you, so will its fulfillment be.[2]

Bill *had* accepted that plan and, as promised, help was always there when he needed it. Zemke also commented, less than two years after Bill's move west, "The most important, perhaps, of all directions or aspects at present in your life is to ground the physical form, to allow yourself to connect with the earth and with the water, to experience a harmony with the basic elements within the world . . . and thus provide a more smooth transition for all the work unfolding."[3]

Bill's first priorities in Tiburon were to settle in, reestablish a sense of stability and security after decades of daily structure, and to meet concrete, worldly needs. Sufficient financial support and anchoring into normal everyday life required attention. Bill was skilled in many ways and adept at negotiating the labyrinth of academic power, but he did not operate comfortably in ordinary daily life. He needed routine and support to function effectively in this world, to keep his feet planted on the earth. For instance, Bill had contributed to his TIAA-CREF retirement fund while at Columbia, but had forgotten to apply for his benefits when he retired. When Pat Hopkins (who entered his life later) found out about this in 1984 through a conversation with Cal Hatcher, she helped him apply for his benefits, significantly increasing his monthly income. Despite chairing a department with a large staff and sizable budget, he was quite detached when it came to personal finances. Jack Luckett corroborates:

> First, he was brilliant in abstract thought and analysis. No question. He could go right to the center of an issue and understand it instantly. And the more abstract it was, the easier it was for him to see right into it. It's why he was such a fantastic psychologist. But he was not well grounded in this world. Now that means relating to food, clothing, directions, appliances, electronic gear, politics, gardening, animals, and children. He did not have a clue about these things. He was not comfortable with and did not understand the governmental political process. He was a great faker. Because of this, he would establish routines in his life, probably because he'd been laughed at earlier. When he found something that worked, he

would stick with it, make a routine of it. He told me that for fifteen years, he ate at the same restaurant with the same waitress at the same table, ate the same meal every night, except when he was asked out by others. I said, "Didn't you ever want to go to a different restaurant?" and he answered that, no, he knew this place, knew where it was. Can you imagine that?

Now Bill didn't really understand food well. When he and Pat [Hopkins] got together as roommates, they agreed to share responsibilities in cleaning and preparing food. Well, Bill never prepared his own food so he was quite nonplussed. He found these frozen enchilada dinners that were good, so he solved the problem. He went down and bought one year's supply of the same kind of enchilada dinner and put them in the freezer. Although that certainly seemed more than a little strange to Pat, to him this was a perfect solution. He would just have those dinners from then on; they were fine, they worked.[4]

Bill's New York acquaintances did say that he could cook one thing—omelets—and if you were invited over, you would have no doubt about the menu. That was the extent of his culinary skill. Because of his basic unfamiliarity with food preparation, he tended to approach it more like an anthropologist than a gourmet and regularly conducted unusual experiments with tastes and food combinations. For instance, years later, Bill and the Lucketts stopped one night at a Haagen Daz store for ice cream, and he ordered maple walnut combined with raspberry tofutti. He had no idea what combining these flavors would be like; this was a foreign world to him. Jack continued:

As for clothing, he relied mostly on his gay male friends, and occasionally others, to help him with clothes. He had no sense of what he should buy. Usually he wore levis that hung down low on his hips with a pullover sweater. One time at one of the garden [ACIM] meetings in San Diego, a fellow took one look at Bill and exclaimed, "My dear, who is your tailor!"

Bill was spatially disoriented. He simply did not understand how to get from one place to another. He liked to go to a meeting that was south from where we lived in La Jolla. Everything to him was linear so I could tell him, "You go down this street until you come to the gas station and turn right; it's like a line." I gave him these landmarks and he was so proud the first time he drove it; it was a major accomplishment. I do know that if he'd ever gotten off that line, he'd have been in real trouble.[5]

Bill took on another challenge when he left New York—to quit smoking. He was a nonstop smoker and quitting was not easy. However, he recognized the need to discontinue the habit, knowing it was preventing long-buried feelings from surfacing. In their stead, he carried cinnamon sticks and chewed on those when tempted to smoke. Bill commented one time that in the hectic New York days, he lived mostly on coffee, which he drank all day long, several packs of cigarettes, and butter pecan ice cream. It's a wonder he lived as long as he did, especially with a heart damaged by rheumatic fever!

Judy, looking out for his best interests, instinctively knew that proceeds from the early sales of the *Course* would go to support Bill when he retired; his receiving a stipend seemed inevitable and obvious. On the other hand, Bill noted, "I didn't expect the *Course* to be a source of financial support. We never thought of that at all. Yet eventually it did happen and it took me a long time even to be comfortable with the idea of living on funds from the Foundation for Inner Peace."[6] Thus, with his stipend from the Foundation, his pension, investments in the stock market, and his capacity to "manifest as needed," he always lived comfortably.

Afterour first visit in Tiburon, a pattern emerged: Bill and I met every couple of months, with phone calls in between. He would come to Denver and stay with my family—my husband and two young boys—and in turn, I would visit Tiburon and stay with him or, later, with Jerry, sometimes to participate in planned events and sometimes for no reason. This schedule continued for about three years. Early on, it felt surreal to watch him sitting on our patio, listen to his tales, or conversely, be included in his daily routine as he settled into California. He had dropped suddenly and unexpectedly into the middle of my life, and it took a bit of getting used to.

During his visits to Denver, "socializing Bill" began in earnest. I wish everyone could have seen him as he participated in that "normalizing process." He was so willing to explore. He especially enjoyed our sons—six and eight when we met; he was fascinated by what little boys could do and got such a kick out of their activities and friends. Although he had studied, tested, and written about children in his professional life, he had very little experience being around them in normal everyday life. As an adult, he was basically unfamiliar with families or the myriad details and responsibilities of family life. Bill would stand in the kitchen as I prepared meals, with little ones running in and out, and often exclaim, "I don't know how you do all this!" It was business as usual; parents learn, out of necessity, to multitask. He himself was a master at multitasking but in very different areas of life.

Because of his lack of experience with young children in their usual environments, he thoroughly enjoyed attending school functions or riding along when it was my turn to drive the car pool. I've not met anyone else who ever saw Bill in that role—riding in a car full of little kids. It was a new adventure for him. He sat in wonder as he listened to their conversations, finding them hilarious and precious. He would look over at me with eyes wide open, a huge grin on his face, as their stories unfolded. Their parents would likely have been less than thrilled to hear their small children candidly revealing private family business. He loved such times, delighting in their complete ease and openness as they prattled on, asking him questions, wholeheartedly including him as a matter of course. They were a marked contrast to his own early experience and to his long-standing inclination to secrecy.

Bill often commented on how very different these children's early years were from his. On one trip to Denver, he watched my younger son energetically ride up and down the sidewalk on his bicycle. I could see the wistful look in his eyes and commented on how this seven-year-old's experience must seem worlds apart from his own at seven, lying in bed gravely ill. He acknowledged the difference, then responded with a broad smile, "Nothing is ever going to get in his way in life!" In addition, both Bill and Helen were true Gilbert and Sullivan aficionados, and he was especially pleased that my older son had a significant role in his elementary school's abridged production of the musical, *H.M.S. Pinafore*. Greg was nine, an age when Bill was still confined to bed, which led to more reminiscing about how different were their early childhood experiences.

I can still see him—tall, handsome, charismatic, and often the only man around—casually visiting with the mothers waiting for their children at the end of the school day, soccer practice, or music lessons, as if he did this every day. Actually, it was probably the first time he had ever been in such a situation, but you wouldn't have known it. Bill had an amazing capacity to seem at home in any situation even when he absolutely was not. These various groups of children took to him at once and all unquestioningly considered him part of their young lives, telling him their stories and competing with one another to hold his hands. Sometimes he read stories to our boys at night, which they loved; they regarded him as a favorite uncle, and in my mind I can still hear the sound of his reassuring, resonant voice coming down the hall.

On a few occasions, we took the boys to Tiburon, always infusing a burst of energy into Bill's world. He watched with delight as they scrambled along the shoreline between his apartment and Jerry's home, a short distance away. This infrequent plunge into typical, busy family life was a source of great amusement—and perhaps some gratitude that he had opted for the single life! Certainly it was different. In retrospect, it doesn't seem a coincidence that Bill came to Denver while my children were the same age he had been while bedridden. In ways we may never understand, I believe some healing of his difficult early years took place through those casual interactions.

Although Bill enjoyed being included in our daily routine, the early morning "get the kids up and off to school" uproar challenged his endurance, and he always remained safely in his bedroom with the door closed until quiet settled over the house. Then we had wonderful long talks in the kitchen, usually followed by a walk. Sometimes Bob joined us for an evening walk and remembered them fondly, "We just walked and talked and exchanged thoughts and information and he was always receptive to whatever was on your mind; he would listen to you. You could talk to Bill about anything and he would have an answer. Somehow the two of us clicked; he was just a dear, dear, friend."[1] Although Bob was not a *Course* student himself, he was a gracious host on Bill's visits; he made sure he had everything he might want or need as a guest in our home. He genuinely cared for Bill—and that was mutual—and even now (we have been divorced for many years), he still talks about him.

So many others I interviewed for this book also emphasized the importance of a walk with Bill, how satisfying it was and how much insight occurred during those casual discussions. Robert Rosenthal, a young psychiatrist friend of Bill's, relates a typical experience: "Often when Bill and I would get together we'd walk and chat. He'd catch me up on the latest 'craziness' going on with the *Course* or what Jerry Jampolsky or other people were doing. But in a way, that was all window dressing. Behind it was a shared sense of presence and peace, just meditating together and sharing the moment."[2] Hugh Prather also mentioned how they always seemed to be walking together somewhere, discussing a range of issues, and how important that was to him. And Jaison Kayn found silent walking with Bill profoundly satisfying:

> Bill and I didn't talk much. It was part of our relationship to be absolutely comfortable together, physically and energetically. We would walk to the bakery on the dock near Jerry's office. It was a casual ritual, going down there every day [when Jaison was visiting in Tiburon], ordering those wonderful custard-filled cream puffs. They were his favorite and, at first bite, became mine as well. Since we were both basically shy people, there was not much to say. We simply sat, watched, and enjoyed our cream puffs. We accepted each other's shyness very easily and did not need to entertain each other. It was more than comfortable; our energies seemed to be quietly communicating something gracious and beyond words. I was probably one of the few people in his life he felt that way about. My sense is that he often felt he had to talk to people more, that most people required that of him. Somehow with me he knew he didn't have to talk because I couldn't either.[3]

ACIM speaks beautifully of the implications of walking together, literally or figuratively:

This brother neither leads nor follows us, but walks beside us on the self-same road. He is like us, as near or far away from what we want as we will let him be. We make no gains he does not make with us, and we fall back if he does not advance. Take not his hand in anger but in love, for in his progress do you count your own. And we go separately along the way unless you keep him safely by your side. . . .

Forgive your brother all appearances, that are but ancient lessons you have taught yourself about the sinfulness in you. Hear but his call for mercy and release from all the fearful images he holds of what he is and of what you must be. He is afraid to walk with you, and thinks perhaps a bit behind, a bit ahead would be a safer place for him to be. Can you make progress if you think the same, advancing only when he would step back, and falling back when he would go ahead? For so do you forget the journey's goal, which is but to decide to walk with him, so neither leads nor follows. Thus it is a way you go together, not alone. And in this choice is learning's outcome changed, for Christ has been reborn to both of you.[4]

Something *was* reborn in those who walked with Bill; it was like coming home.

Bill seemed to need, perhaps more than anything, some comfortable time and space to assimilate his new life and slowly unwind. It was helpful for him to be away from places where the roles of teacher, *Course* scribe, learned professor, or anything else were thrust upon him. On occasion, when we had our private space, he would break down and weep. I comforted him as best I could, at the same time encouraging him to cry those tears so long unshed—tears not so much over particulars, but a lifetime accumulation of pain not fully acknowledged. Nothing specific prompted those episodes; it was more a combination of things. We often spoke of his relationship with Helen, with the *Course*, and the heaviness he carried about it all—the burden of unexpressed life, repressed grief, hiding out. All of us hold onto some secrets, wearying at the very least, and this was especially so for Bill. He constantly lived a dual life: his academic career intermixed with his hidden *ACIM* work, his unresolved love/hate relationship with Helen, his knowledge of various secret CIA projects—very likely carried to his grave—and of course, his never publicly acknowledged homosexual private life. Thus, he could "hide out" in Denver, where almost no one had access to him, and really let go.

Over the years he also engaged in ongoing therapeutic work in Tiburon with both Frances Vaughan and Catherine Riggs Prescott, a close friend he met in 1984, as well as learning from less formal interactions with others. It is easy to see the *Course* operating in his life through a kaleidoscope of relationships and encounters, helping him to identify and release unhelpful beliefs. It's fair to say that all his relationships were mutually therapeutic, though perhaps not recognized at the time.

I regarded Bill as my mentor, as did almost everyone who knew him, and we served as therapists for one another. We were very respectful of one another's capabilities and shared a close connection as colleagues. I, too, remember the importance of our long walks, as we shared our worlds, at once so different and yet so similar. We compared notes about my mother (also named Helen), who at that time was retreating into Alzheimer's disease, and about "his" Helen. He said he had tried for so many years to make her happy, to do or be whatever she wanted, and that it was simply not possible. As simple as it sounds now, it was a significant breakthrough for him to realize it was not his job to make Helen happy, and he advised me accordingly. Her happiness had been his self-appointed responsibility, one she also assumed was his. He used to say that it seemed Helen would never be happy, for she found very little in life even to be acceptable.

It took years for him to grow more accepting of his relationship with Helen, as he released his sense of failure and the need for her approval. Although he recognized it was pointless to continue trying, he didn't find peace with that relationship until near the end of his life. Yet Bill was no different from the rest of us. In my experience, most people learn that being okay, being worthy, having a right to be here, is measured by others' approval; unlearning that lie is essential and often a lifelong venture. He felt disappointed and betrayed because his vision of practicing the *Course* with Helen and having a wonderful friendship didn't happen. He also felt some resentment that she had gotten him into this situation and was not fulfilling her part of the bargain, whatever he perceived that to be. At the same time, he was compassionate with her, aware of her difficulties when she was overtaken by phobias and compulsions. Also, during the last years of her life, after Bill and the Skutches had moved to California, she grew ill with pancreatic cancer. Many who knew her well said she became quite deranged. She was definitely not the Helen everyone had known in her prime.

Once when Bill was in Denver, we were in the front yard watching the children when a lovely dog—a handsome Irish setter—limped into the yard. His paws were raw and bleeding as if he had had a very long, hard run on concrete; he came straight toward us as if on purpose, clear about his destination, then nearly collapsed. Bill had a very tender heart, was concerned about the dog, as were we all, and asked several times what we could do for him. We provided water, food, and a safe place to rest until the owner, whose number was on his collar, returned our call that evening. The dog was very friendly and, despite his recent experience, seemed content to sit with us for several hours until his owner arrived to collect him. Later, the owner told us the dog had been stolen from his backyard and carried off for some unknown purpose. He had escaped his captors and was trying to find his way back home; our neighborhood was approximately on the way.

It seemed purposeful that Bill had this unanticipated encounter with the dog. The episode might seem trivial but it *was* important to Bill. By his own account, he had been under tremendous strain—self-imposed though it may have been—at Columbia, especially during the scribing years; he had spoken of the struggle that seemed the hallmark of his life. Our "outer" life is a seamless whole with the "inner," and both Bill and the dog, after long, difficult journeys, were on the final leg of returning "Home." A lesson from *ACIM* comments on our suffering when we "leave home," in other words, when we refuse to accept the truth about ourselves:

> He seems a sorry figure; weary, worn, in threadbare clothing, and with feet that bleed a little from the rocky road he walks. No one but has identified with him, for everyone who comes here has pursued the path he follows, and has felt defeat and hopelessness as he is feeling them. Yet is he really tragic, when you see that he is following the way he chose, and need but realize Who walks with him and open up his treasures to be free?[5]

W hile planning for one of his visits, I asked Bill if he would allow me to host a reception so that some in the local *ACIM* community could meet him. He said he would be happy for that to happen; he willingly accepted even though he could have said no. On the appointed date, the house and yard filled with people eager to meet him. He responded to their enthusiasm graciously as if being a social butterfly was his favorite thing, once again adapting to the situation. Though he didn't seek it, he understood their desire to meet and visit with him. However, as I grew to know his secret heart better, I learned that being the focus of attention was contrary to his basic nature, and I never put him through that again. In agreeing to the party, Bill was simply being generous, not phony or selling out. He was able to rise to any occasion when he chose.

Bill didn't object to socializing under the right circumstances, but he strongly disliked being put on a pedestal as the center of attention, with expectations attached. Friends from his New York days remembered Bill's great cocktail parties with many people in attendance, including colleagues from Columbia. They also remembered his inventing all kinds of irreproducible drink concoctions of liquor and fruit juices. He was only thirty-four when he joined the Columbia staff, and drinking and cigarette smoking was the norm in his pre-*Course* days. However, I don't recall his drinking anything but an occasional glass of wine when I knew him. Bill was a walking contradiction and could be either vivacious or completely reserved, depending upon the circumstances.

At the reception in his honor, Bill met Bob Beale, another longtime friend of ours. Of all those he met in Denver, he felt most simpatico with Jaison and Bob, both having a sensitive, compassionate nature similar to his. If Bill's Denver "family" was about sanctuary and respite from the various roles he played, these two certainly added to his sense of well-being. I always arranged for them to get together when he came to town, and both occasionally visited Bill in Tiburon.

During that reception and on other occasions, I watched as Bill was inevitably asked two questions: the first about his role in the *ACIM* saga, still a bit unnerving to him, and the second, "Well, Bill, what are you doing now that you're retired and living in California?" He would respond that he was practicing forgiveness as a full-time job, which confused almost everyone—*Course* and non-*Course* persons alike—since forgiveness is often misunderstood even among long-time *ACIM* students. Like so many, he was still sorting out the relative importance of doing vs. being, so he was a bit confused himself. His response of "practicing forgiveness" usually ended the conversation about his career and personal world. Most people would smile, change the subject, or look a bit blank, like, "What does that mean?" Occasionally, however, someone would stumble, acknowledge his response, then ask once again, "But what are you *doing?*" as if practicing forgiveness was simply a clever answer or a dodge.

Normally he was gracious with such questions, patient with the lack of understanding that practicing forgiveness is a full-time job, and if it is not paramount in our lives, nothing else actually matters. Once or twice I saw his eyes flash as if to say, "I'm so tired of answering this question." He probably felt interrogated but knew he was speaking the truth. He realized most inquirers had no idea what he meant and took their questions in stride, but a couple of times they momentarily pushed his buttons.

Even if no one else understood Bill's agenda, he was following his heart, devoting himself as best he could to his own healing. Certainly his crowning achievement was his focus on practicing forgiveness in everyday encounters as his new "career." "I want the peace of God: Many have said these words. But few indeed have meant them. You have but to look upon the world you see around you to be sure how very few they are. The world would be completely changed, should any two agree these words express the only thing they want."[1] Bill was committed to meaning what these words say.

What is this practice of forgiveness to which Bill was now dedicating his life? It certainly isn't what we have learned; the word itself carries a great deal of baggage. First, what it is not:

> Let us review the meaning of "forgive," for it is apt to be distorted and to be perceived as something that entails an unfair sacrifice of righteous wrath, a gift unjustified and undeserved, and a complete denial of the truth. In such a view, forgiveness must be seen as mere eccentric folly and this course appear to rest salvation on a whim. . . .[2]

> The unhealed cannot pardon. For they are the witnesses that pardon is unfair. They would retain the consequences of the guilt they would overlook. Yet no one can forgive a sin that he believes is real. And what has consequences must be real, because what it has done is there to see. Forgiveness is not pity, which but seeks to pardon what it thinks to be the truth. Good cannot be returned for evil, for forgiveness does not first establish sin and then forgive it. Who can say and mean, "My brother, you have injured me, and yet, because I am the better of the two, I pardon you my hurt." His pardon and your hurt cannot exist together.[3]

Perhaps we should call forgiveness "Process X" to distinguish it from the misinformation we have learned. To paint a mental picture, imagine a thatch of many little twigs, sticks, and grass, like a bird's nest or the roof of a building found in many parts of the world. The thatch, being tightly woven, is strong and impenetrable. All those little sticks and twigs, for our purposes, represent our incessant train of thoughts—judgments, future plans, grievances, regrets, defenses, learned behavior designed for our physical and psychological survival, worries, self-images, roles we play, and pictures about how life is supposed to be. This omnipresent complex of thoughts, to which we are seriously addicted, has become like a solid wall that seems to surround us, separating us from the direct experience of life in the moment. We "think" about life rather than experience it directly. *A Course In Miracles*, brilliantly conceived and crafted, is so lengthy because it presents a process for relinquishing these "twigs" rather than a body of material to be learned. We tightly clutch these interwoven thoughts, believing we need them to survive and flourish, and are rarely open-minded on the subject. "Strong and impenetrable" are wonderful attributes if you want to keep the rain out or the eggs in. However, they are a devastating liability if they impede experiencing the present moment, with its inherent joy, peace, insight, and reliable guidance.

The *Course* is designed for the overly active intellects of the Western world. It takes us through a process that systematically dismantles this barrier, allowing freedom and happiness to increase in our daily experience. Forgiveness, as *ACIM* defines it, untangles and removes this accumulated mental debris, the complicated mental filter through which we interact with the people and circumstances in our lives—the blocks to the awareness of Love's presence. When we realize that forgiveness is about freeing ourselves from our self-made prison—one we steadily and unwittingly make ever more secure through ego-driven thought processes—and that it has nothing substantive to do with the "other," then we can proceed to liberation with real determination and gratitude.

So forgiveness is not about ascribing villainy, placing blame or finding who's at fault, and then trying to overlook "bad" actions, but in the broadest sense it is allowing a completely new perspective to emerge on all aspects of the world from personal to global, permitting an entirely different experience of what we are—no small undertaking. When inner conflict is gone, the outer experience of hassle disappears. Love becomes known through all things. This is the centerpiece of the *Course* and the heart of all universal metaphysical teachings.

When possible, my husband Bob and I always arranged for us to attend musical or theatrical events when Bill was in town. He loved these as well as other activities he did not have access to elsewhere. As he grew more willing to explore—literally—we took him to Vail and Aspen, where we attended musical events, visited with friends, or drove up backwoods mountain roads and marveled at the gorgeous scenery. He had lived all his life in cities, inside academic institutions, and had virtually no exposure to the great outdoors, but with his usual adaptability he managed to fit right in on the hiking trails—although short ones, to be sure. We once took him through the Rocky Mountains over Independence Pass, the back way into Aspen and a thrill ride for even the most seasoned mountain travelers. He was awestruck with the scenic beauty and probably terrified, but he never let on. We always discussed potential travel plans with him to make sure they would not be too strenuous. He was a bit nervous at the outset of some of our mountain adventures, because of the high altitude and how that might affect his heart condition; however, he always sincerely wanted to go and we did, with no problem.

On one memorable occasion, Bob and I drove Bill to Santa Fe, New Mexico, along with Bob Beale and his then wife Lucy, to attend the Santa

Fe Opera. Hugh and Gayle Prather, who lived there at the time, joined us for part of our visit, and the seven of us spent a couple of days together visiting, sightseeing, dining out, and attending the opera. It was a riotously funny visit for all concerned and probably for everyone within earshot, as well. Bill had warned us, however, that he always cried at the opera but not to be alarmed—it had nothing to do with us. Other than that, all tears shed were because we laughed so hard.

Aspen, Colorado

During our visits or on the phone, Bill and I rarely talked about the content of *ACIM*. Certainly, we spoke of its effects in our lives, but mostly we just enjoyed the moment, simply being together with appreciation and delight. A mundane accounting of everyday life was richer by far than grand philosophical discussion. Occasionally, however, we did delve into the meaning of certain concepts. Early on, I asked him about a sentence in the text, "Forgiveness is not real unless it brings a healing to your brother and yourself."[4] Since I was fairly new to the *Course*, there was much I didn't yet comprehend, including the fact that intellectual understanding comes *after* the process of forgiveness and not before. Presuming everything was already clear to Bill, I asked him what it meant. He said he had no idea. I was floored and thought to myself, "What do you mean, you don't know what this means?" I now realize that although he knew a tremendous amount about the *Course*, he still retained unhealed grievances that would necessarily cause blank areas or blind spots in his comprehension. When the mind is not clouded with grievances, everything becomes obvious and simple; ultimately, that sentence became perfectly clear.

Bill and I sometimes meditated together, a precious way of relating that many others also shared with him. Both Robert Rosenthal and Roger Walsh have eloquently described their meditation experiences with Bill:

> I recall in particular one meditation. This was probably in the early 1980s in his Tiburon apartment one evening. As we meditated, the room filled with a sense of utter stillness, a dense, loving, overwhelming silence that was a positive presence, not just the absence of noise. In my mind I heard the words, "This is the peace that passeth understanding." It was a concrete experience of peace. A peace and silence so certain, so absolute and impenetrable, it could not be disturbed by anything of this world—the peace of the Holy Spirit.[5]

> Bill actually talked me into my first kensho or clear experience of egolessness. One morning I was sitting with him in a restaurant by San Francisco Bay. We were talking about something spiritual and although I don't remember the discussion, I do remember the experience. As Bill was describing something about the nature of spiritual practice, I felt a dramatic, progressive shift in consciousness. I had a sense of my awareness becoming focused in a simple point, which moved up and up in a spiral

and became disentangled from the workings of the mind. Suddenly there was no exclusive identification with anything. There was clear awareness without any sense of "Roger" or any separate-self sense. There was a sudden recognition that the experience of egolessness that I'd been reading about all this time, a state the *Course* had been trying to get me to experience, is actually not a loss of the ego. Rather, the experience of egolessness is the recognition that the ego never existed in the first place.

As I sat there happily absorbed in this novel state, I described to Bill what had happened. Amazingly, as I described the experience to him, he started having it, too. He moved into the same state and we sat together for an hour or more in this shared kensho experience, which he'd first talked me into and then, simply by describing my experience to him, he had moved into himself. It was a wonderful experience for us both, and it was striking that it was the relationship that had done it.[6]

Regarding the *Course*, I did ask Bill about changes to the scribed material that were referred to briefly in the original write-up about how *ACIM* came to be. This was decades before any serious questions were raised about the editing process. First, he mentioned his amazement that Helen was able to leave the original dictation alone, given her tendency to be a particularly ferocious editor. She thoroughly edited anything that came her way, even a personal note; to be able to leave the material unchanged was astonishing and completely out of character for her. At the beginning of the transmission, if she changed a word because she didn't think it was the right one, she inevitably went back and reinstated it. As the work progressed, she could see the necessity of the exact wording and she specifically stated she didn't want to intrude upon what was unfolding. Bill explained that they deleted their personal material as well as comments about particular individuals, living or dead, that were interwoven with what became the text.

Anyone familiar with the *Course* notices that the first few chapters feel disjointed. Removing Helen and Bill's personal material left gaps in the flow of dictation and some sentences had to be rearranged, but Bill assured me—and I believe him without question—that nothing *substantive* was omitted and that the basic message was in no way altered by their editing choices. Bill's oversight was a governing factor and he gave his imprimatur to all changes. In the beginning, the Author specifically charged Bill to be responsible for the editing choices (with the Author's consent), as Helen still found the entire scribing and editing process too disturbing. Additional factors help explain the disjointed impression; Helen strongly resisted the scribing process in the beginning, and Ken noted she was always trying to impress Bill. This scribing process was no different from other situations where she sought Bill's validation.

Occasionally, sentences were inadvertently omitted (though added back later) during the typing and retyping process, and these weren't discovered until later when compared with Helen's notebooks and the Urtext, the original notes Bill typed directly while Helen read her shorthand notes to him. Sometimes the material didn't come from notes dictated earlier, but came to her directly while Bill was typing. She also occasionally skipped over some notes she had taken, not reading them to Bill at all, because she realized immediately they were personal and should not be included. Helen explained,

> The "text" as it is given is unchanged except for the omission of some of the more personal material which was included only at the beginning. Chapter headings and subdivisions have been added later, but the arrangement of the material, which seemed to fall naturally into these divisions, has not been altered. The "workbook," which was dictated in the form of daily "lessons" is presented as I took it down.[7]

In recent years, I have heard such pronouncements as, "The sacred and secret feminine teachings have been extracted from *ACIM*." This simply is not true; there is no "cult of the feminine" removed from the *Course* and reserved for a special few. Bill set the record straight, telling me that every-thing *essential* about *ACIM* remains as it was originally published.

Finally, if you want to practice the *Course*, you have everything necessary to do so. In the early part of the text the Author states, "I have made every effort to use words that are almost impossible to distort, but it is always possible to twist symbols around if you wish."[8] Because the basic tenets of the *Course* are repeated so many times, you could remove half the content and everything needed would still be in place. Even though the several versions now available are slightly different from the most recent edition of *ACIM* published by the Foundation for Inner Peace, any edition chosen will foster the necessary "unlearning" of the obstacles to peace of mind. Most important, if you fully experience even one lesson, you will have the whole *Course* since it's about forgiveness and radically changing our minds. For an in-depth comparison of the various editions, I refer the reader to an article by Robert Perry on the Circle of Atonement web site.[9]

To broaden his experience with nontraditional subjects he always found interesting, I told Bill about the great therapeutic benefits of Rolfing and he indicated he was up for trying it . Our mutual friend, Jaison Kayn, a world-class Rolfer who personally studied with Dr. Ida Rolf, the genius behind structural integration, was delighted to oblige. I would drive Bill to Jaison's home in Boulder for a session, and he would emerge smiling and grateful. So would Jaison; those sessions were a real win/win exchange for both. Jaison comments:

> Well, it was delightful for many reasons. One is because I just loved Bill
> and wanted to do for him whatever I could. Two things stand out—first,

how much he appreciated it. He totally trusted me and put himself in my hands and was grateful. And he was very aware that it was helpful to him. So anytime I was ready, he was ready. But the biggest thing is that the first time I touched his body, I just saw this light. It was like working on this shell that was full of light. There was this human body and inside that body was this bright, white light.[10]

I asked Jaison if this phenomenon was more pronounced than with others he had worked on, and he replied, "Oh, absolutely! Here was somebody who was full of light, literally. When I gave him bodywork, his flesh was more than receptive; he welcomed me with gratitude. He literally put himself in my hands and asked without words for whatever help I could give. His yearning to heal and to open was tangible to my touch. His ability to yield and to trust was remarkable. His longing to experience defenselessness was always on duty."[11]

Our fledgling *ACIM* group, which had started in August 1978, was still gathering when Bill began his visits to Denver. He always attended our meetings, considering himself very much a fellow student, and was both supportive and curious. One of the early members recalled:

He really seemed to accept us all as students of the *Course* and was glad that we, as a group, had taken on this year of study together. It was not anything he precisely said, but it was certainly his manner. I remember feeling very accepted by him, not special, just accepted. Particularly in those days, I was somewhat in awe of him, thinking, "This man is very bright, he has a Ph.D., he helped put *A Course In Miracles* together, so obviously he's in a league different from mine." But I didn't have that feeling around him at all. There was nothing pretentious or ostentatious about him, nor did he look for flaws or shortcomings; he just genuinely accepted us all. Looking back, none of us really knew what we were getting into. I suspect that in those days we were kind of pioneers. No doubt other people were doing something similar, but I got the feeling from Bill of just being complimented for what we were doing.[12]

As part of his new life, Bill simply liked being in Denver; he felt relaxed and taken care of, as he was actually shy and naïve about many basic areas of life. In Colorado, he could leave behind the academic scripts of New York and escape the patriarchal roles in Tiburon; he could be just plain Bill with as little distraction and pressure as possible. The Prathers, who knew many of the people and circumstances of his Tiburon life, also served as long-distance confidants although he did not visit their home. Most of their encounters occurred while Hugh was in Tiburon helping to edit Jerry Jampolsky's books.

Although I never met Helen, I spoke with her a half-dozen times on the phone, either at Bill's home or mine. He had agreed, when he left New York, to call her every day at noon, New York time, a promise he faithfully carried out. Those daily calls were a kind of test for him, and he diligently practiced not reacting to her provocative comments. "The conversations usually didn't make any sense at all, but the important thing was extending love. Sometimes she would sound very different, very tender, before I would hang up. That was authentic. I didn't understand it, but it was there."[13] He was ambivalent about calling her daily, and although he felt a deep love and commitment toward her, he also felt obligated, angry, and guilty. No matter what he did or said, or how faithful he was about calling, she rarely found it sufficient.

With the daily calls, they would quickly run out of things to say, so occasionally when we were together, he would pass the phone to me and say, "Okay, here, you talk to Helen." They were superficial conversations at best, and I have no idea if she even knew who I was. During one of Bill's Denver visits, however, in contrast to my rather trivial exchanges with Helen, Jaison had a radically different experience—illustrative for all of us. Bill called her at the appointed hour as several of us were chatting. He then passed the phone around so everyone could speak with her, and eventually it was Jaison's turn. He interacted with her for a few moments, then handed on the phone. Immediately after the "group" call concluded, Jaison grabbed Bill and exclaimed,

> Bill, I just heard this voice like it was coming out of heaven! It sounded like it was echoing from inside St. John's Cathedral. It was this majestic, angelic, powerful, soft, clear, feminine, simply beautiful, beautiful voice. How could there be such richness in a voice, and over the phone no less? Her words were something like, "Thank you for being interested," but it was the quality of the voice; I am blown away that nobody else seemed to be impressed by talking to Helen![14]

To Jaison's awe-filled pronouncement, Bill calmly responded, "Oh, she just does that for people sometimes."

Whether it was deliberate or accidental, as she and Jaison talked, Helen accessed the loving aspect of herself that brought forward the *Course*, yet with none of the rest of us present. Even though that was Jaison's only conversation with her, three decades later he still recalls, "I was totally blown away and grateful. It was just an amazing experience."[15] The Voice never interfered with her daily activity but was always there when she "tuned into" that channel, so to speak; her ability to turn it off and on was crucial. She described it as definitely not her own voice, although she recognized it. Most important, that "channel" where the *Course* originated is within everyone, which explains why so many feel a profound familiarity with *ACIM*.

Although Bill was gay, there were women he deeply cared for and considered an integral part of his life, especially after moving to California. I found no evidence from interviews or archival records that there was ever an important woman in his New York life other than Helen. That is not surprising since he always had a male partner while living there and Helen consumed almost all his attention, even during his personal time. It's a wonder he had time for anything or anyone outside his work and preoccupation with her. One of his good friends characterized him as "ambiguously gay," and Bill told Jo, his first and only girlfriend, that he considered himself bisexual even though he was not intimate with women. Others opined that he thought and interacted in the world like a straight man but conducted his private life as a gay man. In his high school essay, he wrote of constantly following his sister and her friends around and about his ongoing fascination with the opposite sex, a fascination that apparently continued into adulthood. In the California era, Bill was attracted to a few other women and with them he had the same intimate yet not intimate relationship he and I had as well. We have all been confounded at trying to explain what that relationship was like. Also Bill was concerned that his homosexuality might reflect negatively on *ACIM*, a sacred trust in his eyes, and spending time with women could provide "cover." Bill cannot easily be categorized in terms of his private life and his ambivalence challenged him, too.

Perhaps he felt safe with women, at least those who were not overly aggressive, just as many women feel safe with their gay men friends, without the complications and expectations of an intimate involvement. Having no romantic agenda leaves room for a deep and abiding friendship. Bill could be very flirtatious, and was capable of giving anyone his complete, undivided attention, evoking a feeling of being valued and cared for. Once when we were walking together in Tiburon, perhaps holding hands, a stranger suddenly stopped and with unusual fervor commented on how marvelous it was to see two people who cared so much about each other. Whatever he "saw" deeply confirmed what I felt, too.

Our time together was always easy, wide open, and without secrets from my perspective (I found out later there were things I didn't know). We didn't project our unfinished business onto one another, which was not a matter of being polite but of genuine openheartedness. And in all fairness, we neither lived nor worked together for extended periods of time, and it is usually in such close, continuous relationships where people begin to abrade against one another, survival strategies begin to surface, and opportunities for self-discovery appear. All of us have had our share of challenging relationships, but mine with Bill seemed more like a reward, a respite from "learning lessons."

The only time I remember seeing Bill angry was in Tiburon while attending the regular nine o'clock prayer meeting/discussion group. Judy and Jerry were unhappy with each other over something, and Bill felt their discord was disruptive. In an uncharacteristic display of temper, Bill picked up the text and slammed it down on the table, saying, "If you two don't stop it, I'm leaving!" like a father admonishing his children. That surprising outburst got everyone's attention. He seemed afraid of anger, his own and others, and like so many, defended himself against it. In my research I've found other instances when Bill displayed anger but I witnessed only that one occasion. Although he rarely revealed his angry side, he was periodically depressed, which usually indicates repressed anger directed against one's self. Hidden anger and upset always continue to disturb one's peace of mind.

A noteworthy and consistent experience occurred every time Bill and I were together, whether in Denver, Tiburon, or elsewhere. About two days after every visit I had an unusual feeling of "more." It did not matter what had happened, who was present, or what we discussed. Something shifted on a level beyond personality or even recognition. If someone had asked, "More of what?" I would have answered, "Everything in general and nothing in particular." It was less about acquiring information and more about clarity—an insightful process. If I had a specific question or an unresolved issue, it was answered or resolved, but not through my effort. With every encounter I discovered a new level of internal power, becoming more aware of myself, larger and more loving. This feeling of literal expanding consciousness was a hallmark of our coming together and it never failed.

Additional opportunities for growth were in store for both Bill and me. One morning in January 1979, Jerry called to say that while meditating he had received a "message" that I should join him, Bill, and a third person, Aeesha, to present a day-long seminar on *ACIM* for the University of California at Santa Cruz, to be held three months later in April. This was a shocking invitation as I had been a *Course* student for only a year and a half. The *Course* does indeed present challenges, and this one raised the bar. Looking back, I can't fathom all I didn't know then, but somehow, by the end of the day, the seminar seemed to be a success and Bill was greatly relieved. He despised speaking before large groups. He thought a group of five or six was the perfect size; that he enjoyed. However, standing in front of a large group produced great anxiety for him. Not only was public speaking threatening to him, but for his first few years after retirement, he was still trying to avoid notoriety about the *Course*. His New York friends indicated that he always hated public speaking while living there too, relying on tranquilizers to get through what he considered an ordeal. Jerry noted on the drive down to Santa Cruz, however, that he seemed more willing when we were together.

After *ACIM* workshop in San Diego, CA

On several other occasions, Bill, Jerry, and I teamed up to present the *Course*, once with Ken Wapnick in San Diego in the early 1980s. I had heard about Ken but hadn't yet met him. Accustomed as I was to making extensive preparations for classes or workshops, the prospect of the four of us spending the next day with hundreds of people, with no collaboration or planning beforehand, made me nervous, to say the least. If Bill and Helen were being rushed in their spiritual evolution, so were many of us. I asked Jerry if we needed to make a plan and he indicated he had one: he would go first, then Ken, myself, and finally Bill. "That's it?" I said, "That's the plan?" "That's the plan," he said, as if that took care of everything, and for him, it did. Jerry was skilled and experienced at letting events unfold, and I, of necessity, learned a tremendous amount from him. I had no choice but to listen carefully and trust I would know what to do next. As Ken, Jerry, and I gave our various presentations, Bill periodically stood up and announced, "I think it's time to do a lesson." He would then read a lesson, inviting the audience to fully participate. He felt that teaching *ACIM* was not his mission, but he was happy to comment on what someone else had to say, and he loved to read the lessons. He could have recited the alphabet and it wouldn't have mattered. People loved listening to Bill—and they loved him.

We ended the day on a happy note, and despite his anxiety, Bill's participation was marvelous. With his beautiful voice and captivating presence, people were spellbound. Over the years, his attitude softened a bit and he became a little more willing to participate, but he was never completely comfortable with public appearances. It was such a paradox, because he was a tremendously effective speaker and people were always greatly moved.

In Denver in late 1979, six of us interested in attitudinal healing formed a center based on Jerry's Center for Attitudinal Healing in Tiburon. Four years earlier Jerry had felt called to provide a forum for practicing the insights gleaned from *ACIM*; he established a program based on its principles for children with catastrophic illnesses. Several other groups and/or individuals were so impressed by Jerry's "experiment" that they modeled centers after his. The Center for Creative Alternatives in Denver was either the fourth or fifth center established, and Bill sat on our board of directors, the only other board of any kind he was part of besides the Tiburon Center. In the mid 1970s, the idea of lay people substantively helping one another was a new idea. Jerry pioneered the formation of lay support groups, and within a short time after implementing his ideas, support groups sprang up like mushrooms.

When we held our center's grand opening in April 1980, Jerry and Bill joined us. Jerry made a wonderful presentation, as always, and Bill remained unobtrusively in the background but definitely present, adding substance to the occasion. We deeply appreciated his willingness to support our endeavor. During the reception afterward, he had a chance to mingle with the Denver students, which gave him yet another opportunity to witness *ACIM*'s impact firsthand and to hear more of its effect on changing people's lives.

Our center started with a handful of support groups, as well as what turned into *ACIM* classes, although they were originally established as volunteer-training classes. Seeking to learn from challenges Jerry had faced, we clearly stated that the services and groups offered were based on principles from *ACIM*, not on a smorgasbord of potentially competing theories. We presumed we would make mistakes, but at least they wouldn't be the same ones he had encountered. We wanted to practice *Course* principles with children or adults with catastrophic illnesses, as Jerry was successfully doing, and in addition, to include anyone in crisis or transition, anyone whose lives seemed unfulfilled. Thus, we decided to conduct a volunteer-training series so those who chose to join us would know what we stood for. Offhandedly, we announced that the series would also be available to anyone wishing to learn more about *ACIM*.

To our surprise, only a few wanted to be volunteers but many were interested in learning about the *Course*. Some apparently wanted to read it but found it difficult. Our *ACIM* overview series, a retooled version of our volunteer-training program, provided clarity about the *Course*'s philosophy, how it worked, what it was and was not for, making the material much more accessible. Although not designed as a substitute for practicing *ACIM*, our classes made it easier to take the first steps of self-study, its original purpose. Beginning in February 1980, we facilitated the series many times during the early 1980s, spawning further study groups for those who wanted to continue group work. It was a great example of proceeding in one direction only to find you have been rerouted elsewhere. Though not our original game plan, the classes turned out to be important venues for teaching what we needed to learn and as preparation for chapters not yet dreamed of.

Jaison Kayn and I originally taught the overview series, and a class was in progress during one of Bill's visits. As we prepared for the evening, we asked him if he wanted to stay at home or attend the class. "I want to come," he answered, "but don't tell anyone who I am." We promised not to disclose his identity, but were certain that someone would find him out. For most of his life, I think Bill was honestly unaware that people recognized something unique about him, and he thought if he didn't say anything, his anonymity would be protected. Since his name was common enough, we introduced him simply as Bill, a friend visiting from out of town and attending just that one night. The classes were long, from 7:30 to 10:00 and often beyond, with a break in the middle. Sure enough, suspecting he was not an ordinary *Course* student, people asked during the break, "Who is that guy, anyway?" We repeated our story that he was a friend visiting for a few days, which was accurate but incomplete. Sensing something unusual, they started to talk to him, and predictably, as he was drawn into conversation, the secret eventually came out, as he was unwilling to lie when the questions became more probing. He still didn't participate outwardly in any way, however, even after being "discovered." Class members asked questions but not of him. I always found it hilarious that he thought he could sit there unnoticed, radiating his light in the middle of the class.

Although Bill and I had shared a platform on a few occasions before and after those classes, I had never taught one with him in the audience. Having Bill there as a smiling student was somewhat unsettling. It felt approximately like preaching the Sermon on the Mount with Jesus sitting in the third row. On subsequent visits, I got used to it, but the first time was challenging, to say the least. Hugh Prather commented that Bill would also faithfully attend his or Jerry's presentations, when they were in Tiburon, and was always interested in what they had to say. Hugh felt Bill genuinely thought he could learn something from him.

Just as teaching with Bill or having him in the audience was a stretch for me, and standing before a group challenging for him, any person willing to confront conditioning, long-held beliefs, and fear of the unknown is courageous. Every small step of self-discovery requires determination, and the *Course* comforts and encourages us as we take them. So did Bill.

Collaborating with Jules Finegold on several books, both Jerry Jampolsky's and their own, had been Bill's first project on settling into his new life. That collaboration extended to include Pat Hopkins, Hugh Prather, and after Helen's death, Bob Skutch. Bill continued some of his own writing; he and Roger Walsh co-authored a revised version of the chapter on personality theory for the *Comprehensive Textbook on Psychiatry*. He also started a novel, but it never went anywhere. Years earlier, more than one psychic reading told Bill he would be living by the water some day, writing children's books with cartoons. Naturally, with his background he found that the most unlikely of predictions, but there he was, organizing Jerry's book, *Love Is Letting Go of Fear*, which included many cartoons to illustrate relevant points about the *Course*.[1] His attention to detail and long history of voluminous writing and editing was very helpful to Jerry and added substantively to his books. Jerry even asked him if he wanted to be listed as a co-author, but Bill declined. He was still dodging the spotlight.

There was plenty on his plate besides writing. Just as his friends wanted to support and nurture him, Bill, in turn, was consistently and generously available for all his close friends, particularly Jerry. Being helpful to Jerry, who was going through some trying times, was a major reason for his moving to California. Years later, as he became less of a "project" for Bill, Jerry jokingly mused that he wasn't sure if Bill had reduced his ministrations because he thought he had succeeded or because it was a hopeless task! Jerry knew perfectly well, of course, how much Bill cared for him.

In Tiburon, in addition to focusing considerable time on writing and self-reflection, Bill served on the board of directors for the Center for Attitudinal Healing, where some issue or relationship often seemed to require his wise counsel. For several months he also devoted time to being interviewed for a video history of *ACIM*, though that first attempt was never released commercially. A couple of years later, a BBC producer who was a friend of Judy's directed the video, *The Story of A Course In Miracles,* which involved more time-consuming filming of Bill telling his story. He also had the daily nine o'clock meetings at Jerry's, attended a weekly *Course* group, and had countless meetings with new people he met through Jerry or Judy.

"New people met through Jerry or Judy" should be emphasized because they occupied no small portion of his time. Jerry was the quintessential Pied Piper, drawing people to Tiburon from all over; some were interested in learning about his center and some were intrigued with him. When I entered the scene, the center was three and a half years old and had already attracted major national publicity; its star was on the rise. And any household over which Judy presides is always a three-ring circus at the very least. The edition of *New Realities* magazine that first announced *ACIM* to the world also featured an interview with Judy:

> As president of the Foundation for Inner Peace, Judith R. Skutch's life in the 1970s can best be summarized as a typical day in her consciousness

exploratorium salon in the Skutch's large New York City apartment. In one room a motion picture is being screened to a group interested in biofeedback. In another are seekers deep in meditation training. In still another room a medical research meeting is in progress.

Skutch herself seems to be in all places at once as she also juggles three telephones connecting people in the consciousness field to each other. And at any given moment, one might find an Edgar Mitchell, a Swami Muktananda, or a Uri Geller on hand, not to mention the usual assortment of mediums, mystics, and scientists—or just friends of friends. To a first-time visitor, it seems a miracle that such a petite lady can keep all of this going at once, in addition to often serving her home-cooked dinners to those gathered.[2]

When the Skutches moved to Tiburon, Judy's inclinations for gathering those at the leading edge of consciousness exploration continued unabated, and their home continued to be headquarters for the Foundation for Inner Peace. When Judy and her current husband, William (Whit) Whitson, established their home, the Foundation functions were divided between their household and Bob Skutch's. When Judy and Whit began overseeing the foreign-language translations of *ACIM* (eighteen have been published and six more are in process), with all the busyness and drama that involved, that comprised only one ring of the ongoing circus. Thus, Jerry and Judy, with their respective households and organizations, were responsible for legions of people—friends, family and extended family, the famous and unknown, movers and shakers of the consciousness movement, those who wanted to offer help, curiosity seekers, and more—streaming through Tiburon. They often included Bill in various activities, either to make sure he felt included and welcome in his new environs or because they sought his advice and counsel. He was one busy fellow. Judy's daughter, Tammy, remembers:

I noticed that when Bill moved to California, he began to relate to many more people in the playful manner that he had always related to me. It was as though the more he practiced the *Course*, and the farther he got from his old establishment life in New York, the more he let loose his indomitable, charming, childlike self.

Dressed up for the dinner parties

After graduation, I didn't see Bill for long intervals. Whenever we did see each other, it was usually for some special occasion or dinner party my mother was orchestrating. Inasmuch as the location and our lives were different, the situation still seemed the same and we comfortably slipped into our playful roles with each other. We once again became participants in a never-ending dinner party in which guests and conversations altered—but the dessert was always chocolate—and Bill would continue somehow to make everything seem more palatable for me.[3]

When I was in Tiburon, aside from visiting with many people and having long discussions with Bill, I would assist him with organizing and editing Jerry's work, beginning with a packet of eighteen cards featuring commentaries on *Course* lessons particularly helpful to Jerry (now expanded to book form: *To Give Is To Receive: An Eighteen Day Mini-Course on Healing Relationships*).[4] Jerry's first full-length book, *Love Is Letting Go of Fear*, was Bill's next collaborative project with him and I occasionally joined him in that effort. At the least, it was another way to spend quality time in each other's company. We enjoyed socializing with others of the Tiburon group and, with Jules in charge, toured San Francisco or the more scenic, rural parts of Marin County. There was never a lack of interesting people to meet or things to do, but relating was what really mattered.

Last but certainly not least, were the really funny episodes interspersed throughout our time together. Bill was a born comedian and would often make hilarious comments that were inside jokes. When other people, especially visiting dignitaries, were around, he might innocently refer to something only he and I knew about, making it impossible to keep a straight face if we made eye contact. Many of his friends also experienced his delightful, playful, and irreverent side, sharing with him a personal joke or watching as he wiggled his ears while looking very serious or proper (no one could figure out how he did that). He was more than willing to lighten things up when he decided someone was being overly serious or self-important.

In Bill's earlier California days, he was not yet driving, and several years passed before he felt comfortable enough to purchase a car and navigate around his neighborhood. In New York he had no need to drive and hadn't owned a car for more than two decades. Therefore, if we went someplace farther afield than Tiburon and environs, someone else drove. When it was time to return to Denver, Jules usually would take Bill and me to the airport. As Jules waited, Bill always came to the gate and stayed with me until boarding time (this was long before heightened security measures), and he seemed genuinely sorry I was leaving. We were very close but that doesn't imply the "specialness" that precludes closeness to others. Over the years, he had other treasured and important relationships as well. The *Course* states: "Under the Holy Spirit's teaching all relationships are seen as total commitments, yet they do not conflict with one another in any way. Perfect faith in each one, for its ability to satisfy you completely, arises only from perfect faith in yourself."[5]

E ven as Bill had struggled during the *ACIM* scribing era, feeling it was so difficult, the purifying effect was under way. The entire process of receiving and typing the material—the discussions and arguments about its meaning and then the editing—forced Bill and Helen to focus on it continually. Even when not doing the lessons or studying, they were under its influence, and by the time I met Bill, much "unlearning" had occurred, though it wasn't yet complete. He was becoming very clear and being with him always felt light and free, even when he was depressed. These "down" periods, when he entertained the preposterous notion that he didn't have much to offer, didn't keep others from enjoying his marvelous presence. He was a "work in progress," still harboring some grievances, but his loving nature was always apparent, his light still shining through, and his help unfailingly available.

It is comforting to know we can be helpful even while we're still getting free ourselves. We need not and should not wait until we are entirely clear before we choose to be truly helpful, which would be like trying to remove the darkness before turning on a light. In fact, doing our best to be compassionate, open, and nonjudgmental is the point, recognizing that correction is not our job but loving is. Shortly after the scribing began, Bill was invited to a meeting on a subject he knew little about. For political reasons, those at the medical center felt it imperative that he attend, and he was most uncomfortable about the prospect. In an instance of synchronicity, Helen took down a passage he found extraordinarily helpful, just as it has been for many others since. It is often recited at the beginning of events or study groups—whenever one needs to remember our true purpose:

I am here only to be truly helpful.

I am here to represent Him Who sent me.

I do not have to worry about what to say or what

  to do, because He Who sent me will direct me.

I am content to be wherever He wishes, knowing

  He goes there with me.

I will be healed as I let Him teach me to heal.[1]

Bill recalled his relief on receiving that special message:

This message helped me recognize that I did not have to rely on my intellectual defenses in preparing for the conference or anything else. All I had to do was to recognize that I was there to be truly helpful and that there would be guidance and help. Regardless of what the assignment might seem to be, I didn't have to plan, I didn't have to anticipate. All of this was very different. I was accustomed to planning, anticipating, having lectures and everything worked out intellectually ahead of time. Here, I think, the lesson in trust is really what is being emphasized.[2]

And a next lesson in trust was about to unfold. In 1981, Bill made arrangements to have Christmas with us in Denver, and all four of us were very excited about his coming. We had planned several special treats, especially related to the seasonal celebratory music; everything was prepared, with his presents under the tree. Then the phone call. The day before his planned arrival, Jules called to say that Bill had had a serious bout of atrial fibrillation, a malfunction of the heart. We were devastated, first out of concern for his well-being, and second, because we were so looking forward to including him in what would probably have been his first truly "family Christmas" since his own early childhood.

The day before, Pat Hopkins, then a consultant with the Center for Attitudinal Healing, had gone by Bill's home after work at his request. They were becoming much better acquainted and had developed a routine of getting together at the close of her business day. He had called her earlier in the day to say he was not feeling quite up to par, a characteristic understatement, and asked if she would take him to the hospital when she finished work. His condition steadily worsened after her arrival and she called the paramedics. They required considerable time to stabilize his acutely dangerous condition, then they rushed him to the hospital by ambulance. No doubt, Pat saved his life. She later assumed the task of handling all paperwork related to insurance, medication, and the details of recovery, which, given his basic unfamiliarity with such matters, would have been more than overwhelming to him. She was literally a God-send.

Bill returned to Denver only once or twice after his near-fatal collapse. Our Center for Creative Alternatives had teamed up with the Mile High Church of Religious Science in Denver to sponsor a workshop featuring Jerry and Hugh Prather in April 1982. We had a sellout crowd, and while planning that event, Jerry and I intuitively felt we had some joint work to do. Three weeks later, I went to Tiburon and we brainstormed about the nature of possible projects. For the next two years, Jerry and I worked closely together in a number of areas, which entailed frequent visits to Tiburon and ongoing contact with Bill. Thus, between 1978 and 1985, I was there many times.

During his first four years in Tiburon, Bill's life was busy, especially for a retiree, but not extraordinary. His days were not filled with particularly grand or exotic events. He worked, meditated, wrote, visited, recovered from his cardiac difficulties, helped friends, and faithfully walked. Because his daily routine sounds so ordinary, it doesn't convey the magic so many felt on being around him. Therefore, before continuing with the chronology of his earthly adventure, here are more details of his major positive characteristics and their life-altering impact on others, as well as the "demons" that plagued him—all the challenges, fears, and concerns that had to be forgiven.

And for all of us drawn into his energy field and who feel part of his lineage, our job is to continue our own forgiveness. The world can't wait for us to be "ready." As with Bill, we can be helpful while we're still "in process," and we must. The stakes are very high and ignoring our calling could be disastrous.

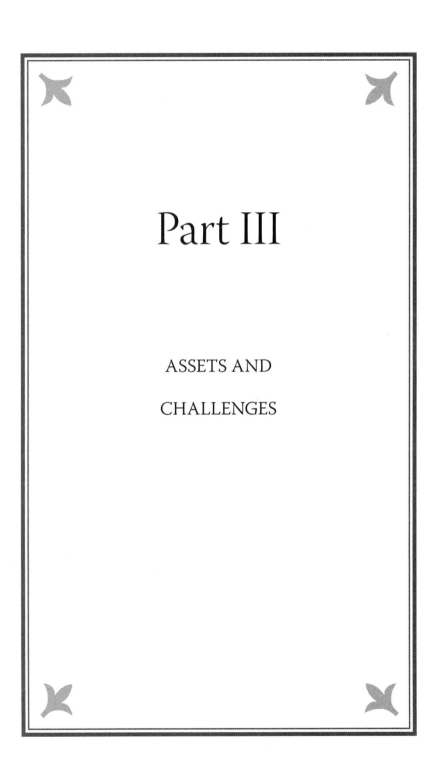

Part III

ASSETS AND

CHALLENGES

There is no doubt Bill's external life history is fascinating, but more important, it ultimately provides éntree to his inner experience. Bill was highly regarded, widely known, and included in assorted "Who's Who" lists of the academic world. As should be obvious by now, he was brilliant, erudite, painstakingly meticulous, sophisticated, dignified, and a great lover of music and theater. Those persons interviewed for this book added their assessments—gracious, courtly, a real gentleman, compassionate and encouraging, an impeccable man. He was also reserved, nonconfrontational, and rarely emotionally expressive. Catherine Prescott, a good friend, observed:

> Bill was an old-fashioned, almost Victorian transplant into this century. He had very formal, perfect manners and protocol. I saw him in a lot of different environments and he never lost that really charming and debonair quality. In many ways he was a real chameleon. I think he was many things to many people.[1]

He could be ultrawitty and was a universally acknowledged master of the pun, even a double pun. And because he was so smart and sophisticated, his ability to be funny was on the leading edge of the bell curve. As with many, his humor could also be a defense, a way of deflecting a subject that got too close for comfort, a distraction from his own pain. He was courageous, having steadfastly continued with *ACIM*'s secret unfolding in the face of potential disgrace and loss of employment.

Bill was also private, shy, deliberately compartmentalized, and secretive, often keeping various relationships separate from other friends and colleagues. His ability to compartmentalize was ideal for someone who had worked for the CIA and held diverse positions at Columbia, especially for a gay man, given that our society was much less tolerant several decades ago. Incidentally, Bill would not have discussed his sexual preference even if he had been heterosexual, considering that déclasse and none of anyone's business. He used to joke, "Keep your life a muddle and no one will ever know what's going on." In his reading in 1980, Leroy Zemke described a characteristic of the indigo blue color in Bill's aura:

> This color also indicates that you can be very secretive, that you have a way of sharing what you feel you can share, but if you choose not to share, no living person will every draw it out of you, period. That color indicates nobody gets through and that is between you and God. . . . You are not about to open yourself to the place where you're almost going to be put on an operating table, to be taken apart piece by piece. This color represents your not wanting to share yourself with the world, or even with close or intimate friends.[2]

Although it sounds contradictory, he was also very open, authentic, warm, friendly, casual, unassuming, gentle, kind, and as a friend mentioned earlier, intensely sincere. He operated from a deep sense of integrity, which partially accounts for the instantaneous sense of safety almost everyone felt around him.

Regarding his challenges, Bill could be depressed, ungrounded, restless, and argumentative; he required routine in order to function effectively in many areas of life. He could also display an edge when his passive aggressive nature was aroused and was perfectly capable of analyzing another's ego, seeing what was inconsistent or unworkable. In the presence of loud or pushy people, whom he found distressing, he would "back up" emotionally.

When upset, he could be uptight and not at all funny. Not knowing much about the world outside academia, he tended to observe life rather than fully participate in it. For the most part, I never personally experienced his "down" side, but to complete the picture, others' experiences and observations deserve inclusion.

Almost everyone was disarmed by Bill's transparency, which was profoundly effective. One might ask how this squares with being secretive, but the answer is easy. He felt the need for privacy at the human level and to keep secret his thoughts and actions, but he couldn't hide his energetic presence. The unalterable truth of him, his loving reality, was always apparent. As part of his inclination to secrecy, he rarely expressed a strong personal opinion or commented on political issues or current events. I never heard anyone attempt a political or other controversial conversation with him. Jack Luckett shared his thoughts about Bill's sense of patriotism: "He knew he was lucky to be born a white American male but he wasn't sure about the gay part. We used to go to 4th of July celebrations in La Jolla, and when well done, he found them moving. I think sometimes he found my gung-ho Marine commitment amusing, but he admired it as well."[3] His wife Layle added, "You knew Billy very well and know he was not passionate about much except opera and Mozart! I'd call him 'neutral' regarding patriotism. Certainly he was not a flag-waving, 'America first' kind of a guy, but he appreciated being born here. Maybe he was too removed from human 'life-in-time [and space]' to concern himself with feeling superior over his choice of birthplaces."[4] Jack concluded, "Bill was as complex as a Chinese puzzle but had a strong desire just to be normal."[5]

A Course In Miracles states that what we perceive in others is up to us; we can see them through eyes of love or fear and our "perception is a choice and not a fact."[6] That said, it is fascinating to note that almost everyone I interviewed described their experience with Bill in nearly identical terms—

repeatedly emphasizing a few signature traits. These comments, for the most part, were offered by those who knew him in his post-Columbia years, and thus after he had been strongly influenced by the *Course* for more than a decade. *ACIM* was working on him even while he was working on it.

What does it mean that the *Course* was "working" on him? Bill knew very well that one doesn't "take the *Course*," as one might take an algebra or chemistry class. The point is not to learn how to get one's way or acquire facts or strategies more effectively, but to unlearn our early programming. Some persons have labeled *ACIM* a mind-training course—indeed, it is and thank goodness for that! From birth, our minds are trained to believe in separation, self-absorption, and lack, not only through our families but through all our societal encounters—educational, political, religious, and through the media. That training—unhelpful and inaccurate but not necessarily deliberate—to regard ourselves as smaller and less deserving or important than we really are, must change if we hope to experience any peace of mind. The consistent practice of *Course* principles drives long-standing, limiting beliefs from our original mind training into conscious awareness, so we can decide whether to be bound by them or not. It's as if we have all been born and raised in a cult, with the ego as the tyrannical leader, requiring absolute allegiance. Since we know of no other way of being, we presume this is the only way to live. *ACIM* acts as a "deprogrammer" for our ego-directed brainwashing.

Socrates famously declared that the unexamined life is not worth living. In modern parlance, if we refuse to look at the mental/emotional conditioning we originally learned for survival, we become like reactive robots unable to make appropriate choices, basing our lives on an irrelevant past rather than living in the here and now. *A Course In Miracles* is a spiritual technology, celestial cleanser for the soul, cleaning our vision so we can know surely and directly we are safe, loved, and valuable—now and always.

The introduction to the workbook states:

> The purpose of the workbook is to train your mind in a systematic way to a different perception of everyone and everything in the world. . . .
>
> This will require no effort on your part. The exercises themselves meet the conditions necessary for this kind of transfer.
>
> Some of the ideas the workbook presents you will find hard to believe, and others may seem to be quite startling. This does not matter. You are merely asked to apply the ideas as you are directed to do. You are not asked to judge them at all. You are asked only to use them. It is their use that will give them meaning to you, and will show you that they are true.
>
> Remember only this; you need not believe the ideas, you need not accept them, and you need not even welcome them. Some of them you may actively resist. None of this will matter, or decrease their efficacy. But do not allow yourself to make exceptions in applying the ideas the workbook contains, and whatever your reactions to the ideas may be, use them. Nothing more than that is required.[7]

Notice there's not a word about carefully learning anything, only daily practicing in the face of one's disbelief. And practice Bill did, but what was he practicing? The last section of the text, "Choose Once Again," was one of his favorites and he took it to heart. "Trials are but lessons that you failed to learn presented once again, so where you made a faulty choice before you now can make a better one, and thus escape all pain that what you chose before has brought to you."[8] He was determined to notice the times when he lost his peace—times that threatened his self-image or when things weren't unfolding as he thought they should. As swiftly as possible he would choose to let them go, realizing he was the author of his own distress. One can almost see his original mind-set being released and these new, yet timeless, values being adopted.

Bill's inner life can best be explored in three ways: through quotes and illustrations from members of his extended *ACIM* family who knew him well; through his own words; and through revealing comments made by the Author of *A Course In Miracles.* My task is to facilitate joining these "voices" to reveal the most comprehensive picture possible of Bill's inner life. The reason for providing an inside view is that his inner life and ours are so alike. Even though the externals of our lives may look entirely different, the internal process of release is the same for everyone.

Remember the observation about Bill's being as complex as a Chinese puzzle? In choosing to release his grievances, quiet his mind, and live defenselessly, Bill allowed the love that was the ground of his being, and of everyone's, to appear effortlessly. He was letting go of the learned "untruth" about himself. The word Bill's friends most often used to describe him was *presence.* Although inadequate, it is the closest available. Something happened around him; one felt lighter, more expansive. Some expressed it as a calming and radiant quality; others said it was like the room became electrified or filled with an exuberant energy. In any case, it was a great influence in people's lives and left an indelible mark. Zemke speaks eloquently about this quality that everyone observed:

> You have three shades of rose red [in his aura]. This first shade is a very pale pastel shade. It is the color of divinity incarnate in the form of love. You bring that energy forward through your being. This is the divine essence or divine loving force transmitted into the earth. Then there is another step-up of that color and it is mixed with a lot of white, indicating transformation through love, the capacity to transform people, life circumstances, through love, and this is the mark of a very advanced teacher or soul. Then still another color attached to this rose spectrum is a rose-white, a blend of the two so subtle that it seems more white than rose, and this indicates the connection to the divine that at times is so

strong and so clear that there is no way you can translate that information in words. It is simply a transmission that occurs on an energy level of your being and gradually filters into form in whatever way is best. It happens without your doing anything about it consciously and is responsible for the attraction that people feel. Many of the people who experience this with you do not understand what they are experiencing. They just know they want to have it. They want to be near you, be around you, close to you.[9]

The following excerpts from many interviews help identify and explain more fully Bill's prominent qualities as listed at the beginning of this chapter.

If *presence* was a term universally ascribed to Bill, several noteworthy subsets derive from it. A sentence from Dante's *Paradiso* succinctly captures so many people's subjective experience of him: "You are my sire, said I: you give me heart freely to speak my thought: above myself you raise me."[10] Or a more modern translation: "You give me full courage to speak; you lift me until I am more than myself."[11] That was Bill, and it most fully articulates his greatest gift, the most noted aspect of his way of being—his unsurpassed capacity to support and accept almost anyone or anything. I say "almost," because in his last decade there were still a few loose ends of forgiveness not yet handled and some persons could still push his buttons. Offering acceptance has a noticeable, substantive healing effect both on those who give and receive it. It speaks in ways far more compelling than words that we are not judged, that we are completely acceptable as we are and deeply cared for. Within the light of Bill's acceptance, frantic or mindless thought could settle down, accompanied by a deep sense of relief. Imagine no need to defend, impress, convince, or dominate. People relaxed in his presence. Bill's acceptance had the instantaneous, profound effect of orienting people to their own innate value, and the expansion was automatic. The *Course* speaks of the healing effect that practicing forgiveness has on others:

> The power of witness is beyond belief because it brings conviction in its wake. . . .
>
> Now in the hands made gentle by His touch, the Holy Spirit lays a picture of a different you. It is a picture of a body still, for what you really are cannot be seen nor pictured. . . . Show this unto your brother, who will see that every scar is healed, and every tear is wiped away in laughter and in love. And he will look on his forgiveness there, and with healed eyes will look beyond it to the innocence that he beholds in you. Here is the proof that he has never sinned, that nothing which his madness bid him do was ever done, or ever had effects of any kind. That no reproach he laid upon his heart was ever justified, and no attack can ever touch him with the poisoned and relentless sting of fear.[12]

No wonder people were so drawn to him! It was like being absolved at the confessional, not as a ritual but as an absolute and incontrovertible fact. Many still speak of the magic of being around him and the unforgettable experience of being unconditionally loved. Praise for him is so consistent that it might tend to sound worshipful, precisely what he would not want. "Fair and balanced" reporting would require my listing as many complaints of Bill as glowing reports, but I would have to manufacture them. The representative quotes below, echoed by many others, express the power of his influence:

Jaison Kayn reflects, "He was comforting in the sense that if there were pretenses, it didn't matter to him whatsoever. He was also going to stabilize the situation beyond any pretenses, any situation. He knew what was true and you could just take that lead from him."[13] Bruce Gregory, a friend from New York, remembers:

> After a visit with him, I felt so free and at ease. Something about Bill's expansive, liberating "just be happy, just be loving, don't worry" quality

took by osmosis. That is the answer for all of us, so barriers were loosening and crumbling. He was able to see more and to love more and when you're around that, when you're not highly defended, you have this wonderful sense of loving acceptance as well as encouragement; it just fans the flame of spirit. Bill was very, very gifted in that sense. He would listen, was compassionate and encouraging like, "Don't let that bother you, it's okay, don't hold onto it."[14]

Judith Skutch Whitson comments on that first fateful luncheon with Bill and Helen, "I was quite uncomfortable with Helen, or I should say slightly terrified, because I didn't know which social skills to use with her. She was an anomaly to me. You didn't know if you were getting through. You didn't know whether you should be open, closed, chatty, quiet—at least I didn't know. But with Bill I was so relaxed because I felt so comfortable with him."[15]

Although Bill knew that teaching the *Course* was not his mission, he fully supported other people's efforts on behalf of the *Course*. Hugh Prather noted,

He was open to almost any approach. Once at a meeting in La Jolla, Bill was just as happy as a Cheshire cat sitting in this absolutely far-out, "woo-woo" California atmosphere. Some people would say things I know he didn't believe philosophically, yet he was completely accepting of whatever they had to say, their attempts to heal, the songs that they would sing.

Also, I was impressed with his gentleness, his openness—he would talk about anything you wanted to talk about—his lightheartedness, his humor, and of course, he was very intelligent with that sort of eastern sophistication, which being from Texas I'm sometimes intimidated by, but not with him. It was a relief to find him so open and friendly and accessible. I just connected with him right from the beginning.[16]

Catherine Prescott remembers,

He was so generous with me and my children in the sense of making me feel secure, his kindness when I moved to Marin County was just over the top and I needed it. I was a single mother and scared! I never felt more deeply empowered by another human being; he helped me know in a profound way that I was okay. I could move toward self-love or self-acceptance because he showed his humanity so much, being willing to be the bumbler. He put no weight on degrees or fame or anything. He was not impressed. That was interesting. He was also funny and cynical and made comments about everybody, including himself. He was always self-deprecating and always "we're just people." Aside from his funny, really ironic humor, as far as character, he was the actual living proof of unconditional love. His kindness and tender heart came through everything.[17]

Bill finding peace of mind

Diane Cirincione, Jerry Jampolsky's wife, always felt supported with Bill,

There was a time when, like so many others, I was consciously exploring the depths of my own spirituality. He gave me encouragement and support, not because he said, "I'm going to encourage and support you," but our interaction simply gave me permission to be me and find my voice. He did that for a lot of people. He had the ability to validate your being without having to say anything, to help you feel good about yourself—perhaps the greatest gift anyone gives anybody. It's as if he said, "If anyone needs permission to be themselves, I grant it," only it wasn't done at a conscious mind level. It happened automatically around him. If I had an issue, something I wanted to work on, he would say, "Why don't you do that? Just change it all. Change it in your mind." I went, "Oh, okay, why don't I?" He was free and unattached to the whole thing, a very empowering person, not to overuse an old word. I found him to be equally loving to everybody. I think he loved a lot of us, his love was strong and that was very important. I never felt judged by Bill in any way, shape, or form. He had a way of being kind of egalitarian, not elitist at all, and of course, I loved his humor.[18]

Carlagaye Olson, who became a close friend of Bill's in the 1980s, fondly recalls,

You know, the most important moments with Bill were those personal ones. There is nothing I can condense into some words of wisdom, except to say that he was so incredibly accepting, just that feeling that this was a family and we were unconditional members of that family and there was nothing in him that said, "I pick you and not you." You know how the *Course* says our only problem is the feeling of worthlessness? Well, just being in the presence of someone you admire a great deal . . . I don't know anybody else who could have provided that experience.[19]

My older son, Greg, recalled from his experience as a young boy,

It didn't matter what he said, or what we did. I just remember what it was like to be around him—that was the key. When he was in the house, you could feel it. You could breathe a sigh of relief like there was a way home. There was something about his presence that was so comforting and reassuring and had nothing to do with what he said. I always felt an endearing sense of calmness. He brought a sense of safety, which is the key point. People will naturally gravitate toward individuals like that because they want that sense of safety and peace and tranquility. It's an unbelievably powerful feeling. Most people have some hard edges; he seemed to have soft edges with nothing that made you feel rough or constricted or uninviting. When you were near him, everything was a little bit finer, a little more okay, more resolved, none of which quite do justice to what it was like to be around him. There was something about Bill that was almost angelic.[20]

LeRoy Zemke made some interesting far-out observations about Bill in the early 1980s. He indicated that he represented a new kind of awakened cosmic teacher, a living example of what's possible—a guru, but not in the traditional sense of the word. As he tuned into Bill, he picked up his awakened heart-center energy, a deeply integrated sense of holiness, almost a saintly quality. Bill would have had difficulty accepting any of that, certainly balking at the guru idea, but the final outcome of his life gives credence to those earlier observations.

Frances Vaughan remembers, "He took himself lightly, but he never made light of other people's concerns. His presence was very even, even during times when he was not well or when he was struggling with some of his own issues. He was still able to give others loving attention."[21]

16

So what were the issues he struggled with? The same as ours—grievances, of course, and feelings of guilt and failure, as well as the defenses that hide the pain and distress they cause. Despite his outward demeanor and his obvious loving nature, he still had some long-held notions about himself to release. Bill may have been kind to others, but he was hard on himself, troubled by perceived deficiencies. It's amazing that he could have had such a profound effect on others while still battling with his own guilt, testimony to the two starkly different modes of living in this world. Just as Helen could alternate between polar opposites—bowing to her difficult, demanding ego *and* accessing the love that created the *Course*—Bill, too, could operate from an unconditional loving space or be caught in the grip of self-doubt. And just as *ACIM* dictation was not compromised when Helen didn't feel good, so too, love is present along with confusion about lack of worth.

There are three avenues we can use to discern the challenging aspects of Bill's interior life. First is the direct material in the Urtext that addresses both his assessment of his unworthiness and the defenses he employed to cope with it. The purpose of the *Course* is to illustrate how to release entirely the notion of unworthiness, rather than provide more sophisticated strategies for keeping and dealing with it. Second, throughout his life, Bill elicited certain behavior patterns in others, which allows great insight into what he feared or found troubling in himself, although perhaps unconsciously.

"Unacceptable" behaviors in others, of course, reflect our own unfinished business and condemnation of ourselves. Third, he specifically commented on certain characteristics he found objectionable in himself and others; no detective work required here.

The Author of *ACIM* was firm and unequivocal in the messages to Bill and Helen about what they needed to look at, release, and make different choices about—attitudes they needed to trade in for a happier way of living. Bill was a master of ego discernment, but the Author of the *Course* was a step ahead of him, and after reading the personal commentary in the Urtext, one can see why neither Bill nor Helen wanted this personal material, disclosing their most basic fears and shortcomings, to be part of a public record.

A significant digression is called for here related to the Urtext. Why was the personal material in it deleted? In addition to the potential embarrassment to the scribes, the Author specifically stated it should not be included. It is important for both new and seasoned students to realize the Author requested that specific or personal material be removed to avoid confusion, rather than thinking this was done unilaterally by Helen, Bill, or Ken. Where she had a personal investment, Helen did interfere to a degree, contaminating some of the very earliest material (and *only* the earliest) with her own biases, because she was not yet a totally clear channel. Such material was inconsistent with the actual *Course*, and Ken referred to these parts as "Helen-isms." The scribing was very informal, especially in the beginning; the form was not sacrosanct. Ken Wapnick writes in an unpublished manuscript, "The History of the Manuscripts of *A Course In Miracles*":

> What is most important to consider about the public exposure of these earlier manuscripts [the Urtext, the Hugh Lynn Cayce version, and a couple of others] is that regardless of the version you read, you will receive the essential teaching of the *Course*. In that sense, no real harm has been done.

In another sense, however, the situation is unfortunate because people could be misled and at this point, nothing can be done about it . . . except, perhaps, to clarify what inquiring students may be reading. Let me cite some examples. There is material in the Urtext about sex and sexuality, an area that will almost certainly pique the curiosity (if not prurient interest) of students. Thus, for example, one will read that homosexuality is essentially a pathology (the traditional psychoanalytic view) and that the only purpose for sex is procreation, two positions that are antithetical to Jesus' own teachings in the *Course* about seeing all forms of the ego's world as the same, the correction to the ego's first law of chaos that *there is a hierarchy of illusion*. To believe that these would be the words and thoughts of Jesus is as preposterous and unthinkable an idea as to believe that I could influence Helen as to what belonged in the *Course* and what did not. It should be obvious that these beliefs belong to Helen and not to Jesus. Helen had her own biases about sex, and unfortunately they came through in these early passages. Yet those who believe that every word in the Urtext is sacred and are Jesus' words can use statements like these to support their own preconceived notions. This same issue holds, though perhaps with less emotionality, with material related to Edgar Cayce, Freud and other psychologists. . . .

Thus, it became very clear to me in the years I knew Helen that I should take with a grain of salt some of the things she said or wrote as coming from Jesus, and this clearly included the early Urtext material. Unfortunately, there are also some things there that if you do not know the context, you will not understand what they refer to, or what they mean. This inevitability means that those who were not present and did not know Helen and Bill will misunderstand much of what is found there.[1]

Helen did recognize this periodic corruption of the material where her biases intruded and discussed it with Ken. She may also have talked with Bill about it, but that is only conjecture as their relationship was so often discordant. A short while into the text, Helen's resistance relaxed; the dictation flowed evenly and no longer included dialogue or personal material. Bill often commented on how difficult scribing the *Course* was for both of them; being thoroughly examined by the Author makes "difficult" seem, at the least, an understatement. Both Bill and Helen called on considerable courage to continue their scribal commitment while being in the "hot seat" with the Author.

A few examples from the Urtext reveal both the specific nature of some of Bill's issues, remembering they allude to his state of mind at the onset of the *Course*, and how universal they really are. They concerned his fear that he was not going to succeed without being special in some way and that without specialness everyone would see his unworthiness, and thus failure. (By the way, Ken indicated that the quotes I have chosen for inclusion in this book are valid, not ones where Helen's personal opinions bled through.) Despite his outer success, Bill still harbored resentments and was plagued by a lack of self-worth. Sound familiar? The following material comes from the early part of the Urtext, which was deleted from the first six chapters of the published text. The Author was equally firm with Helen, but her issues are not the subject of this book. (Bill capitalized some words as he typed Helen's notes to denote emphasis, but I have changed them to italics.) This message for Bill was relayed to Helen.

> His real specialness does *not* stem from exclusion, but from inclusion. *All* my brothers are special. He should stop interpreting this as "all except Bill." This is ridiculous! Tell him that the implied lack of love that his version contains is way off the mark and misses the level of right thinking entirely. He *must* heal his perception in this respect.[2]

> You and Bill *do* have special talents which are needed for the celestial speed-up at this time. But note that the term "speed-up" is not one which relates to the *transcending* of time.

When time is abolished and all of the Sons of God have come home, no special agents will be necessary. But do not underestimate the power of special agents now, or the great need there is for them. I do not claim to be more than that myself. No one in his right mind (a term which should be especially noted) ever wants either more nor less than that.[3]

At the end of a long dissertation on the confusion about communication and knowledge, the Author listed four general statements about the misuse of knowledge (as we understand the word, not as the *Course* uses it), and then specifically called their attention to this list:

> 4. Knowledge can also be misinterpreted as a means of possession. Here, the content is not physical and the underlying fallacy is more likely to be a confusion of mind and brain. . . . The fallacious use of knowledge can result in several errors, including:
>
> a. The idea that knowledge will make the individual more attractive to others. This is possession-fallacy.
>
> b. The idea that knowledge will make the individual invulnerable. This is the reaction formation against the underlying fear of vulnerability.
>
> c. The idea that knowledge will make the individual worthy. This is largely pathetic.

Both you and Bill should consider type 4 [all of the above] *very* carefully. Like all these fallacies, it contains a denial mechanism, which swings into operation as the fear increases, thus canceling out the error temporarily, but seriously impairing efficiency.

Thus, you claim that you can't read and Bill claims that he can't speak. Note that depression is a real risk here, for a Child of God should never *reduce* his efficiency in *any* way. The depression comes from a peculiar pseudo-solution which reads:

A Child of God is efficient.

I am not efficient.

Therefore, I am not a Child of God.

This leads to neurotic resignation and this is a state which merely *increases* the depression.[4]

However uninviting these messages were, Bill did take them to heart and diligently practiced reaching out to others. As he took the steps offered him in the *Course*, he became more than willing to spend a great deal of time with many people in order to help them. He lavished attention on those with whom he had strong connections, as well as in more casual encounters. For many of us, he was our greatest cheerleader, inspiring us to take our next steps, both internally and externally, and helping each to let go of whatever was in our way—modern-day disciples, perhaps. As one person stated, "I just can't imagine anyone else playing that kind of [inspirational] role and for so many of us!"[5]

He was also willing, as a demonstration of love, to do things he really didn't care to do, but he honored those who asked, if his guidance so dictated. Do not mistake this for being wimpy, having no boundaries, or being unable to say no. For sure, when Bill felt it was not right for him to do something, nothing in heaven or earth could move him from his position. He really lived this admonition:

Suppose a brother insists on having you do something you think you do not want to do. His very insistence should tell you that he believes salvation lies in it. If you insist on refusing and experience a quick response of opposition, you are believing that your salvation lies in *not* doing it. You, then, are making the same mistake he is, and are making his error real to both of you. Insistence means investment, and what you invest in is always related to your notion of salvation.[6]

As one example, Jerry Jampolsky remembered this favorite: "You know he never exercised and I thought maybe if I bought him a jogging suit for his birthday, he might get interested in walking and doing things like that. He said, 'No way am I going to do that, but I'll tell you what I'll do. I'll let you take one picture of me with that suit on.' He took it off and never wore it again. He wasn't going to a gym."[7] Actually, he did walk every day, sometimes more than once, and he enjoyed that a great deal; it made possible the wonderful experiences so many had on those walks. But true to his word, he never went to a gym.

Jogging suit—present from Jerry

Jerry was also aware of the great love and brotherhood they felt for one another, exemplified by Bill's willingness to serve on the board of the Center for Attitudinal Healing, which was "the last thing in the world his ego would want to do. I remember his infinite patience with me. I asked him a thousand questions and later came back with more. His willingness to do his best to listen to the Voice was amazing. What I remember about him was that steadfast commitment. He was like a rudder on a ship going straight in the direction toward God."[8]

Jaison Kayn remembered:

> He would never think of speaking himself, but as other people asked it [to speak] of him, he would. That was one of his forms of generosity, as if to say, "If that's what you want, then I'll talk." Another thing he gave me was the sense that if there was anything he could do to make me comfortable, he would. He mostly did that with his presence in terms of reassurance, not verbally. He honored people for who they were and let them know that there was nothing about them that he judged. He supported your being.[9]

Bob Beale occasionally visited Bill in Tiburon:

> One of the things I loved about him was his gentle manner and that he subtly offered some really powerful insights, always made in low-key statements, and I was very receptive to listening. Sometimes people try to give you advice or insights and they come on fairly strong and one instinctively pushes back. He never made emphatic statements and I had no feeling of wanting to push back with Bill. It was a delight to experience his gentle manner. I can distinctly remember when it was time to leave, I would go up that hill from Tiburon over to San Francisco and things would really just start to vibrate. All of a sudden I'd really get what Bill said.[10]

Bill always modeled the wonderful way we can be helpful to each other without being oppressive or giving advice or fixing. How comforting it is when information comes through the loving presence within, rather than from the ego's critical perspective of, "Here is what's the matter with you, so shape up." It's not that Bill saw things and then had to work to overlook them; somehow they fell off the radar screen for him. He touched people deeply because it was his goal to be aware only of their underlying love, and he was determined to let go of judgment. It was not in keeping with his goal of unconditional acceptance to try to change a person or buy into their fears.

Bruce Gregory met Bill at the Skutch home in New York, which he described as "Miracle Central." He left Manhattan in 1979 and moved to rural Arizona, where he worked in a prison. Being closer then to Tiburon, he visited Bill occasionally.

> Those visits with Bill, though small in number, were quality times with a gentle, settled soul who was kind enough to hear out my challenges in my personal and work life in a small town that was friendly but openly critical of anyone who wasn't "normal.". . . He also provided such kind support as I tried to integrate my spiritual yearnings with the fact of being gay in a world that did not really understand or accept either.

> Bill was able to exude acceptance and normalcy and even a little feistiness about my self-acceptance. I can't say that I resolved my issues completely with his help, but I certainly did come back to my new home after my visits refreshed and with more peace of mind, along with the magic of self-acceptance and acceptance of others, even in their bigotry. That was a miracle for me, in that I saw no need to fight or struggle to change the minds of others to accept me as I was. It was more important to accept them as they were. I then found that this started to translate into acceptance of the inmates I worked with in my substance abuse groups.[11]

Although there are many examples of how Bill's supportive attitude led people to greater forgiveness, and thus to a more rewarding and helpful life, excerpts from Bruce's essay are typical.

> I'm sure that when I asked God if I should go with my friends out to Arizona for this new life in forming a small spiritual community of

friends, and the answer I got was "Go!" that some interesting plans for my healing were put in place. I had spent my life avoiding any kind of bullies, after a rough encounter in the third grade, leaving me with a firm but tearful decision to "never trust anyone again." That firm rule had never really been challenged until my move to Arizona. When I went for a job, there were only two available: skinning coyotes (seasonal) and counseling inmates at the local prison. I wanted neither, but I had to earn money to pay off my part of the mortgage. The prison paid better and was steady pay, so that's what I chose.

My first day on the prison yard was a nightmare, as I got all sorts of comments and catcalls and whistles from the inmates. Not a great beginning, especially when I really didn't want to be there. But since skinning coyotes was definitely worse, I knew I had to find a way through this. I went home that night to the peace and quiet of our new home and tried to sort it out. I figured that the inmates had responded to my fears, and found an opportunity to feel stronger than me by comparison, especially in their one-down position in prison. I decided then and there to choose to go beyond my fears of the inmate bullies and focus on my desire to be of help in whatever way I could. I went back to work the next morning, and I never had another negative encounter with them in the twenty-seven years that followed. In fact, one of the highest compliments I've ever received came from a fellow counselor, who told me that if ever a riot were to break out among the inmates, he was planning to stand behind me because no one would ever hurt me.

Bill helped me to develop this inner calm from his own example. And when I was asked to work with medium-custody inmates, a rougher, tougher crowd, I found myself dealing with personal attacks again, this time in the classroom from those who didn't want to be there, but were required to be "for their own good." At this point, again with some time spent with Bill under my belt, I found myself not caring about the obvious barbs intended to put me down, but caring more for the inmates' well-being. It was a new-found freedom that came from this that eventually led to a greater acceptance, appreciation, and even joyous love for the inmate "bullies" that I had so assiduously avoided all my life.

> Understanding his [the childhood bully's] background as well as my own attack thoughts helped me to break down the barriers I had built toward everyone and forgive my "bully." I've never met him again, and yet I have met him in so many others, especially in prison. Even the inmates have told me, "I know you. You're the person I used to give such a hard time to." We both knew that we were speaking of substitutes, later in life, but we could see that we were both moving beyond our old roles. So I thank Bill for his loving encouragement not to be afraid. I know it meant a lot to have that deeper part of me recognized and energized by his knowing gaze.[12]

Bill had not always been consistently supportive and accepting. For instance, one of his friends at the CIA told of going to lunch without him after they had specifically planned to get together. She apologized and indicated that she and her friend had simply forgotten about his going, but that it certainly wasn't deliberate. Bill replied that that was worse, interpreting her explanation as an obvious rejection, though perhaps not on a conscious level. He told her, "We go to lunch together but then at a subconscious level I'm not someone you want to be with." She still remembers being quite taken aback by that comment because he was serious, and not playful, about feeling rejected.

A famous magician of the early twentieth century, David Verner, aka Dai Vernon, spoke of the deep hunger within us for the "numinous"—divine power, creative energy, spiritual elevation. We love the idea that something mystical and unexplainable can occur. A true magician can project and change the experience of those he influences. In that way, Bill was like a magician, although it was not contrived but automatic. Through his openness to them, he could invite people into a sense of Self and was delighted as he witnessed that occur. Frances Vaughan speaks of a particularly important aspect of Bill's acceptance:

> One of Bill's gifts was a presence that enabled people to grow. He was very accepting. He never tried to impose his own views on anybody. I would describe his way of being as an absence of personality noise. He created a safe place for people to be who they were. He was definitely very attentive to whomever he was with; it was as though he didn't need to take up any room. By making a space for you to fill up, he made you feel that you could just be who you are.
>
> When I talked to Bill I felt he really listened and could understand what I had to say. That was one of the nicest things about him. He wasn't full of his own agenda or ideas about the way things should be. He provided a spaciousness and a quality of listening that was very deep. I felt he gave loving, non-interfering attention to everyone. That is a great gift that can be very healing.[13]

These observations include several critically important ideas. First, we all know individuals who take up a great deal of psychic space, who seem to take all the air out of a room, who dominate with "I, me, and mine—it's all about me." No one warms to that person and yet we all believe that we require some degree of self-promotion to be happy, secure, and prosperous. However, if you ask someone to elaborate on how that happens, you will not get a valid answer. We have fallen into the trap of believing that taking up space is good and necessary, competing for it through attempts to be special. The philosopher Douglas Harding often speaks of "disappearing in favor of the other person," another way of stating Bill's capacity for open acceptance. It seems a paradox that the more wholeheartedly present we are for others, the more we "disappear," the more everyone gains. This contradicts our earliest programming of how to "stake out our territory." If we gathered up all the "I, me, and mine" thought patterns and rolled them up to almost nothing—figuratively speaking—our happiness would increase. Focusing on the other, rather than self, is a major component of forgiveness. One caution: taking up no space does not mean withholding, hiding, or defending. Keeping things bottled up for fear of being unacceptable is hardly a no-space situation. Feeling inferior with the need to hide can result in one's being an irritable, high-maintenance person, indeed.

A second important aspect of the acceptance Bill demonstrated was his capacity to listen fully, to give another his undivided attention regardless of the subject matter; this is healing for both parties. The one being listened to feels completely and unconditionally accepted, and it quiets the mind of the listener, bringing both into the present moment—the only time a change of mind can occur. Undivided attention also clears the mind enough so that guidance or intuition about what to do or how to change perspective becomes possible. Counterintuitively, "taking up no space" incurs no sacrifice whatsoever. *ACIM*, understanding that we believe this change of outlook is dangerous, states:

> Therefore, the period of overlap is apt to be one in which the teacher of God feels called upon to sacrifice his own best interests on behalf of truth. He has not realized as yet how wholly impossible such a demand would be. He can learn this only as he actually does give up the valueless [ego self-promotion]. Through this, he learns that where he anticipated grief, he finds a happy lightheartedness instead; where he thought something was asked of him, he finds a gift bestowed on him.[14]

Deeply listening to others is an act of love. Where we think that genuinely deferring to others will bring us loneliness and unhappiness, instead we find ourselves included and revered. The following passages from the Urtext indicate some of Bill's errors that he corrected through deep listening and engaging with others.

Tell Bill the reason he was so strained yesterday is because he allowed himself a number of fear-producing attitudes. They were fleeting enough to be more will-of-the-wisps than serious will-errors but unless he watches this kind of thing, he *will* find the notes fearful, and knowing him well, will mis-distantiate. [In short, he would keep the notes at an intellectual or emotional distance inappropriately.][15]

You, Bill, have not made consistent efforts to change your mind except through applying old habit patterns to new ideas. But you have learned, and learned it better than Helen, that your mind gains control over *itself* when you direct it genuinely toward perceiving someone *else* truly. Your lack of vitality is due to your former marked effort at solving your needless depression and anxiety through disinterest. Because your ego *was* protected by this unfortunate negative attribute, you are afraid to abandon it.

When you have given up this voluntary dis-spiriting, you have already seen how your mind can focus and rise above fatigue, and heal. But you are not sufficiently vigilant against the demands of your ego that you disengage yourself.[16]

Do not disturb yourself about repression, Bill, but *do* train yourself to be alert to any tendency to withdraw from your brothers. Withdrawal is frightening and you do not recognize all the forms it takes in you. . . . You, Bill, will learn somewhat differently because you are afraid of all complete involvements, and believe that they will lessen *you.* You have learned to be so much more clear-sighted about this that you should be ready to oppose it in yourself *relatively* easily. As you come closer to a brother, you do approach Me, and as you withdraw from him, I become distant to you.[17]

Detachment is essentially a weaker form of dissociation. This is one of the major areas of withholding that both you and Bill are engaging in.[18]

Tell Bill that his delaying tactics are holding him back. He does not really understand detachment, distantiation, and withdrawal. He is interpreting them as "holding himself aloof" from the Atonement.[19]

There is much evidence that Bill often felt trapped, an interior experience but one he tried to rectify in his outer world. For instance, he always preferred to sit by a door at meetings or in an aisle seat at the theater or concert hall, any place that facilitated a quick escape. Ken noted Bill's propensity for standing in the doorway of Helen's office as they met during the editing phase, not only as an escape route but also to retreat to his office for a cigarette, another type of escape. Also, when one is uncomfortable in a situation and can't "escape" geographically, it is common simply to detach from it and disappear emotionally, a defense universally employed until one realizes it doesn't bring happiness or peace of mind. Bill used that strategy as well.

Bill is better at understanding the need to study the notes than you are, but neither of you realizes that many of the problems you keep being faced with may *already* have been solved there. You do not think of the notes in this way at all. Bill does from time to time, but he generally says, "It's probably in the notes," and doesn't look it up. He believes that, although he reads them over, they cannot really help him until they are complete.

First of all, he cannot be sure of this unless he tries. Second, they would be completed if both of you so willed. You vaguely know that the course is intended for some sort of preparation. I can only say that you are not prepared.

I was amused when you reminded Bill that he, too, was being prepared for something quite unexpected and he said he was not at all curious about what it was. This disinterest is very characteristic of him when he is afraid. Interest and fear do *not* go together as your respective behavior clearly shows.[20]

Bill's behavior is not chaotic because he is not so much goal-divided as not goal-oriented. Where Helen has over-invested in many goals, Bill has under-invested in *all* goals. He has the advantage of *potentially* greater freedom from dis-tractability, but he does not care enough to use it. Helen has the advantage of great effort, but she keeps losing sight of the goal.[21]

Bill has very intelligently suggested that you both should set yourself the goal of really studying for this course. There can be no doubt of the wisdom of this decision for any student who wants to pass it. But, knowing your individual weaknesses as learners, and being a teacher with some experience, I must remind you that learning and wanting to learn are inseparable.[22]

B ill's sense of humor ran a close second to *presence* and un-conditional acceptance as his most-mentioned outstanding characteristics. In the Urtext, the author commented:

I wish he would decide to use that talent of his [for making puns] con-structively. He has no idea how powerful it could be. Actually, it does come from the unconscious and is really a distorted form of miraculous perception, which he has reduced to word twisting. Although this can be quite funny, it is still a real waste. Maybe he'd care to let me control it, and still use it humorously himself. He doesn't have to decide it is one *or* the other.[1]

Bill must have surrendered some control over that talent because he could be simply hilarious. Whit Whitson, a superb wordsmith himself, noted, "I was soon captivated by Bill because he struck me as a voice of balance and sanity packaged in dry wit. The more I listened to his views about the *Course*, the more my respect grew for it and for the whimsy and sparkle of his mind."[2] His innate lovingness, combined with his wonderful ability to be lighthearted, was indeed sparkling and compelling. Everyone, without exception, recalled with delight their times of rich, heartwarming laughter with Bill.

LeRoy Zemke's reading confirmed this trait, even though Bill was an unknown client at the time: "You have a remarkable talent to aid you in this, and it is your capacity to draw upon the wit and the clarity of your own mind that stems from warmth and from your capacity to see a sense of the ridiculous in all that life offers. . . . Use it amply whenever it applies and you will find that whatever you have to teach, this will be the tool that will aid you in the work that needs to be done."[3]

And aid us all, it did. Getting a handle on Bill's humor moves you very close to his essence—it was one of his ways of loving. He was never malicious with humor, which is often a thinly disguised cover for a put-down, but not with Bill. His really funny way of being was not at someone else's expense. Bill laughed at the absurdity of life and found nothing too sacred for his lighthearted touch. It was all amusing—his work, the science of psychology, people, situations, or sex. Predictably, when people started taking themselves or a situation too seriously, he became an impish, irreverent jokester, as if to say, "Lighten up, everybody!"

Happy to be alive in 1982

Fast forwarding to the La Jolla era, Bill occasionally enjoyed the company of some lady friends there, although they were never actual romances. Jack Luckett recounted that sometimes, when someone from Tiburon would visit and one of those women were around, Bill would "hold and kiss her and act as if this was a real huge romance; he thought it was a great kick [to shock the visitor] because he had a little bit of a trickster in him."[4] Jack's wife Layle remembers a great story many of us can identify with, having been in similar situations with Bill:

I heard about a poetry reading way across San Diego on the far east side of town. We found the small, old frame house and entered to find a small room jammed with chairs and people. We found seats far from the aisle, a very bad sign for Billy in case escape was required. Also, we learned that the house had no back door—the back overhung a steep canyon—and that there was only one bathroom, but we persevered.

The first reader, a man, started out reading something terminally boring in airy-fairy Victorian style with full expression and an almost nausea-producing rhythmic beat, sway, and facial expression. Soon, Billy and Jack found this hilarious, but couldn't escape! We didn't dare look at each other for fear of setting off explosive laughter! They tried not to be rude, but they were holding back so hard that little snorts were escaping their noses and mouths. Finally both—on either side of me—had their faces in their laps shaking. I was bored, but oblivious, so thought they were emoting. Naturally, this event went on for about ninety hours until we were finally released. Imagine how fast we got out of there, never to return. Jack can still get almost hysterical remembering this.[5]

Hugh Prather remembers,

Well, I can tell you, everything about him was this deep connection with God combined with his advice not to take it all too seriously—one of the primary themes of Bill's life and the great gift he gave the world. Every conversation I had with him had an effect on me because I was taking the *Course* very seriously and you just couldn't do that with Bill. I wish everyone could have felt his very lighthearted approach to the *Course*. As a matter of fact, I think one of the reasons he kept telling these stories, pointing out the absurdity of everything that had gone on when the *Course* came, whether done consciously or not, was for the effect it had of lightening me up on the whole subject. Additionally, he just thought it infinitely amusing that the CIA had financed so much of their work, and he always joked about the typewriter—the CIA-funded typewriter that typed *ACIM*.[6]

Incidentally, the CIA never orchestrated the production of the *Course* in any way. There is some misleading speculation to that effect on the Internet, but anyone who knew either Helen or Bill or has the slightest knowledge of the material would find that patently absurd. This profound and transformative work could not possibly have been faked or planned by even the best of intellects, no matter what the purpose. And for those who knew Helen, the notion that she could be coerced or manipulated into doing something she didn't want to do is also ridiculous. When she said no, that was it.

Among his stories from Columbia, Bill delighted to talk about being co-editor of the *Journal of Abnormal Psychology* from 1965–1971, the years of *Course* dictation. He periodically rejected articles that were "not sufficiently scientific," and, of course, he found this situation ridiculous and very humorous.

In the early 1980s, a woman who was writing a spiritually based sex manual, which she believed was being dictated by Jesus, started corresponding with Bill to inform him about messages she was getting from "Jesus." Being a bit nonplussed and not knowing quite how to respond, he finally wrote her back after receiving several letters and said that he, too, had talked to Jesus, who told him they should not communicate for five years! Once again, this particular use of humor was not to denigrate the woman but to infuse a greater sense of lightheartedness into the situation.

Most of us take everything so seriously, but this was quintessential Bill. Whit Whitson remembers,

> I often told my children when they were growing up, as a first principle you really should be more than you seem. And that to me was Bill in spades. On the surface, he was a good-looking guy and with just a little exposure one found there was something in Bill that was gentle, that was tolerant; his punning, his propensity to humor, the light touch were very important to me. I just enjoyed him, especially the laughter—we laughed a lot.[7]

During the mid 1980s, the Unity Church in Hawaii sponsored a large *ACIM* conference and invited those of us from the early *Course* days to be presenters. By this time, it's obvious that being besieged by adoring fans was not Bill's favorite situation. One evening, the church treated the entire group of participants to a cruise lasting several hours. Bill's major goal quickly became to find someplace private. The Prathers, Bill, my husband Bob, and I found a little bench up near the bow away from the festivities. As we sat down to chat with no one around, Bill said, "It's so good not to be one with my brother, with whom I am one!"

ACIM was dictated during the cold war era with the Soviets, and "brinksmanship" was a word often used then. Bill used to refer to practicing the *Course* as "celestial brinksmanship." After all, it asks that we take on faith a very different way of living, and it seemed to him that he was plunging into the unknown, not knowing exactly what experiences he might be precipitating. Humor enabled him to "take the plunge" more gracefully. He was aware of his human frailties but was able to see through and not invest in them; he advised all who would listen to do the same, to laugh at their own judgments. As important as *ACIM* was for him, and as dedicated he was to practicing, he still could witness the entire project from a distance and find it all amusing. He closed many a conversation with a smile, saying, "I know it's hopeless, just not serious."

A lthough Bill was a superb speaker, he seriously did not like it. This certainly is an anxiety-producing situation for a professor and the Author addressed it a number of times. These passages from the Urtext address his fear of teaching and the problems caused him by his defenses.

The role of a teacher, properly conceived, is one of leading himself and others out of the desert [i.e., ignorance or unawareness]. The value of this role can hardly be underestimated, if only because it was one to which I very gladly dedicated my life. I have repeatedly asked *my* pupils to follow me. This means that to be effective teachers they *must* interpret teaching as I do. I have made *every* effort to teach you *entirely* without fear. If you do not listen, you will be unable to avoid the *very* obvious error of perceiving teaching as a threat.

It is hardly necessary to say that teaching is a process whose purpose is to produce learning. The ultimate purpose of *all* learning is to abolish fear. This is necessary so that knowledge can happen. The role of the teacher is *not* the role of God. This confusion is all too frequently made by parents, teachers, therapists and the clergy. It is a real misunderstanding of both God and His miracles. Any teacher who believes that teaching is fearful *cannot* learn because he is paralyzed. He also cannot really teach.

Bill was quite right in maintaining that this course is a prerequisite for his [upcoming teaching assignment]. However, he was really saying much more than that. The purpose of this course *is* to prepare you for knowledge. So is the real purpose of *any* legitimate course. All that is required of you as a teacher is to follow Me.

Whenever anyone decides he can function only in *some* roles but not in others, he cannot *but* be attempting to make a compromise which will not work. If Bill is under the misbelief that he is coping with the fear problem by functioning as an administrator and a teacher of interns, but *not* as a teacher of students, he is merely deceiving himself. He owes himself greater respect. There is nothing as tragic as the attempt to deceive one's self, because it implies that you perceive yourself as so unworthy that deception is more fitting for you than the truth. Either you can function in all of the roles you have properly undertaken to fulfill, or you cannot function effectively in any of them. This *is* an all or none decision. You *cannot* make inappropriate level distinctions within this choice. You are either capable or not. This does not mean that you can *do* everything, but it *does* mean that you are totally miracle-minded, or not. This decision is open to *no* compromise whatsoever. When Bill says that he cannot teach, he is making the same mistake that we spoke of before when he acted as if universal laws applied to everyone except him. This is not only arrogant, but patently untrue. Universal laws *must* apply to him, unless he does not exist. We will not bother to argue about this. . . .[1]

I emphasize this only because I do not want you to allow *any* fear to enter into the thought system toward which I am guiding you. I do *not* call for martyrs, but for *teachers*.

Bill is an outstanding example of this confusion, and has literally believed for years that teaching *is* martyrdom. This is because he thought, and still thinks at times, that teaching leads to crucifixion rather than to re-awakening. The upside down nature of this association is so obvious that he could only have made it *because* he felt guilty.[2]

Bill may claim (and he has certainly done so in the past) that the *professorship* was thrust upon him. This is not true. He wanted it very much and also worked hard to get it. He would not have had to work so hard either if he had not misunderstood it. . . . Bill could not be afraid to teach unless he still believes that interaction means loss and that learning means separation. He stands guard over his own ideas, because he wants to protect his thought-system as it is, and learning *means* change. Change is always fearful to the separated, because they cannot conceive of it as a change toward *healing* the separation. They *always* perceive it as a change for further separation, because separation *was* their first experience of change.

Bill, your whole fear of teaching is nothing but an example of your own intense separation anxiety, which you have handled with the usual series of mixed defenses in the combined pattern of attack on truth and defense of error, which characterizes *all* ego-thinking.[3]

In addition to describing him in consistent terms, a number of people had similar first impressions when they met Bill. Layle Luckett, excited to meet the man who brought *ACIM* forward, said, "After the next Thursday night class, or maybe it was at a Christmas party, I met Bill—this long, tall string bean—and I looked up into those deep brown eyes and I do not remember anything he said. I don't remember how he was dressed; I just remember deep brown eyes. It was so compelling, so mesmerizing."[4]

Frances Vaughan recalls: "The first time I met Bill, I didn't pay much attention. I thought he was just another visitor from New York. But the second time I met him, I really saw him and was astounded by the light that I experienced as coming through him. There was something about his simplicity, his being nothing special, while at the same time seeing the love, the kindness, the generosity of spirit, and a sense of humor that touched me deeply."[5]

I was fascinated by these and other responses because it was so like my own, as well as the experience of a number of others. Sarah Whalen-Kraft, a dear friend since childhood, had quite a startling experience on her first meeting with Bill, and given that she is an accomplished editor and writer, I asked her to share her thoughts on that first encounter. Here is an excerpt from that essay—a synopsis of the effect Bill had on so many, and why.

A Reminiscence of Bill Thetford

In March 1980, Carol invited me to attend a presentation about the *Course* given by Jerry Jampolsky, a widely known author and teacher of its principles, and Bill Thetford, the man who had transcribed *ACIM* in the late sixties and early seventies. She had often spoken of these two, and I very much wanted to hear them, regardless of my lukewarm interest in the books. So it was on the morning of April 12, I drove to Denver for the day-long event.

It was held in a rather small, old church in a quiet neighborhood. I was a bit early, and as I entered the foyer, Carol came over to greet me, saying she wanted to introduce me to Jerry and Bill before things got started. Jerry is a delightful, radiant person whom I have since heard several times, always with pleasure and gratitude for his great understanding of the *Course*. He was already engaged with other participants, so after introducing us, Carol steered me toward a tall, slender man standing alone to one side. In contrast to Jerry's ebullience, this person was rather restrained and unassuming, with a gentle easiness of manner about him. Carol introduced us, then darted off, and we started to shake hands and exchange the usual "I've heard so much about you" pleasantries. Then a most extraordinary process suddenly began dominating what was happening.

As we shook hands, Bill began speaking, but while I looked into his kind, friendly eyes, his words receded and a powerful jolt of recognition rushed through me, simultaneously with the thought, "But I know you! We've already met before!" Immediately following I felt intense anxiety and a devastating sense of loss, accompanied by thought of "But where? What happened?" and a desperate longing: "I can't bear to lose you again!" Then my entire being flooded with light and peace and the realization, "Of course I know you—you are my Self and I'll never lose you again."

The experience receded as quickly as it had come; all had taken place within a couple of minutes at most. We had both been talking and were still shaking hands as Bill finished whatever he was saying, completely innocent, I'm sure, of the upheaval he had precipitated. I thanked him rather incoherently, turned around, walked over to the sales table, and bought the *ACIM* set on the spot. I literally don't remember anything else from that day, except that they spoke and I was at peace inside.

I started the *Course* that day, and it has changed my life, joining the knowledge and experiences I had gained from Eastern traditions with a new understanding of Jesus' eternal teachings, which had been in my life since childhood. In the process I have come to understand also what happened that day.

Bill apparently was a very modest "teacher of God," the *Course*'s term for one who has chosen to see another as himself. He was reluctant to be "out front," preferring a behind-the-scene advisory role in promoting *ACIM* principles and seeing his role as scribe as his most important contribution. Considering the *Course*'s transforming effect on countless thousands worldwide, this is an accurate assessment. I'm told, however, that Bill didn't see himself as important or even especially good. I believe that even though he was a learned, sophisticated man, his greatest strength by the end of his life lay in his innocence.

The Vedic tradition of India is where I first understood that Truth—the Veda, or Knowledge—is universal, eternal, and always present and available. It manifests in a particular time and place because of the willingness of a few to minister to the spiritual needs of the many. For a while this specific form of Truth spreads and flourishes, but often it becomes too far removed from the original inspiration and is diluted or lost. A true teaching, however, will inevitably revive and once again transform people's lives, as *A Course In Miracles* is demonstrating for thousands who had become dissatisfied with traditional Christian structures. Wherever this renewal process begins, it is because even one or two individuals are willing to allow changes in their perception of each other and the world. They are not perfect, but they consistently seek to suspend judgment, see another's interests as not separate from their own, and forgive. Those who make this effort witness to the Truth, and as they accomplish their goal—and all do eventually—they are able to bring others to their own healing within, sometimes knowingly, often inadvertently.

Bill Thetford was such a witness. After the *Course* was transcribed and published, he continued for the remainder of his life to try to live its principles on a daily, neverending basis. This is surely the most difficult and fearful task, it seems, but it is ultimately all we are asked to do in this world, for the process of forgiveness is what removes "the blocks to the awareness of love's presence," in the *Course*'s words. I doubt that Bill was ever fully aware of the power that his willingness and commitment gave him, but I was only one of many recipients of the fruits of his labor. For one moment he suspended all prejudice, judgment, and expectations of me, providing a mirror unclouded by egoic perceptions and needs. In that clear mirror he showed me Who I really am—and opened the door to the way home. As we return to an innocent perception of each other, the Christ comes forward and reveals the Self that is always present. An old gospel hymn sings, "Jesus, lover of my soul, let me see my soul at last." Thanks, Bill—I got it![6]

Bill was a walking miracle, innocently loving, exerting an enormously powerful healing influence while not realizing what he was providing. His gift was innocence, not specialness, and that came from being willing to change his mind. What more need be said about the unutterable power of perceiving one another, and ourselves, as innocent at our very core, despite what our senses observe? The choice is universally available to everyone. Thus, despite his ambivalence about teaching, for many Bill was the greatest teacher they had ever known.

Throughout the *Course* we are told in every possible way that attacks must stop and that defenses are not only unnecessary but counterproductive. They do not make us safe but only add to our sense of danger, producing exactly what we are trying to avoid. Like everyone, Bill had developed his own defense strategies—primarily withdrawal from others, holding in and holding back, which result in depression, apathy, and a stubborn insistence on "being right."

ACIM is very clear that physical birth is not our beginning and physical death is not the end. In this life—a chapter in the ongoing continuity—defenses develop early and take place within the context of "family," however that is construed. Bill seems to have had a loving relationship with his mother. She read to him and took care of him while he was ill; apparently, he had no particular issues with her. His father, on the other hand, was his challenge. Bill rarely mentioned him, perhaps even feared him. He was a working man and often absent, and it seems Bill experienced him as not being present for him physically or emotionally. Bill confided that he had felt "the wrong child died," a haunting, guilt-ridden statement about his beloved sister's sudden passing when he was seven. Deeply traumatized by her death, he said that, at his sister's funeral, his father, who adored the little girl, seemed to convey that Bill should have been the one to die. No one knows if that was the father's intention, but he did shut off from his son, and six months later Bill became seriously ill. He also remembered his father berating him later on for being a financial burden because of that illness and ultimately becoming ill himself through worry and grief. Jo, his college girlfriend, knew both Bill's parents and commented, "His father was sort of a strict, rigid gentleman. I don't think Bill ever really related to him well. His mother [who worked two jobs to help supplement their income], I would say, was probably over-protective and pampered him. . . . His mother would fix us these beautiful picnic lunches to take with us when we would go bicycling."[7]

No wonder Bill was always in the "prepare to escape" mode, being relentlessly preoccupied with his own imagined guilt. "If you did not feel guilty, you could not attack, for condemnation is the root of attack. . . . For it is guilt that has obscured the Father to you, and it is guilt that has driven you insane."[8] He carried forward the burden of guilt and projected it onto others, causing him much unnecessary pain along the way. Catherine Prescott remembers, "We used to talk about yielding, about how there was the tendency of his ego to yield to whatever power was in his space. . . . But what was underneath that was his guilt about being alive when his sister had died so young. And so he just became smaller rather than bigger. It was like he thought if he could just make himself small, then it was okay for him to be alive. He admitted to being deeply traumatized by her death."[9]

The following extensive commentary from the Urtext about his relationship with his parents in particular, and parenting in general, is instructive for everyone.

> As you have so often said, no one has adopted *all* of his parents' attitudes as his own. In every case, there has been a long process of choice, in which the individual has escaped from those he himself vetoed, while retaining those he voted *for*. Bill has not retained his parents' political beliefs, in spite of the particular kind of newspapers that constituted their own reading matter in this area. The reason why he could do this was because he believed he was free in this area.

There must be some acute problem *of his own* that would make him so eager to accept their misperception of his own worth. This tendency can *always* be regarded as punitive. It cannot be justified by the inequality of the strengths of parents and children. This is never more than temporary, and is largely a matter of maturational and thus physical differences. It does not last unless it is held onto.

When Bill's father came to his new office and "destroyed" it, it is quite apparent that Bill *must* have been willing to let it be destroyed.[10] The many times that he has commented on this event alone would suggest the extreme importance of this misperception in his own distorted thinking. Why should anyone accord an obvious misperception so much power? There cannot be any real justification for it, because even Bill himself recognized the real problem by saying, "How could he do this to me?" The answer is, *he* didn't.

Bill has a very serious question to ask himself in this connection. We said before that the purpose of the Resurrection was to "demonstrate that no amount of misperception has any influence at all on a Son of God." This demonstration *exonerates* those who misperceive by establishing beyond doubt that they have *not* hurt anyone. Bill's question, which he must ask himself very honestly, is whether he is willing to demonstrate that his parents have *not* hurt him. Unless he is willing to do this, he has *not* forgiven them. . . .

Parents do not create the image of their children, though they may perceive images that they do create. However, as we have already said, you are not an image. If you *side with* image-makers, you are merely being idolatrous.

Bill has no justification whatever for perpetuating *any* image of himself at all. He is *not* an image. Whatever is true of him is wholly benign. It is essential that he *know* this about himself, but he cannot *know* it while he chooses to interpret himself as vulnerable enough to *be* hurt. This is a peculiar kind of arrogance whose narcissistic component is perfectly obvious. It endows the perceiver with sufficient unreal strength to make him over, and then acknowledges the perceiver's mis-creation [about himself]. There are times when this strange lack of real courtesy appears to be a form of humility. Actually, it is never more than simple spite.

Bill, your parents did misperceive you in many ways, but their ability to perceive was quite warped, and their misperceptions stood in the way of their own knowledge. There is no reason why they should stand in the way of yours. It is still true that you believe they *did* something to you. This belief is extremely dangerous to your perception and wholly destructive of your knowledge. This is not only true of your attitudes toward your parents, but also of your misuse of your friends. You still think you *must* respond to their errors *as if* they were true. By reacting self-destructively, you are *giving* them approval for their misperceptions.[11]

As noted above, insistence on feeling unworthy is associated with arrogance and narcissism, not with humility. We come into form with our inclinations already intact, and conditioning commences at birth and even before. Most of us learn at a very young age to be afraid of "being seen" or of others discovering what we're really like, so we fortify our defenses, the prime one being the mask we hide behind. Hiding convinces us we really do need to hide, as if our survival depends on it, and we are not open-minded about this. It is crucial to look directly at what we fear is wrong with us because this fear is nothing more than one end of the spectrum of beliefs we hold about ourselves. Those beliefs, both positive and negative, collectively constitute the ego, which is a convenient verbal handle for what *ACIM* is designed to address. The *Course* states clearly that everything true about us is completely loving and harmless. As this material poured forth, exposing their defenses, one can imagine Bill and Helen's shock; did they ever wonder why they had ever asked for a better way?

From years of teaching, counseling, and simply living, I can testify that virtually everyone suffers from a sense of deficiency accompanied by the need to hide it. It is not possible to go through the early maturation process without acquiring some belief in inadequacy by the age of five or six. Years ago, a man came to see me about an emergency in his life, having never previously sought professional counseling. After a short while, he asked, "Do very many people who come to see you feel kind of unworthy?" I answered, "How about 100 percent?" (This is true even if they are not aware of it.) Of course, he felt much better knowing he had a great deal of company, including Bill.

Stated another way in the *Little Book of Runic Wisdom:*

> An Oracle does not give you instruction as to events. An Oracle points your attention towards those hidden fears and motivations that will shape your future by their unfelt presence within each present moment. Once seen and recognized, these elements become absorbed into the realm of choice. Oracles do not absolve you of your responsibility for selecting your future, but rather direct your attention towards those inner choices that may be the most important elements in determining your future.[12]

The key phrase here is, "hidden fears and motivations that will shape your future." While fear and guilt remain hidden, they powerfully disrupt our peace of mind, causing us to experience our world as threatening or, at the least, unsatisfactory. These unconscious fears shape our lives and we are helpless to effect real, substantive change until we look straight at them, acknowledging the pain they engender. Thus, what is hidden must be brought to light for healing.

> Do not hide suffering from His sight, but bring it gladly to Him. Lay before His eternal sanity all your hurt, and let Him heal you. Do not leave one spot of pain hidden from His Light, and search your mind carefully for any thoughts you may fear to uncover. For He will heal every little

thought you have kept to hurt you and cleanse it of its littleness, restoring it to the magnitude of God.[13]

As a restatement of this idea, many Eastern traditions teach that happiness and peace of mind require destroying the *vasanas*, variously defined as mental images, latent tendencies, memory-stores, past impressions, and predispositions, in other words, the self-limiting ideas we hold. Those early traditions referred to the necessity of "scorching the seeds of tendencies." The *Course*, keeping ancient company, restates this as removing the blocks to the awareness of love's presence. All viable traditions of self-knowledge include facing our early conditioning in order to be released from it, thus restoring peace of mind. Everyone is reading from the same page.

Just as Bill's defenses were transparent to the Author, we can deduce other examples of self-judgment not yet relinquished from his relationship difficulties, both before and after moving to California. Since relationships with others reveal the relationship we have with ourselves, the hassles he experienced in New York and beyond clearly pointed to fears and expectations about what he thought he deserved, though perhaps unconsciously. Every "difficult person" in his life was a red flag pointing to his own self-condemnation, mirroring judgments he may have been unaware of, or unwilling to face. They sat there, staring back at him, each representing some facet of his guilt. What we complain about in others always indicates what we need to own in ourselves.

So what did Bill complain about, even minimally? One of his greatest issues, played out through relationships, was his objection to being "forced" to appear as something he wasn't. Certainly, no one can coerce anyone in any way unless all parties cooperate in that process. From his perspective, he felt he was told who he was rather than allowing that to reveal itself and also that there were agendas and expectations about his having to be a certain way. Of course, these merely revealed his own expectations and agendas for himself, which at times he conveniently forgot. His anger about not being accepted for who he was provides a specific clue about his own failure to accept himself. Who has not engaged in that behavior somewhere along the way? "Whenever you consent to suffer pain, to be deprived, unfairly treated or in need of anything, you but accuse your brother of attack upon God's Son."[14] *ACIM* never lets us off the hook, always bringing all our distress back to our own self-attack.

If Bill felt others made demands of him, trying to push him into a mold that didn't fit, he needed to look no farther than his own inclinations. If he labeled some persons as "pushy," we can be sure he harbored, even in a latent state, some guilt or fear about his own pushiness. Catherine Prescott commented, "The pushy part of Bill was that he wanted everyone to be happy. If I complained or felt burdened, he would say, 'Come on, Usha [Catherine used to be called by her middle name, Usha], let's go and forget about it. Let's play instead of being overly responsible, or overworked and negative.'"[15]

Also, it is common for those who don't honor themselves to be considerate of everyone else but not themselves; this failure to include themselves is often disguised as a false notion of humility. Catherine remembers,

> On one hand, he wanted to be kind, to say yes, to be good and loving and generous. He was such a fountain of giving, of pure generosity to everyone, and when he had to set limits and enforce boundaries, it was quite devastating to him. He had to sort out what might be hurting someone else and what was hurting himself. He worked with that a lot. He could have written the book about "When I say *no*, I feel guilty," and rising up from that was really his challenge. He often would say, "It's the guilt, it's the guilt."[16]

Then there was possessiveness. He felt that some, chiefly Helen, wanted to own a piece of him for themselves. Bill had created a tremendously constrained and constraining environment for himself, as is evident in how consistently events unfolded, and he was always trying to break free of that constraint. In the meantime, people who seemed to restrict him appeared throughout most of his life—the "wherever you go, there you are" principle at work. His "inner jailer" was always on duty, playing out its role, from his subjective point of view, in his relationships.

Catherine recalled another aspect they worked on together:

> He was breaking out of the heaviness of New York and was intolerant of anything that wasn't really free and joyous and up. He wanted a more uplifting experience and was pretty intolerant of, frustrated by, heaviness in himself and others. He was trying to escape from it, thinking, "Oh, my God, now I'm a hippie!" It's as if he were getting out of jail, and it reminded me of his getting out of the bed after his scarlet fever. It was almost like he was jailed as a kid. He wanted to reconnect with the seventeen-year-old; he was more "adultified" and skipped being a carefree teenager. The chains were breaking and his spirit finally flying free. That wanting to play is who and what his spirit quintessentially was/is. He did it, he did the work. He really processed it through.[17]

Neither Bill, nor the rest of us, can escape this very direct statement related to our "challenging relationships": "Learn this, and learn it well, for it is here delay of happiness is shortened by a span of time you cannot realize. You never hate your brother for his sins, but only for your own. Whatever form his sins appear to take, it but obscures the fact that you believe them to be yours, and therefore meriting a 'just' attack."[18]

In contrast to some behaviors and attitudes to which he was still blind, other areas of his discontent were clear. He really despised his bouts of depression and moments of irrationality and condemned himself for them, considering them a real deficiency on his part. He felt terrible after a display of anger, which stirred up much self-doubt and self-loathing. He also felt remorse for the comments he had made in 1982 about Ken in his autobiographical interviews. When Ken read the notes and asked Bill about them, he responded very differently, telling Ken that now he realized he had inherited a most difficult task, which he had performed admirably under the circumstances. Not only had Bill developed a broader perspective, but he detested conflict.

He also did not like glamour in relation to the *Course*—deliberately courting the "rich and famous"—in fact, couldn't stand it. When he saw people feeding their egos through *ACIM* association, he reacted to it, indicating an unhealed fear of his own. You cannot have an aversion to something unless you already feel guilty about it. According to Catherine,

> Actually he hated it [the glamour], but yet, funny enough, when I interviewed him [for a TV pilot], he loved it and laughed about it, saying he "looked good." He had that vanity way down underneath—way, way, way down. He was so good-looking, so charismatic, and so amazingly modest and humble. I think that [a love-hate relationship with glamour] was a juggling act for him.[19]

In the early California days, as Bill was coming to terms with his involvement with *ACIM*, he sometimes voiced concern that it would be misused, misunderstood, trivialized, presented by people who didn't necessarily know what they were doing, or generally corrupted. We discussed this at length and, although it was not my experience with him, others noticed he became upset when people misused the material, preaching concepts he thought were superficial or incorrect. He was clear that *ACIM* is basically a self-study course and did not like the idea of churches or organizations being formed to promote it. This has, indeed, occurred, rendering an important service to many. He continued to shift his position on this, however, recognizing that so long as he was attached to its being used a certain way, he wasn't learning his lesson. Despite his private concerns, he never advocated preventing the varied uses made of it or fighting something already implemented, trusting that there are no mistakes and that learning can come from any situation. By the end of his life, he was very accepting of anything done with the *Course*, realizing it now had a life of its own and couldn't possibly be contained. There simply was no way to control what people might do with it.

He also felt some pain that the relationship with Helen wasn't how it was supposed to be. She was back in New York, sick and angry, and he was in California, out of "prison," with a new set of friends and opportunities. Bill felt strongly they were supposed to work on their healing together, so not successfully applying *ACIM* teachings with her was still a major disappointment. And if he blamed Helen for that, he also blamed himself.

I t is evident by now that Bill's hallmarks were his almost unparalleled ability to accept and support others and his fabulous sense of humor inviting everyone to lighten up. Their effect was healing—of body and spirit—both for Bill and those around him. There was often no conscious discussion of or focus on healing; it just happened. For some, it was merely being in his presence, for others it was hearing his voice; but in other cases, he intended for healing to occur. He never stated directly what he thought ought to be healed in a person. Layle Luckett remembers, "One thing I learned about myself during that process is that there is a wonderful indirect way of teaching [and healing]. Bill would usually tell us some story that would illustrate a point. For instance, he would never say, 'Forgive your mother,' but he'd talk about some instance of forgiveness."[1]

Under any circumstances, the *Course* speaks eloquently and often about our own need for healing and why and how that is the only requirement for being truly helpful to everyone else. It also emphasizes that relevant healing is of the mind, and that with a healed mind, a healed body and/or situation can follow. Healing the body is never the direct focus of *ACIM*. "Come to the holy instant and be healed, for nothing that is there received is left behind on your returning to the world. And being blessed, you will bring blessing. . . . Thus is your healing everything the world requires, that it may be healed."[2]

No one who subscribes to the worldview of dualism, who believes he is an entity separate from virtually everyone, can possibly make any sense of this statement, but those who had the good fortune of spending time with Bill did experience it directly, whether they understood it or not. Understanding is much less relevant when results occur right on the spot. *ACIM* promises that as we practice forgiveness, we automatically become a healing presence for those around us. Not only did Bill's change of mind affect him but also those he was with. He recognized the *Course* was about both teaching and healing, but the healing part was more attractive to him than the teaching. He always emphasized that healing was not tied to some special skill, but was the automatic result of releasing grievances—a gift available to every man, woman, and child who chooses a defenseless, forgiving way of relating. Hugh Prather remembered,

> Certainly, I would always regain my perspective when I was around Bill, because one of the things, as I'm sure you've found on your spiritual journey, is that it's all so simple, so simple that it's almost embarrassing. It just gets down to a matter of "Are you going to do it [let go of grievances] or not?" So his effect on me was how to make things unimportant. Something is important only in the sense that it provides an opportunity to know peace. Bill was a living example of the *Course*, rather than someone who teaches it or talks it. He actually lived it; that was his real intent.[3]

Jack Luckett spoke of the healing that occurred when Bill was present: "He did not have to lay hands on people. He did not have to give them a diagnosis or something like that. His mere being was enough to alter something in their consciousness. What he actually did was to remind people of who they were, and with that reminder, they had the power to do what they wished."[4]

In another instance Jerry remembers, "In Hawaii, a woman with a lot of orthopedic problems asked for a private audience [with Bill], and following that, her pain disappeared. Bill had trouble thinking it had anything to do with him, as if it almost threatened him. I think that kind of thing happened a lot."[5]

Judy also recounts a healing that took place in her kitchen. On one of the many occasions when fascinating guests filled the Skutch household, Judy was preparing food while others enjoyed the lively company elsewhere. As she cooked French fries, she found herself a bit out of sorts about missing all the fun. While busy feeling sorry for herself and not paying attention to her work, she spilled hot grease on her hands. Bill heard the racket that ensued and came in to see what was happening. Completely serious, he asked if she wanted the burn and, of course, she said no. He held his hands above and below hers without touching them and the burn disappeared miraculously.

Carlagaye Olson recalled a life-changing moment of resolution while visiting Bill in La Jolla years later.

> When Bill moved to La Jolla, Jules [Finegold] and I went down to help him get settled. Jules had to return home, but I was still there, so Bill insisted that I stay in his room and he'd take the guest room. I felt treated like visiting royalty. In the morning when I woke up, I looked up through the clerestory window and the word in my mind was *both*—a simple word. I went down to the kitchen, he was already up, and I told him of this wonderful experience of the word *both*. Now whenever I feel any anxiety arise within me about my worth, my lessons, anybody else, I use that word, *both*, and just calm right down. The gift Bill gave me was passing into some place where I don't have to choose.
>
> It's not about here or there, or this or that, or them and me, where everything is pivotal about making the right choice. All of that went away. It's *both*—just take a deep breath. In that feeling of being so honored with Bill, I finally got a word that would reduce me to grace.[6]

Another of Carlagaye's stories illustrates not only Bill's healing influence on her—indeed, their mutual healing—but also one of the foundational premises of the *Course*: that we must be willing to look at our "dark side," our own unforgiving, judgmental thoughts.

Bill, Jules and I started doing our field trips together in the spring of 1981. I would arrive at 11:00 a.m., our meeting time, and we'd go someplace for lunch. Jules was our leader and he would line up things for us to do in the afternoon; we would take field trips to see unusual or natural sights. Bill, of course, was not a nature boy, not liking to be off the sidewalks, so we didn't get too adventurous. He then would take a nap later in the afternoon for his meditative time. [Then they would have dinner, often with others, and attend the Tiburon *ACIM* meeting.] I was a very strict *Course* fundamentalist and that was very attractive to Bill, because there was such a spiritual sideshow going on. He liked it if I made comments in the group.

Time during the day with Bill was very playful, but the drive back home every week from Tiburon, leaving at 9:30 and getting back at 11:00 p.m., was filled with just incredible reactions I was having—negative reactions to myself, to other people. My ego and its reactions to everyone and everything were incredibly intense! Things were bubbling up and I was responding in a very heightened way. I would have this wonderful day of fun and affection and then I can't tell you the things that got dredged up in me. We would have so much fun and laugh and laugh and then I'd come home with this creepy, horrible ego and I would realize, "My God, this is really an incredible process going on and it doesn't happen with people other than Bill!" I was such an imperfect student. Intellectually, I was fine with it, but the practice of it! So everything that was unlike Jesus in me would come up on those drives home and I was so grateful for being with Bill, because I came back every week into those loving arms of acceptance and then every week I would drive home seeing the worst in me. I just can hardly explain that!

The relationship with Bill helped to settle me down, get quiet, and realize this is all happening internally. It's happening to everybody and it's taking its own course. I think I trust more in the whole deep process rather than expecting extraordinary things, events, and circumstances. Somehow it was a very gracious thing, a very blessed thing [to know him] and none of the words that say, "It was a great honor to be with him," sound right. That has too much of a worldly cast, but there was grace involved in being with him.[7]

If this isn't a perfect example of how *ACIM* works, I don't know what is.

What is healing but the removal of all that stands in the way of knowledge? And how else can one dispel illusions except by looking at them directly, without protecting them? Be not afraid, therefore, for what you will be looking at is the source of fear, and you are beginning to learn that fear is not real. . . . Do not be afraid, then, to look upon fear, for it cannot be seen. Clarity undoes confusion by definition, and to look upon darkness through light must dispel it.[8]

The *Course* dredges up that unconscious material for review, so we can choose whether to hang on to guilt or release it. It's like comforting arms around us, with a voice saying, "Okay I'm going to be here with you while we look at these ugly thoughts." Bill, to me, thoroughly personified the process of being there for so many as their dark sides surfaced. And, as promised, awareness expanded and healing happened.

The following is an excerpt from a dialogue between a student and Ramana Maharshi (Bhagavan in quote below)—an awakened Indian master who passed away in the 1950s. It addresses the phenomenon, from the Eastern perspective, of how healing one's self facilitates the healing of everything else.

Question: While sitting near you, what sort of mental state should we have so as to receive the transmission from your pure being, or Self?

Bhagavan: Keep your mind still, that is enough. You will get spiritual help sitting in this hall if you keep yourself still. The aim of all practices is to give up all practices. When the mind becomes still, the power of the Self will be experienced. The waves of the Self are pervading everywhere. If the mind is at peace, one begins to experience them.[9]

The noise within us decreased around Bill, and the loving "waves of the Self" could be felt. From my perspective, Ramana's teaching of nondualism echos that of *ACIM*, and Bill thought so too. Ramana taught that attainment of Self-realization requires: a) diverting the mind from its object and ceasing the objective view of the world; b) bringing an end to the mind's internal activities; c) rendering the mind characterless; and d) resting the mind in pure *vichara* (inquiry of "who am I?"). When one looks closely, we see this as a restatement of removing the blocks to the awareness of love's presence. And like the *Course*, silence and stillness of mind is a prerequisite. Hence the need for mind training, which *ACIM* both refers to and provides. Noise and confusion subsided *around* Bill because it was reduced *in* him. As his focus on the intellect as a source of power and wisdom diminished, his mind grew more quiet. And, of course, when our intent is our own healing, we receive all the necessary assistance without fail.

In the early 1980s, an unlikely event—but not uncommon when we are serious about practicing forgiveness—occurred at a presentation by Hugh Prather and Jerry Jampolsky at a Religious Science church in San Diego. There was a good crowd of over three hundred, including Bill, who sat in the back and frequently sneaked out for a smoke. The Lucketts remembered:

> Shortly before lunch, Jerry or Hugh suggested that we each hug someone next to us. Billy tried to run, but got snared in the doorway by another escapee, a blonde woman who hugged him intensely (naturally) and forever! Then they leaned back and looked at each other. He exclaimed, "Jan!" as she screamed, "Bill!" They knew each other from Columbia. Her husband had worked for Bill and she had done her Ph.D. there. They had

all been best of friends but then had a bitter falling out, I think because her husband had divorced her and moved in with Bill. She hated Bill intensely! At this point, she was in some cancer treatment. Imagine all the venom she'd stored up. And out of all people on earth, here these two were in each other's arms at the end of a whole morning's highly inspiring talk about forgiveness. As the past melted, they instantly forgave themselves and each other on the spot and spent some time together. Billy was actually very healing for her, though she eventually died of cancer. What a demonstration and what a kick-off for moving to San Diego over five years later![10]

As for healings that took place related to Bill's speaking voice, Leroy Zemke commented:

Immediately now is another step, which has also been initiated elsewhere. There is before you a work that involves the uses of the voice, the uses of the mechanical energies of the material world involved in the engineering of sound. You are to involve yourself in the projection of voice in many different ways that can be utilized to inform the teachings already in print. It is simply another way to demonstrate the source of the power, the essence of Holy Spirit. . . . You have a quality of healing that is transmitted through your being. Your words become as tools through which this force, or focus, is directed. And all who hear them will experience a sense of direction and feel the vibratory patterns of their own being resonating with those flowing through you. Many will experience healing—some instantaneous, others through gradual forms of healing—but the process is the same.[11]

Bill had a beautiful voice through which much healing automatically occurred, something of an embarrassment to him, but he was also mindful that it was his gift and always had been. Jerry recalled:

For me, when he read passages from *ACIM*, there was a vibration in his voice, different from when he was just talking to you, that was the vibration of God and I bathed in that. It allowed people to experience the peace of God and I'm not the only one, I'm sure, who felt that. He was like an older brother. He was wearing the "cloak" of Bill Thetford, but as far as I'm concerned he was a manifestation of the Christ spirit.[12]

Judy recalled a situation that was typical of how people responded to Bill's voice, particularly when he read from the *Course*. She had introduced him to some friends, both of them psychologists and students of Assagioli (an Italian psychotherapist who developed the technique known as psycho-synthesis); they were well known in their field and had helped a great many. About twenty minutes into the visit, the woman, who was very matter of fact and down to earth, asked Bill if he would mind reading something from *ACIM*. Both Bill and Judy were surprised, as no one had ever made that request. He asked if she had a preference about what to read and she answered no. Judy recounts:

> Bill opened the book at random, read for about fifteen minutes, and I saw the tears flowing down this woman's face. She was holding her husband's hand and I could still see her silently weeping, which was so powerful for me! When Bill put the book down, he suddenly saw them sitting there—he really did get into what he was reading—and the woman said, "I've heard the voice of God." She wasn't trying to be flattering. She meant, with his reading, she heard the voice of God, and when they left, she asked if he could be persuaded to record his favorite parts, which he later did. When he read the *Course*, it was transporting.[13]

Bill's own healing, always related to relinquishing the ego, was a work in progress. He was still "unlearning" the storehouse of conflicting impressions he had amassed and was still partially an "unhealed healer." The *Course* writes a great deal about "unhealed healers" because, obviously, it came through two experts in traditional psychotherapy. They must have been shocked to have their life's work so roundly dismissed as unhelpful, at least as they assumed it should be practiced, in the section entitled "The Unhealed Healer":

> The ego's plan for forgiveness is far more widely used than God's. This is because it is undertaken by unhealed healers, and is therefore of the ego. Let us consider the unhealed healer more carefully now. By definition, he is trying to give what he has not received. If an unhealed healer is a theologian, for example, he may begin with the premise, "I am a miserable sinner, and so are you." If he is a psychotherapist, he is more likely to start with the equally incredible belief that attack is real for both himself and the patient, but that it does not matter for either of them. . . .

> A therapist does not heal; *he lets healing be.* He can point to darkness but he cannot bring light of himself, for light is not of him. Yet, being *for* him, it must also be for his patient. The Holy Spirit is the only Therapist. He makes healing clear in any situation in which He is the Guide. You can only let Him fulfill His function. He needs no help for this. He will tell you exactly what to do to help anyone He sends to you for help, and will speak to him through you if you do not interfere.[14]

Once when Bill was in Denver, he and Bob Beale had lunch with a well-known, "larger than life" financial guru. Bob remembers Fred (not his real name) as a self-promoting person with a strong ego, who talked at length about his accomplishments. Finally Bob said,

> "Fred, this is Bill Thetford who is one of the two scribes who created *A Course In Miracles.*" That didn't particularly impress Fred, who knew what it was but so what? Bill added, "Yes, I was part of the team that brought that in," and started to be a little boastful. Then he just stopped, as if he thought, "I don't really want to do this," and said no more in that vein. It was an interesting meeting, watching him rise to the bait and then let it go. Bill started to relate on the same level as Fred—not a very pleasant one—and then he stopped. He just let it go and I thought that was commendable, to say the least.[15]

Here is a marvelous object lesson—in mid-sentence you can choose to let something go when you realize your error. Bill did that frequently and remarkably well from the beginning. During my early visits to California, I saw him bow only once to an obvious ego inclination, as he showed me various books he had contributed to and more than one academic "Who's Who" in which he was listed. It was almost as if he wanted to reassure himself, and me, of his value—"See, I really did do wonderful work before I left the academic world"—vacillating between wanting to be special and wanting to give that up. One friend said, "Bill's only self-promotion was a conspicuous undersell."

Bill truly desired to give up the ego-enhancing needs to be right or to prove his value and he worked very hard at not taking things personally and recognizing what did and did not matter. Hugh Prather remembers,

> Right from the beginning there were little things he would say, making it obvious that not everyone agreed on what had actually happened [in terms of the *Course*'s history]. I remember one detail. He said, "It's now been decided that it only lasted eight years. It actually lasted ten, but it's been decided that this process took place over a period of eight." He made several comments like that, but the interesting thing to me was that he didn't care. It was just fine for it to be eight years, whatever it was; he saw that it was not important; he had no ego in the details. He was happy to accept whatever.[16]

Leroy Zemke noted how important music was to Bill's healing and sense of well-being:

> Music, incidentally, is very, very much a trigger for you, and in former lives you have been involved musically. It has been very much a part of your training as a priest in Egypt, in Tibet, in India, and also when you have lived in Europe, particularly in Italy and Austria. There is a very strong, strong musical attachment. Voice comes forward particularly and

instruments like the piano and stringed instruments are very, very, very, strong. [Bill took both voice and piano lessons when he was young.] There is a very powerful, powerful tie to that and it is a very transformative energy in you. Whenever you really need to touch that [healing] dimension of yourself, you can simply go to music.[17]

As he dedicated himself to his healing through forgiveness, Bill continued to become more transparent and open. Catherine Prescott, with whom he spent much time in therapeutic exploration, commented on his noticeable healing:

He became happier, looser, less burdened, way more energized. We did voice dialogue work on his rheumatic heart condition and realized that part of him was still frozen from back then, so we woke that up again. It was almost like soul retrieval for the part of himself he had dedicated to his mother, to be sure she didn't lose her third child. He and the sister made a contract, with her death, that he wasn't going to live fully. That was the core of the work. So we looked at what it would it be like to wake up every cell in the body, get out of that rigid frozen state, and live fully. I feel that was part of his moving down to La Jolla. He became way more joyous. He always had such a great spirit, even from the beginning, but it was like he was wearing some kind of a mental straightjacket. He was really in a psychological shutdown and it felt so wonderful to watch the blooming.[18]

And bloom he did. Judy remembers reminiscing about Bill's "olden days" at Columbia with a colleague who declared, "I can't believe that the guy who smoked five packs a day and drank coffee all the time is the same gentle, loving, peaceful Bill we know now. *ACIM* works!"

Whit Whitson noted in his remarks at Bill's memorial service,

It was then my privilege to watch Bill's transformation into a healed healer. As he disciplined his mind to perceive the world and himself through the lenses of the *Course*, he became the personification of the process of inner growth. His courage and his pain were masked by his inspired sense of humor. His humor was a gentle expression of his compassion toward the glory and the absurdity of the human condition. He was a master teacher and while he would not wish such recognition, preferring anonymity, the day will come when his work in pioneering the PAS and helping Helen channel the *Course* will receive worldwide recognition. Knowledge sets us free. Bill truly understood the ego. His knowledge set him free and beckons each of us to follow.[19]

A nother defining characteristic that Bill possessed was a simple, uncomplicated wisdom that was anything but simple-minded or elementary—quite the opposite. And, with the dwindling instances of ego involvement mentioned earlier, Bill was the poster child for genuine humility, intellectual and otherwise. Frances Vaughan referred to his being "wonderfully nothing special."

> He was a very important mentor to me. One thing about Bill that not everyone saw was his incredible knowledge and understanding of psychology, philosophy, and comparative religions. He was extraordinarily erudite and well read. He never flaunted his intellectual brilliance, yet he really had a profound, universal understanding of human beings and the way we grow and change.[1]

A friend from Florida said, "I loved his careful, clear mind, so precise but so well buffered with kindliness, and I can easily appreciate how you would be drawn together in friendship." Another unusual and compelling trait was his willingness to grant wisdom where he found it. He was always very happy to give everybody credit for their capabilities, regardless of their "official" credentials.

Jaison Kayn spoke for so many when he noted:

> He was more than just a dear friend who was there to listen; it was his very simple and direct wisdom. I was comforted by the knowingness that he had. It's nice to know someone who was that clear and alive and

personally caring of me. One time we were actually in your backyard and he was enjoying Shanna [Jaison's dog] and he just looked at me and said, "Well, isn't she your alter ego?" Bill didn't wear his knowledge at all, but if you asked him something, he would give the clearest, brief summary of anything—the Vedanta, the Urantia book, or whatever. This guy was a library, not only of knowledge, but a library of very precise understanding. He was so tuned in without the outward appearance of it, almost as if he were surprised that it came out.[2]

Sometimes that wisdom could be very direct and short. One of Judy's favorite stories is about a time when she was utterly furious with Jerry and caught in the grip of her own anger. Not to put too fine a point on it, she was having a fit! She called Bill and ranted to him about Jerry's various shortcomings. Bill's calm response was, "Are you willing to see your brother sinless?" She shouted that no, she was not! He said to her, "When you're ready to do just that, you will feel much better," and hung up.

Pat Hopkins recalls, "Also, while he had a brilliant mind and a naturally elegant way of speaking, he never clobbered you over the head with his knowledge or the power of his intellect. He was truly the most modest, gentle man I've ever known."[3] Another example of Bill's confirming wisdom was this response to Bob Beale:

One early morning while we were on that trip to Santa Fe, I jogged around the national cemetery there for about forty-five minutes or so, and after returning, we were all having breakfast and I said, "You know Bill, when I was in that cemetery I got a sense that a number of the spirits of those people buried there were around. And it seemed like they were talking to me so I just decided to have a conversation with them. I told him Sergeant So-and-So said this and Captain Jones said that, calling them by name." I remember Bill saying, "Well, of course, that's what happens." He didn't elaborate on things, just giving such amazing confirmation.[4]

That quiet, behind-the-scenes brilliance manifested in other ways. Whit Whitson noted,

> When we were at parties or elsewhere, Bill and I would see someone come in and watch their body language to try to fit that personality into the PAS, not dissecting the person but playing with the basic structure of the PAS as applied to that person. Then we would embellish it. It was as if we had found the basic Christmas tree and then decided what kind of baubles would be hung on that kind of Christmas tree [in terms of fine-tuning the exact details of that particular personality type, after noting the basic personality components]. Bill knew so much more about it than I did that I would sit there fascinated. He enjoyed that kind of intellectual discourse because at the level of analyzing the ego, he was the best.[5]

Whit also commented that Bill possessed a talent for evaluation that was almost psychic and always empathetic. However, that particular demonstration of his talent remained private, shared only with Whit in Tiburon, who could appreciate Bill's ability from his own experience with the PAS. Hugh Prather noted,

> Another thing that was very interesting to me about Bill's life was that he never used *ACIM* to his benefit, where all the rest of us have. To one degree or another, we've made money off the *Course*; we've increased our reputations with it. I don't think there's anything wrong with that, but it was just remarkable that Bill never once used the *Course* to enhance himself or put money in his pocket in any way, nor did he have any interest in doing that. In fact, he had great reluctance.[6]

Roger Walsh commented on his first impression of Bill:

> The one that immediately comes up is that he was so shy. It took me a while to appreciate that it was an extraordinary degree of humility. He was unduly self-deprecating but I came to appreciate that that was just a very genuine and deep form of humility. When I first saw the *Course*, I

opened it up and saw those words "God" and "Holy Spirit" and said, "No thanks." One time, Bill and Jerry were making a presentation on *ACIM* at the American Psychiatric Conference in San Francisco. I remember going to the gathering afterwards and meeting Bill there and literally having the thought, "Well, if this guy's into it, I'm interested." . . . He served the purpose of opening doors for me in the sense that I came from a very hard-core scientific, materialist, reductionist, anti-spiritual background and he was someone who I could not pretend to be brighter than, and yet who himself had come around to appreciate this material, so I appreciated it. Here was someone with a very impressive intellect who was impressed by it. It's one thing when people who may not be so analytically or critically inclined get into something but another, indeed, with someone whose credentials are impeccable, whose intellectual and skeptical faculties are good.[7]

At Bill's memorial service, Roger additionally commented on the deep impact of Bill's choice to leave no legacy. Although so many devote enormous amounts of time to creating a legacy and identifying their lives with it, Bill's intention was to leave no personal footprint but simply to be ordinary.

> Bill's life was a model of the opposite. He had already created a legacy, one of priceless worth, and worked very hard to make sure he was not identified with it. Bill could have symbolized many things—an extraordinarily successful psychologist or a really successful person of the world, or a spiritual symbol as someone who was the source and creator of this most important spiritual text. He didn't do any of the things I would assume to be part of making an important spiritual contribution—lecturing, writing books or papers on *ACIM*, appearing on TV, giving interviews. He stayed home most of the time, studied the *Course*, and tried to make his relationships whole, humbly and unpretentiously practicing the material. That, I find, is just an extraordinary example.[8]

One aspect of Bill's wisdom was his willingness to acknowledge what he didn't know, despite all the knowledge he possessed. If you believe you should already know it all and must not reveal that you don't, protecting your image as an accomplished self becomes job one—a terrible trap. In contrast, Jaison Kayn noted,

> Bill, clearly being human at the time, had all his normal human stuff to deal with too, just like the rest of us. And he never tried to pretend that wasn't so. The feeling he conveyed was that he was in this soup like all the rest of us, and enjoyed being with us. I also had the sense that he liked being included [in our Denver group] because in a certain way he was shy and naive about some things. I expected someone who was the authority, but he was very open about his confusions and doubts. Everybody assumed he knew everything, but he was just another guy trying to figure life out. Sometimes he was the opposite of the guy with all the answers and would get that look in his eyes like, "I haven't got a clue, don't ask me." He would defer as much as possible, put everybody else in the middle of things and have them speak because he didn't want to be the center of attention. He didn't want to be the big cheese at all, but when he spoke, everyone listened. He did not like having that much responsibility, but he accepted it as if he knew his gems were seeds that he needed to scatter. He also knew he was giving more than information or wisdom; he was giving support and encouragement, an act of love that would help people believe in the message and do their inner work. When he spoke, there was no preaching; it was all about practice.[9]

Catherine Prescott remembered,

> He seemed very egoless to me, I will say that. I'm sure he had one, but he was so humble himself. Probably the worst [in terms of the ego revealing itself] was in those sessions where he got in touch with the angry side of himself. He would blow up and then feel remorseful and disgusted with himself. I think he was finishing up some work with Helen, and of course,

we talked about all that nonstop. He always reflected back, wondering if he was a good or a bad person.[10]

Many of us had conversations with Bill about who the intended recipients of the *Course*'s teachings were to be. Hugh Prather said,

> I remember one of the things he brought up right from the beginning was his confusion over why *ACIM* was so popular. I think he interpreted the guidance he and Helen received as meaning this was for them and maybe a few others and that wasn't the way it was turning out. Even then, it was obvious that it had, in a sense, taken off. I remember his telling me that Helen's guidance was that the *Course* was only for about two hundred people, so he thought there was some sort of conflict here. It was as if it seemed obvious to everyone else that it was for everyone. He didn't have any proprietary sense about this; I didn't pick up that he was in any way resentful, simply amazed and perplexed as to why this had happened. That was a deep concern to him [early on], but it left him in the latter part of his life.[11]

Perhaps Helen was right. Maybe, comparatively speaking, only a few people in the world really want to dedicate themselves to letting go of all grievances, totally accepting all aspects of their lives without reservation, and living without resistance. The other millions of *ACIM* students, either directly or through its surrogates, are proceeding in their own perfect and helpful way toward accepting the *single* goal of peace of mind, moving from understanding what the *Course* says to applying its principles in more and more situations. Therefore, it is both for a few and for everyone. How unusual and reassuring when everyone is right!

Personally, I knew only a couple of people who were uncomfortable in Bill's presence. One woman didn't actively dislike him; she just thought he was socially inept and somewhat dull and boring. When I discussed this with a friend, he said, "I think she saw in Bill the very things that I saw, but had a different label for it. I saw that he knew how to handle himself, was obviously socially skilled so that he could participate, but he wasn't completely comfortable with it. He just did the best he could. He did prefer to be quiet, but to me, that wasn't boring, that was fabulous!"[12] His attempts to let go of ego, not call attention to himself, and practice forgiveness in every possible way paid off. He was just "ordinary Bill" in the end, but the most extraordinary person most of us ever knew.

B ill's ability to turn directly to God manifested, among other ways, in his excellent sense of guidance, his ability to follow his intuition or hunches. The *Course* clearly states that spiritual direction is always available and actually leading us, but most don't believe they have that capability. *ACIM* teaches that, "The Holy Spirit's Voice is as loud as your willingness to listen. It cannot be louder without violating your freedom of choice, which the Holy Spirit seeks to restore, never to undermine."[1] Quite simply, we have chosen not to listen and can change our minds whenever we choose. Bill helped many make that decision.

Bill himself often meditated in order to access his connection with God. When Bill felt things were getting stuck for himself or others, he would recommend doing a *Course* lesson or meditating. Hugh commented on Bill's meditation process:

> I would peek at how he was meditating. He would pray quite deeply, then open his eyes and sort of look around, and then he would close his eyes and meditate. He would go back and forth in that way. There are some lessons in the early part of the workbook where you open your eyes and it was interesting to see. But I remember being struck right from the beginning at how deeply he could turn to God. It's as if the ego side, or the outward side, of Bill was filled with doubt and laughter and vulnerability with a wonderful, very interesting, appealing personality, but he could click that off, put all that aside, and turn very deeply and directly to God.[2]

Long before *ACIM*, Bill had deep faith in something, always knowing things would work out somehow. He had an inner sense of being prompted or led, tapping into omnipresent wisdom, as all of us can when we believe it possible; he didn't quite know how to use that talent, not knowing where it came from. It didn't seem very scientific or a likely subject for testing or evaluation, so in his younger years he usually ignored it or at least didn't talk about it. One of the greatest limitations we adopt early on is that only what we apprehend with our senses is legitimate and all else is suspect. Of course, quite the contrary is true.

Bill told many of us this story, one of his favorites, about "things working out" and acknowledged that it had a very profound effect on him (this account taken from a 1984 interview with Bill in *New Realities* magazine):

On Easter Sunday in 1970 I had agreed to take Jean, an elderly woman artist, down to dinner in Greenwich Village with some other artist friends. It was a very cold, stormy, wintry day with sleet and high winds—unusual for that time of year. Being without a car, I realized I was going to have a lot of trouble getting a taxi and so I meditated briefly about what to do. I got a clear message that I was to go to the corner of 78th Street and Fifth Avenue, near where I lived, at exactly 3:15 and the problem would be taken care of. I had enormous resistance to doing this but I put on my stormy weather gear anyway, walked to the corner, and tried to hail a cab. Since I was in competition with all the doormen on Fifth Avenue, it seemed utterly useless.

Then for just a moment I closed my eyes and let go of my troubled thoughts, saying to myself, "Thank you, Father, it's already done." And for an instant I truly believed that. When I opened my eyes, a chauffeur-driven limousine had stopped right in front of me at the corner and the driver rolled down his window and asked, "May I help you, sir?" This, as anyone who's been to New York or lived there knows, was a highly improbable happening.

I was very tempted to ask him why he had stopped for me, and then I realized that this would be an inappropriate question; I was simply to accept this gift. I got in and we drove over to Jean's and picked her up. She was absolutely thrilled that I had come to pick her up in a limousine!

The interesting thing, too, is that I didn't discuss a fee with the driver. He simply took me without any question and when we arrived at our destination, I asked him how much it was and he said something ridiculous like five dollars. I think I gave him several times that amount out of enormous gratitude and relief.[3]

He recounts another instance of "just knowing":

Louis [Schucman] once told me that one of the profound experiences of his life, that made him believe in the reality of "this *Course* stuff," happened a number of years ago when he called me one day and said, "I would like to see you privately." I remember that particular occasion quite well, because of what took place. It just occurred to me that Louis needed at least $1,000. Without any further thought, I wrote a check to have ready for him so that when he arrived he wouldn't be embarrassed about asking for it. When he got to my office and started telling me about having some temporary difficulties with his business, I said, "I thought maybe you were having some problems, so here it is." It blew his mind.[4]

Many people commented that one of Bill's major gifts was his ability to suspend the ego and let the Voice speak through him, not just when he was reading from the *Course* but in his normal daily discourse. This does not mean he went into a trance state, but simply that in everyday interactions he was inspired, calmly and naturally, to make just the perfect comments to help someone, often without his knowing that had occurred. And this capability was in addition to the inherent healing quality of his physical voice. During our Santa Fe trip in the early 1980s, Bob Beale remembered,

We really had time to just hang out with Bill. I don't know that Bill was the kind of guy who just hung out, but nevertheless, that's what we did. I distinctly remember we were all having lunch on the patio of a restaurant when Bill turned to me and, not as part of the conversation, said, "Bob, you need to trust your presence and you don't, you know. And if you'll just learn to trust your presence, you'll find that you'll do what you're here to do." At the time it seemed an odd statement but it really resonated with me and I've never forgotten it. It was just "trust your presence." There was something about the simplicity of his comment and his tone of voice, very gentle and loving, that reverberated like a ton of bricks.[5]

Over the years, Bill would speak of his life adventures, especially those related to guidance, not boasting but with amusement and fascination about the way things worked out. He witnessed unlikely events unfolding and was completely intrigued by them. One of his favorite stories was about making financial arrangements to move to Tiburon. He was still weighing his options about moving and was reluctant for several reasons. He thought to himself, "Well, if I have $10,000, I'll go," feeling he needed extra financial assurance. Soon he was inwardly prompted to buy some IBM stock options. "I didn't have the money at all, and no one in his right mind would do anything like this, it was extremely risky. But right after I bought them—the same day—the stock began to shoot up. I made the $10,000 I needed within twenty-four hours."[6]

Despite his eminence as a professor, Bill always considered himself a student and sought wisdom from a wide range of sources, from the "far-out" to the more traditional. He explored anything that could be therapeutic or that facilitated self-discovery. In LeRoy Zemke's personal readings, which

Bill found helpful in gaining new perspectives on his unfolding life, he speaks of another aspect of the indigo color in Bill's aura:

> This is the color of the unknown, the part of you that reaches into the unknown, always seeking to draw in more of what you do not know. It is that dimension that is never satisfied, always yearning for more. As its external effect, it causes you to search out unusual things, unusual ideas or to attract them into your life. This causes you to draw unusual friends into your life pattern, unusual people from very different walks of life, some of whom are very incongruous with others, but all of whom have very special, almost what might be called spiritual or holy qualities about them.[7]

Bill had immersed himself in mystical and metaphysical teachings once the *Course* began, because he felt certain its premises could not be unique and he was correct—universal wisdom is just that and not the exclusive province of *ACIM*.

A year or so before he died, Bill and the Lucketts went to see Adele Tinning, the "table tipper." She was an older woman who lived in a little old house in southern California and was renowned for her ability to make a huge oak table levitate—to vibrate and tap out answers. She asked Bill to identify who was tipping the table as it spelled out a name that was unfamiliar to all present except Bill—it was Helen's secret name for him. (I cannot find anyone who knows what that name was.) He was astounded and convinced of the validity of Tinning and her methods. He then asked Helen a series of questions, via the table, and received answers. Clearly, Bill was not shy about privately pursuing the unusual and he loved the unexplainable, the ineffable. With his usual play on words, he used to joke about trying to "eff" the ineffable, discover the undiscoverable.

Both Bill and Helen sought answers and reassurance from unlikely sources, meeting with two well-known British psychics and visiting Hugh

Lynn Cayce in Virginia, just before the *Course* began and several other times as well. Though Bill was not interested in organized religion, parapsychology and psychic phenomena had long caught his attention. Hugh Lynn had highly recommended the work of Eileen Garrett, the world-famous psychic, and Bill felt a strong intuitive urge to speak with her. He had heard she never went out publicly, but nevertheless, he had a persistent feeling he was supposed to meet her. "I had also heard she was ill most of the time and impossible to meet," he recounts, "that she spent a great deal of her time in southern France. I thought I would certainly not call her office; it didn't seem like the thing to do. But there was something in the back of my mind urging me to meet her."[8]

Sometime in 1968, he received an unexpected announcement from the American Society for Psychical Research about a lecture on mediumship to be given by experts in the field.

> When I saw this announcement, I thought, "I must go to this," even though I never went to ASPR meetings. It seemed strange that I would want to do that, but I thought this was an important occasion. When I walked in for the meeting, I was aware of something different in the atmosphere. A number of people came up to me and talked in a way that suggested that they thought I knew something about psychics or that I had psychic abilities. People seemed to be reading my aura and there was a lot of strange stuff going on that I wasn't accustomed to. I sat in the back of the hall and during the speaker's presentation a woman in the front row asked questions. I thought, "That must be Eileen Garrett," yet I had never seen her. I was just sure that this was who it was. . . . At the end of the meeting I did something that was very out of character for me. I went up to her, held out my hand to introduce myself, and said, "Mrs. Garrett, my name is Professor Thetford from Columbia and I think it is very important that I talk to you." She turned around, looked at me with total attention, held my hand for a moment and said, "Yes, you must come. Call

and make an appointment."[9]

Within a week, to the astonishment of her office staff, Bill had an appointment with the "impossible to meet" Mrs. Garrett and was amazed that it had been so simple. His next hurdle was to induce Helen to go with him to meet Garrett. She panicked at the idea of seeing her and discussing dissociated states, but ultimately he succeeded in, as he called it, "dragging her down there [to Garrett's office]."

When Bill and Helen met with Mrs. Garrett, she was gracious, charming, calm, and very reassuring to Helen, calling her a "fragile little flower" and indicating that she (Eileen) needed no details about the manuscript they referred to, but that she would publish whatever they had taken down because of its source. In her mind, there was no question about its authenticity. Bill said her most important comment was that "if we went in the direction of the *Course*, if we followed it in our personal lives, we would both be gloriously happy, but if we fought it, we would be sick. She repeated that. It was obvious that she saw something about the character of the *Course* even then in 1968."[10] Bill believed she was the greatest living psychic, and for her to confirm its legitimacy and to repeatedly emphasize the need to practice it made a strong impression on him. He was deeply reassured because he and Helen could talk to so few people about their extraordinary project. In retrospect, their meeting Eileen seems destined, just as was mine with Bill and the process was so similar. We cannot avoid meeting those who are to be in our lives, no matter how convoluted the process of our coming together may seem.

Another confirming experience for Bill occurred in London and involved the famous English psychic, Ronald Beasley. Beasley read auras, the energy field that we are and emanate. He commented that Bill's and Helen's auras were remarkably similar, a very unusual situation, and told them personal information he could not have known, which they found most impressive.

Beasley concluded by saying they were wasting their time, "You shouldn't be involved in the university life; you should be involved in healing."[11]

Since the *Course* was clearly about both healing and teaching, Bill sought more information about unusual healing practices, just as he investigated various mystical traditions. He had watched Kathryn Kuhlman, a widely known faith healer, on TV and thought she was a bit hysterical but sincere, prompting him to seek her out. They managed to acquire front-row tickets for one of her events in New York and were captivated at seeing her in action up close. Bill recounts:

> It was a highly charged emotional atmosphere. At the beginning, Kathryn came out on stage and went through a warm-up period. She was really coquettish and, to my mind, inappropriate, especially for her age. She wore a white dress and made little jokes, gradually warming up her audience. This went on for a while, then gradually something began to happen. She became more serious and started talking about the power of spirit. I was aware of the moment when things clicked—changed. She became quite different, another consciousness had taken over. That was presumably what she was waiting for. It takes enormous courage to get up before thousands of people and wait for that to happen. When it happened, there was a feeling of authenticity about it. She was no longer this sort of silly, somewhat hysterical woman, but a power and spirit that somehow came through. When she started calling out healings in various parts of the audience, people would come down and line up. It was amazing; she would just touch people and they would fall over. This went on for hours. Time didn't seem to make any difference. None of it seemed contrived; it was all quite startling. Some of it may have been suggestion, but I don't think it was all suggestion. It's easy to dismiss this kind of thing, but Helen was very moved by it, too. Helen even dropped all of her blasé defensiveness, and I was very touched. We felt a tremendous spiritual power that was generated somehow. Kathryn was acting as a common battery, I guess; she was the focal point of this energy. It was

very, very impressive. It went on all day, so by the time we left I felt both exhilarated and drained.[12]

If Bill sought out-of-the-ordinary experiences, the reverse was also true. Cal Hatcher, Bill's confidant as the *Course* was being scribed, recalled an incident. "Father Ben" in this tale was Bill's graduate student who arranged the first meeting between Helen, Bill, and Ken Wapnick.

> Ben had come up to Columbia and taken his doctorate under Bill in psychology. Ben was confessing to Cardinal Cook. He was a character to me, and would come up there in his long brown robes with his cross swinging on him. My office was on the first floor at Columbia Presbyterian [Hospital] and sometimes he'd throw little pebbles at the window to get my attention. One day he came by and was throwing pebbles. There was a little concrete ledge there and an iron fence all around the office building I was in. I raised the window and Father Ben was standing out there with these two ladies in habits, nuns. He said, "I want you to meet a friend of mine." I invited them to come in to talk. "We don't have time," he said, "but this is Mother Teresa and this is sister So-and-So." Well, I didn't know who Mother Teresa was, but my assistant, who was Catholic, said to me, "You dim-witted Protestant, you wouldn't know anything." So Mother Teresa was there. She was short, and so was standing up on the concrete ledge with the other sister. We were just talking back and forth, and they were on their way to see Bill and Helen. The famous Mother Teresa from India was on her way to visit Bill and Helen![13]

Bill said that while they were transcribing the *Course*, he had prayed that he might meet a living teacher, someone who embodied these teachings of love. He had been "led" to a book about Mother Teresa, and shortly after, circumstances conspired to facilitate a meeting with her. She was then establishing a branch of her order in the South Bronx, the worst of all crime-ridden poverty areas in New York. He was invited to meet her there and of that invitation, Bill said,

Initially, I felt apprehensive about actually having my prayers answered, since I was not sure that I was up to meeting a living saint. However, when this tiny woman graciously met us with palms extended, I felt an almost instantaneous sense of relief. It seemed as if I had always known her. Completely selfless and without pretense, she radiated the joy of total spiritual commitment. Later, when she turned to me and said, "Doctor, wouldn't you like to come to India? There is so much you could do to help the poor," I felt an almost irresistible impulse to answer, "Yes!" . . . To me, her life is a demonstration of the importance of total dedication and complete consistency on the spiritual path.[14]

Later, she came to see Bill and Helen; they visited on more than one occasion. As Tammy Cohen conducted interviews about Bill and the *Course* et al. in the mid 1990s, several would begin a sentence with, "Bill was no saint, but . . ." and proceed to comment on his gentle ways, his generosity of spirit, or his refusal to indulge in character assassination. Those I interviewed or others who knew him in California never included the initial qualifying phrase, but mentioned only his positive traits. His westward move proved to be a specific line of demarcation in how most people saw him. It also marks that time when, perhaps guided by the several meetings he had with Mother Teresa, he lived more and more that "total dedication and complete consistency." Years later, Roger Walsh commented,

There will doubtless be mythologies that try to make a saint out of Bill and perhaps other *Course* founders. If we mean by "saint" someone who has resolved all their psychological and spiritual difficulties, then Bill was certainly no saint and never pretended to be. However, he was someone who worked as hard as possible to have a full spiritual life. Perhaps, in the end, that's a more realistic view of what a saint is. But labels aside, Bill was clearly a model of sincerity and integrity, and who can even guess how many millions of people his life will touch?[15]

Bill's guidance was as clear about saying no as saying yes. Layle Luckett remembers,

> A great learning for me was in being less directive and less controlling. Bill wasn't a guy you could control. We used to go out almost every night. He had a very powerful intuition and sometimes he would balk. He would open the door and just say no, he wasn't going. We knew not to push. For sure, when he said he wouldn't go, we should have stopped in our tracks, because it would be the worst play you ever saw.[16]

His close associates knew about his inner inquiry for any decision, large or small. When anyone made a request that he felt was not for him, Bill usually modeled the ideal response, simply saying, "No, that doesn't work for me," with no need to justify, explain, or make excuses. He made it clear there was nothing personal in refusing, it was simply his guidance.

Another legendary talent was Bill's ability to get tickets to any event he chose. Stories abound about all the times he showed up at an opera, play, or other special event, and someone would always sell or give him a ticket(s). Almost everyone who knew him well observed this remarkable skill in action—and it was a very specific action. He never had subscriptions to the Metropolitan Opera while he lived in New York but always attended whatever he wanted. He was likely to note that at 7:12 p.m. it would be time to go to the box office to get tickets. He always seemed to have a precise sense about when to go on his ticket-acquiring quest; and he wouldn't get just any tickets but the ones he preferred. As with all of us, the more something happens, the more we trust the process and the more frequently it occurs.

Pat Hopkins recalls a special trip to New York with Bill to visit some of his old haunts:

> The highlight of the trip for both of us, however, was hearing Jessye Norman sing her Metropolitan Opera debut in Berlioz's *Les Troyens*. Bill worked the magic he was famous for among his friends by somehow man-

aging to obtain center-aisle orchestra seats to a sold-out performance. No matter how popular the event, or how long he waited to purchase the tickets, I never saw Bill fail to get excellent seats for anything he wanted to hear or see, anytime he wanted to go. It was absolutely amazing! He used to tell me it was God's reward for being willing to help bring the *Course* though. Even though he always laughed when he said this, I'm not at all sure he was joking.

On that particular occasion, we had been sitting in our hotel room reading the morning newspaper when Bill suddenly said, "I think we should go down to Lincoln Center about 2:30 this afternoon and look around." Not a word was said about opera tickets—we already knew there were none available—and Bill was never one to state the obvious. So we had some lunch and went down to Lincoln Center a little before two. We strolled around looking at the Chagall murals and some photographs and musical scores on display in the opera hall. I didn't even realize Bill was gone until I turned around at one point to say something to him and saw him walking toward me from across the room. He had a gleeful expression on his face and I knew that he had done it again. Sure enough, in his hand were two center-aisle orchestra tickets for that evening's performance. It was a thrilling performance! . . . I remember looking at Bill during a particularly moving aria and realizing we were both in a kind of altered state. It was a transcendent, joyful occasion, one I'll never forget.[17]

Another example involved Ice Capades tickets. Jack Luckett had bought three tickets sometime in advance of a particular performance, only to find they would be out of town. He gave them to Bill, who then invited a couple to go with him. As it turned out, another friend was going to be in town at that time and Bill invited him also. His initial invitee reminded Bill that he had only three tickets, but he reassured him that was no problem, all four would go. Jack recounts:

They drove to the sports arena with only three tickets. There were thousands of people surrounding this place, and they were walking across the parking lot when a man on a bicycle comes riding toward them, riding through all the people, through all the cars and right up to them. . . . Bill said, "Do you have a ticket for me?" And the guy answered, "Yes." Bill asked him how much it was and the man mentioned an amount. Bill reached into his side coat pocket and pulled out the money and handed it to him—the exact amount. It was not the amount of the ticket, but to the dollar, he had the amount the guy was asking for the ticket. As he handed it to him, he said, "Thank you, I was waiting for this," put the ticket in his pocket, and they went in. As it turned out, this fourth seat was very close to where they were sitting in that huge sports arena.[18]

Though it may sound trivial, the same dynamic applied to parking spaces. Ease in finding parking spaces per se is hardly cause for celebration, but the state of mind it reveals is. I was with Bill more than once when we needed to find a space in a very crowded area. As we approached, I would suggest we start looking and Bill would say, "No, there'll be a parking space waiting." One time near a crowded plaza, a vacant spot appeared right across from our destination—it was as if it was invisible to all the others looking for one. That often occurred for Bill; he was intuitive and open to such things and took great delight in their happening. Although he knew very well that miracles arise from a miraculous state of mind, he wasn't always there; he wasn't constant. But when he knew he was "on," it always worked. Hugh remembers,

And yet he didn't think he'd led a charmed life or had special powers and was just as aware when things didn't work out. It's not like he thought there was someone making everything smooth for him. He did not subscribe to a race of chosen ones, and the whole subject of manifesting— that somehow our spiritual path gives us powers ordinary mortals don't have—whereby the Holy Spirit opens personal doors so you get the right job, the right car, money, success, and parking spaces was immensely amusing to him. We shared a tremendous amount of humor about all this . . . and he delighted in talking about it. It was part of his open-mindedness. Despite his being somewhat cynical about our personal ability to manipulate the world, he was completely open to psychic phenomena that show the unreality of the world, which is not quite the same thing.[19]

If intuition worked while he was "on" and not at other times, he was very happy that Helen's intuition was not always reliable. One unusual challenge that weighed on him in his first years away from New York was Helen's prediction, made around the time *ACIM* was first published, about when both she and Bill would die; she saw the date on her own tombstone (she was off by a year) and indicated Bill would follow her within a year of her passing. Since she had died in February 1981, everyone, certainly Bill, felt some apprehension as the anniversary date approached. It came and went without incident, and everyone let out a collective sigh of relief; Bill survived Helen by seven and a half years. Ken Wapnick has noted she could be notoriously wrong when she had a personal investment in a prediction. That was her psychic facility misfiring, rather than the Voice that authored *ACIM*. Only with nonspecific, nonpersonal *Course* material was she always absolutely clear.

Even though Bill had followed his guidance or intuition about moving to Tiburon, that didn't imply his time there would be the proverbial bed of roses. It was simply the locale for his next round of inner growth and releasing defenses. He mused, "I guess too, sometimes, we also really have to go to the ultimate despair in order to break through; at least I do. It seems to be the way it went, and that may be the only way I can learn. I felt I had to struggle with everything, including the *Course*. It was very hard to be on this path without the notion of struggle, which seemed so predominant, but I loosened up a bit."[20] All learning isn't difficult or painful of necessity, only resistance makes it seem so. Along with the more challenging situations, Bill also had some wonderful, happy times in Tiburon.

A friend of mine coined the phrase, "trading up to grace," to describe the process of relinquishing the ego. Bill was increasingly able to set aside the distractions of the world and his own illusions; he moved steadily toward his goal—peace of mind—through each opportunity to let go of fear and, indeed, trade up to grace.

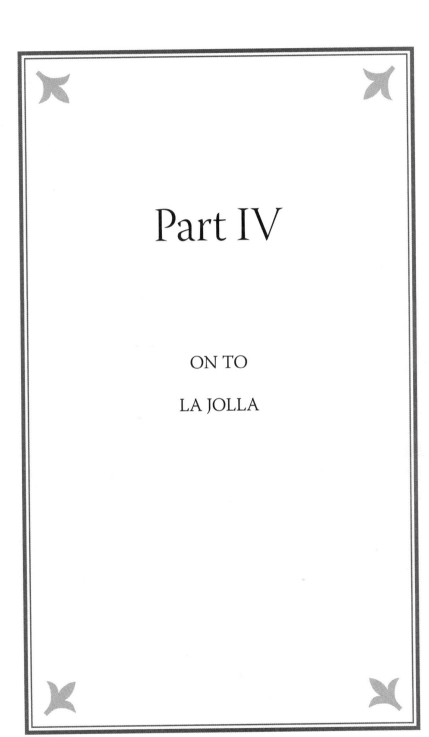

Part IV

ON TO

LA JOLLA

22

In 1982, as Bill recovered from his near-fatal heart episode, his friendship with Pat Hopkins continued to deepen. Pat remembers from that time, "Sometimes I would join him and Jules for dinner and our conversation would continue through the evening hours. It was obvious that our friendship was becoming more intimate, but it did not feel like falling-in-love romance. Rather, it was more a recognition of something I do not know how to describe, something that gave us both comfort and a deep sense of kinship."[1]

I find it fascinating that so many people referred to that feeling with Bill; they variously likened it to a sense of kinship, being part of a family, an indescribable connection, recognizing an old friend or even one's self, or a feeling of coming Home—nothing words can accurately convey. Incidentally, it's reassuring to know that no matter who you're with, the feeling of "being included in the family" increases as you practice forgiveness.

In late spring, Bill suggested they become housemates. Pat had a long daily commute to Tiburon from Santa Rosa, her home at the time, and Bill recognized his need for companionship, so for both practical and emotional reasons it seemed a perfect fit. From a broader perspective, it was also a perfect opportunity for both of them to continue to acknowledge some unfinished issues and to choose to let them go. The *Course* is crystal clear that the purpose of all relationships is our healing, whether we ever come to that awareness or not, and this one was no exception.

Pat and Bill had much in common. They both loved classical music—

Mozart for Bill and a more balanced repertoire for Pat—and it was the centerpiece of their respective lives, second in importance only to their spiritual practice. Both were also very bright, intellectually gifted, and loved reading and discussing what they read, including much mystical and spiritual literature. They also shared a common sense of the absurd and had many a good laugh over the local "soap operas" within their community. As a primary focus from 1982–1985, Bill, Pat, and Jerry spent a great deal of time together writing *Good-bye to Guilt,* attending the daily 9 a.m. meetings, interacting with their friends whose common bond was the *Course,* and attending to the business of the Center for Attitudinal Healing. All three were on its board of directors. During times when not serving on the board, Pat was a consultant to the center and later a temporary acting director. She also helped Jerry establish an ancillary organization, the Foundation for Spiritual Alternatives, so as she said, she was the "ham in the Bill/Jerry sandwich."

In preparation for moving in together, Bill had opened a box of memorabilia and, with some resistance, looked through it.

> I found samples of absolutely everything, like reprints of old papers going back over thirty years and a report I had written when I was studying brainwashing. . . . I also found a certificate that the War Department presented to me for my work on the atomic bomb, as well as some scattered personal notes from the *Course* that Helen and I had taken out. There were also some old birthday cards that Helen had written and pictures of both my parents. It was a review of "This Is Your Life" going back to the middle 1940s, all jammed in a box. I found my reaction very strange. I was sad and obviously had resistance to looking. I threw out a lot of it in preparation for the move. So in cleaning house, I reviewed all the madness that one accumulates. . . . House cleaning is good, but I have the feeling that there is something that I don't want to look at or something is missing.[2]

In his relationship with Pat, Bill would continue that housecleaning, moving yet another step toward his liberation. Despite all they had in common and their great admiration for one another, Pat indicated that "nevertheless, living together did not always go smoothly for us" and that their time together was "the best of times and the worst of times, to quote Dickens."[3] This is exactly what one might expect from a relationship so important to their mutual growth. I've always thought we learn our lessons with our closest friends, who agree at some level to be the mirror to our own fears, though at the time it can feel decidedly unfriendly. The people we live with provide the setup for deep and essential work, if we choose. Bill followed his own unique path to waking up as he built and maintained various relationships throughout his life that delivered exactly what he was willing to deal with at any given moment. The introduction to the *Course* text says, "Free will does not mean that you can establish the curriculum. It means only that you can elect what you want to take at a given time."[4] We do have to unlearn our fear and guilt. We can drag our feet or dedicate ourselves in a cooperative manner to discovering those beliefs masking as truths. Clearly, Bill and Pat's relationship had the same purpose: mutual healing, regardless of whatever reasons or needs seemed to draw them together. Bob Howe recalled, "I remember sitting down there in his condominium when Pat was living with him and they were arguing about which way the toilet paper should be on the holder. And the paper towels. Each one had their own inner secrecy and you kinda knew they had their own thoughts, their own way of doing what they wanted to do, and how they wanted to do it."[5] They were perfect companions for the work at hand, and their time together was an essential part of his curriculum (and hers), a releasing, clearing, and burning away of old grievances and outworn beliefs. Regarding that curriculum, Pat reminisces:

As the surviving co-scribe of the *Course*, I believe Bill felt an enormous responsibility, I would almost call it a burden, to be both modest, which was his nature, and to do everything he could to live and exemplify it. I still feel that Bill felt very strongly that he was holding the iconic, the symbolic, essence of the *Course* after Helen died. While he did extraordinarily well with not being inflated by those projections, I think he still felt them. At times, I felt this cost him enormously in terms of his own personal life; he was very divided between a fulfilled personal life and what he felt he needed to be for the *Course*, putting certain constraints on our relationship, as well.

It is hard to know, however, whether this sense of constraint I felt came solely from Bill's desire not to compromise the *Course* in any way, or from the guardedness he felt compelled to maintain most of his life about his homosexuality.[6]

I believe that beyond guardedness about being gay and resistance to the iconic role he felt he should fill, Bill simply had an internal sense of constraint from birth. Jaison Kayn picked up on that when he visited Pat and Bill shortly after they had moved in together:

The only time I ever saw Bill a little nonplussed was when I went to see them just after they started living together. Pat and Bill were standing in the kitchen of his apartment and I was close by in the adjacent dining nook. All of a sudden the room was filled with soft rose-pink energy. I saw it everywhere and felt it inside myself, as well. It was astounding! Fortunately, I had had an experience of this just the week before and knew what it meant. It was the presence of love urging us to open to expansion. Before I could stop myself, I felt the energy move me into the room and open my mouth. I started telling Bill to trust getting closer to Pat, which for me was—well, I never say things like that. I could feel this sweet rose-energy presence saying to them, "You have something important to do together." Bill was clearly nervous and upset. I think he felt inadequate and overwhelmed, but I could tell that he knew he was being given a gift he could trust. It was about their hearts joining. It was clear that their hearts were on the verge of joining into some remarkable commitment that neither of them had experienced before. I don't know if he saw the energy, too, but I certainly felt it and Pat seemed grateful because she knew. Her heart was ready to give him whatever she possibly could. For Bill, it was like asking a person to step off the curb blindly, knowing that rush-hour traffic was about to begin, yet also knowing the danger he felt was his own fear and that he would somehow be okay.[7]

Robert Rosenthal speaks for many in seeing their relationship as imperative to Bill's stepping forward.

I think when Pat Hopkins moved in with him, that was Bill's attempt, at a deep psychological and even psycho-spiritual level, to move through his grief. And maybe not just the grief from Helen, though that was the most significant, but a deeper, lifetimes-long grief. . . .

I think that he and Pat had an old connection, that they had agreed to come together at that time so she could help him get through his fear and grief. Bill was the happiest I had ever seen him with Pat, at least in the beginning. I believe their relationship allowed him to move beyond his unfulfilled expectations about Helen.[8]

As an interesting aspect of Bill's multitasking talents, or perhaps of his "don't fence me in" proclivity, Bill established new, significant relationships and maintained others while he and Pat lived together. About the time Bill and Pat were becoming better acquainted, he met Carlagaye Olson. They became close friends and their Thursday "play-days" with Jules were noted earlier in terms of the healing Bill often seemed to precipitate. Bill and Carlagaye occasionally got together on weekends, when her husband Steve also joined them. When Catherine Prescott moved to town in 1984, she and Bill also became very close. At first, he saw her regularly in her professional therapeutic role, but that ultimately morphed into a more personal relationship, as well. Bill's other meaningful relationships created a win/

win situation, as Pat also cherished having her own space.

Those of us from out of town also maintained our friendships with Bill. He and I got together on my visits to Tiburon as well as periodically talking on the phone. His original core group in Tiburon remained central to his life in California, and his capacity to genuinely care for many individuals at the same time was very deep and remained to the end of his life. Bill could be with a person, in love, rather than being "in love" with a person, and each relationship seemed to foster another important aspect of his self-discovery.

As Pat and Bill began their fourth year sharing an apartment, both were often gone. In 1985, Pat started traveling to do research for the book she co-authored with Sherry Anderson, *The Feminine Face of God,* and ultimately moved into her own apartment in January 1986.[9] Bill was spending perhaps a third of his time in La Jolla, visiting there from 1982–1986 on an increasingly regular basis. Several months after they moved in together, Bill and Pat had gone to La Jolla, and after that Bill made extended visits, sometimes with Pat and sometimes alone. They had discovered a quiet, well-run motel, and either he or they stayed in the same room on each trip. He loved the greater ease of the southern California lifestyle and established a pattern of going there for at least three weeks, then returning to Tiburon. After several weeks, he started to feel a bit lonely and less energized, so he would head back south. He talked about vacillating between Tiburon and La Jolla, or more humorously, teetering away from Tiburon and leaning toward La Jolla. Clearly, something was drawing him there. It would be the last venue for his healing, representing a major breakthrough—an outward sign of another significant step in his evolution.

Robert Rosenthal recalled, "I think the next important transition for Bill was when it became clear that the relationship with Pat was not going to work out. From the way I understood it, Bill really wasn't capable of a full sexual relationship with a woman. And so the relationship, as close as it was, was always left incomplete—a halfway relationship. Celibacy may have worked okay for him, but probably not for her."[10] From Pat's perspective on their time together, "We were like family, but not sisterly-brotherly, and we were partners, but not in the traditional sense of the word. To this day, I don't know how to describe our relationship."[11] She also told me, "I know it was hugely and immensely important; I would say that both our lives were significantly enriched, but I couldn't give specifics."[12]

Hugh remembers getting together with them after they stopped being housemates:

> Well, he saw the humor in it [their learning experiences] and at the same time I think it [times of not getting along] was distressing to him, but he didn't hang on to it. Neither of them did. They had been very close friends and became very close friends again. They would tell many funny stories about what had happened when they were together and what went on in that apartment; it was just a riot![13]

He also observed, as Bill was vacillating about his move,

> He was several years making that decision [to go to La Jolla], which was a very deep one. It was on his mind for a long time, and I'm certain that at that point he saw his own ego clearly, which was sort of the eastern, sophisticated, New York professor, classical music, classical education-type thing, which he shared with everyone else he was surrounded by there, with the exception of Jerry. [Jerry was California born and bred and attended medical school at Stanford.] But Pat, Jules, Frances, Roger, and Judy shared his same worldview. That was the unconscious part of Bill's ego in the beginning. In other words, he just presumed everyone would love Mozart and opera; that was a given or a fact. His whole personality, that whole eastern thing, was quite unlike this lighthearted self.

My understanding in conversations, and from my own observation, was that he saw that in order to let go of his ego he was going to have to turn it upside down. He would have to stand it on its head. He was going to have to get out of this situation and put himself in a completely different, nonintellectual environment, which he did. He had a tremendous capacity for acceptance and was able to accept and enjoy it immensely; that's when his ego dissolved at a remarkably fast rate.[14]

Gayle Prather additionally noted: "He did agonize over that decision to move to southern California. I guess it was because, basically, he really was going to be saying good-bye to his past because everybody, despite how he or she may or may not have felt about it, deferred to Bill as the patriarch. He was the head of the family, and I don't think he could shake that role as long as he was in Tiburon."[15]

Bill and Judy - ACIM 10th anniversary 1986

Bill's situation was transparent to everyone watching him. Many echoed Hugh's and Gayle's comments, recognizing the heavy intellectual emphasis in Tiburon, his attempts to escape it, and his inability to take his next step until he was out of that environment entirely. In his own way, he was dissociating himself from normal rules of behavior, of self- and other kinds of evaluation. He had told his stories long enough and had chosen not to pursue a more public or authoritative role with the *Course*, nor a more conventional, professional career. In terms of an outward focus, he had done what he came to do. Also, Roger Walsh felt that part of the pull to La Jolla was to be with people, primarily the Lucketts, who solely devoted themselves to practicing *ACIM*. Although his Tiburon friends were all *Course* students, they had divided loyalties, including careers, organizations, family responsibilities, or other worldly matters.

23

In October 1986, Bill moved permanently to La Jolla. He had released much in Tiburon and done a marvelous job, as Frances Vaughan stated earlier, of learning to "take up no space," inserting virtually no "personality noise." However, not wanting to be egocentric can sometimes be a cover for emotional repression; he retained some old inhibitions and defense patterns when it came to self-expression. La Jolla was about sorting this out so he could more easily express his loving, gracious energy without reservation. He knew, as did those close to him, that the healing uniquely possible through his friends in southern California would be the major focus of the rest of his life. Forgiveness was still "job one."

Bill's companions—better called playmates—for "letting go on the fast track" were his close friends, Jack and Layle Luckett, whom he had been visiting since the early 1980s. They met in Tiburon in 1978, when Jack was director of the Center for Attitudinal Healing. After a short while, the couple felt drawn to the San Diego area and relocated there. The Lucketts served as Bill's gateway to the joyous part of himself, because they were certifiably the most lighthearted of his companions. The label applied to them was "wild and carefree," and almost literally arm in arm, the three of them traveled the last part of Bill's path together.

Wild and carefree? Here was a couple with unlikely credentials for being Bill's playmates. When they met Bill, Layle was teaching MBA students in San Francisco and working on her Ph.D.; Jack was a retired Marine colonel, also retired from careers as a criminal lawyer and assistant district attorney in Los Angeles. They were devoted *ACIM* students and loved music and the theater. Who could be more suited to assist Bill move from an academic/intellectual orientation to its opposite end of the spectrum than ones who had already done so themselves?

If San Diego was as far from New York as one can get in this country, so was life under the Lucketts' tutelage. They were the perfect catalysts for Bill in tying up loose ends, moving toward greater openness and freedom, and releasing what yet weighed him down. He relaxed and enjoyed life in La Jolla, loved the lighter atmosphere and just being a regular member of the "Garden," the Lucketts' *ACIM* group. A local friend found a condo for him, and Jules and Carlagaye moved his possessions and set things up there. His friends carefully watched his comings and goings to La Jolla, weighing in with observations about what would be his last and final move, and unanimously approving it, as if anyone else's opinion mattered. Bill was following his famous right-on intuition.

Pat's observation echoed those opinions:

> What I did feel was that he was reliving the childhood he hadn't been able to have. I thought that was terrific—doing such goofy and uncharacteristic things that he wouldn't have been able to do in the Bay area because of inhibition and projections, too many roles. The Lucketts were such a wild and carefree couple; they were fabulous for him. I think his homosexuality had much more spaciousness there, going to places where I think he felt in the company of his own.[1]

The "company of his own" referred not only to the myriad new friends and acquaintances from dozens of *ACIM* groups, but to the gay community there and its much more open atmosphere. Jack commented:

> We always had a strong gay contingent in our groups and we took Bill to many *ACIM*/gay meetings. We also observed him with his own gay friends. As you know, Bill possessed a quiet but intense magnetism that

impressed and attracted women as well as men. He was uniformly cordial and warm to men, women, straight, or gay. He was not at ease with children or loudmouths. He was a celebrity in the gay male community, because of what he had accomplished in life. He did not try to impress or boast regardless of who he was introduced to. That was part of his unique charm. When we were with Bill and a male friend on a date, going to the theatre, the circus, or dinner, he was always very attentive and super concerned that his escort was treated well and had a good time. Bill had many gay friends but few, what we would call today, close relationships. His past lovers as well as casual friends were loyal and respectful right to the end. How lucky we all were to share part of the life of a real avatar.[2]

Because it is unusual, a number of others also mentioned that Bill remained friends with and was revered by past lovers and intimate associates. It's almost as if he lived parallel lives—his straight life and his gay one—with very little overlap. He was known to have a dozen or so gay friends in La Jolla with whom he spent more time, but no one knows any names or details. Judy remembers that he never hid his homosexuality from any of her family nor from Helen's, but publicly he was very discreet.

Long before Bill moved to La Jolla permanently, he attended *ACIM* groups there, both the Lucketts' and several others. At first, Bill didn't actively share, but gradually he joined in. Even though he had been mostly an observer in many activities throughout his life, here he really started to play and participate, and he got such a kick out of it. Some members of the Garden group were dancers, and they finally persuaded him to join in the dancing. He had danced some in his youth but not often as an adult, and then only under very private circumstances with very close friends.

Jack forbade attendees to ask Bill anything about the scribing the *Course*, as that trapped him in his past, but they could ask him anything about his current life. Treating him like anyone else was a stretch for everyone; however, when Jack set those limits, Bill relaxed and became increasingly available and confident. In addition to dancers, there were a number of singers in the group and that encouraged him to experiment both with reading and later singing *Course* selections. According to Jack,

> When he started reading the *Course* in the first person, everyone else was freed up to do it. He started singing the *Course* and that just broke a dam; it was a very big moment. He really joined the group. People realized they could just walk up and hug him. He was no longer just a quiet figure that had all the authority. He was Billy, nobody special, a member of the group. He still had the authority, but it was more accessible; he was just one of us and that is what he wanted. He did not want to be above or below, in front of or behind. It was, I think, a major healing. There was a very playful little kid in there, one who hadn't played, and this part of him had a chance to come out in a safe space.[3]

Bill learned more about how to express his perspectives on everything; for him, all subjects offered something lovely. Friends in Tiburon and beyond, who kept a watchful eye, noticed his gradual but steady unburdening. What a treat for those who participated in Bill's unfolding! One fortunate Garden participant, Jim Jeffries, remembered Bill's generosity, recounting that on one occasion Bill unexpectedly pressed something into his hand as the meeting concluded and said, "The Holy Spirit directed me to give this to you." When Jim got in his car, he looked and there was a fifty-dollar bill. From then on, Jim called him "Fifty-Dollar Bill," delighting him with the pun.

Sometimes disagreements arose about what a passage meant and Bill would not join those debates. Jack remembers, "So as a being of pure love, which is really what he was, . . . he did not feel that he had to tell other people how, because he knew they needed to do it in their own way and not to rely on others. He never took on the teacher/guru role, but was always in a supportive role. He supported everyone . . . and he was never threatening—never, never, never."[4]

One particular incident about Bill's giving advice, however, has literally traveled around the world. I have heard this story retold in a number of ways, and it has also returned to Jack and Layle in somewhat altered form. Here is the actual eyewitness account.

> We had a friend, Wayne Germaine, a very sweet person, who moderated a small *ACIM* beginner's group—maybe a half dozen people—at his home on Tuesday nights. Bill would go to that meeting, I think to support Wayne, although, oddly enough, there were many meetings he wouldn't touch with a ten-foot pole. He wouldn't moderate, wouldn't say a word. Wayne told Bill, in a conversation away from the meeting and in a totally different social context, "I don't know how to handle this situation. It's come up two or three times and it's baffling me. [This incident occurred at one of the few meetings Bill had missed.] Somebody will say something about the *Course* and then someone will say something that's the opposite, and then they will start arguing and I'm not supposed to correct my brother. I don't want to have fights in my group, but I don't know how to handle these aggressive people who are arguing about the meaning of the *Course*." Bill simply looked at him and said, "Tell them to tear out the page. There is nothing in this world worth arguing over."[5]

Quite a statement from a man who had argued with Helen so vehemently for so many years! Layle continued,

> We started laughing when this issue came up because we knew one of the guys [provoking the argument]. We didn't know the new person, but the other one was a regular in our group, a person who was extremely adamant about his position and how something had to be done. Bill and Jack and I knew him very well, and Bill was howling because he knew this guy would get into an argument with somebody instantly. This was after maybe six years of our facilitating meetings every day, so we knew how to cope with this, but it caught Wayne unaware. It was Wayne's sweetness

to admit, in the first place, that he just couldn't cope with the argument, and Bill's answer was absolutely priceless. It came out so quickly with no forethought whatsoever.[6]

This story has captured people's imagination, as this King Solomon-type wisdom was so typical of Bill. His message was to follow the *Course*, don't put it on a pedestal, and don't deify it or make it a holy text. He did not rigidly worship the literal meaning of *ACIM*, although he understood it profoundly. Speaking of the worshipping issue, Jack recalls a time when a short person used the text for a footstool. Some visiting students of another *ACIM* teacher were distressed at what they considered a lack of respect for the sacred book. All teachers have their own style, which is perfect for their students, but the style in La Jolla's Garden group was definitely not to worship the *Course*, but to steadily practice its teachings.

A rumor circulated during Bill's early time in La Jolla that reinforced the Lucketts' "wild and carefree" reputation; it held that he attended nude *ACIM* meetings at their home. This was an exaggeration as there never were nude meetings in the Garden groups, so named because they took place in the enclosed back patio of the Lucketts' beach cottage, which was made of concrete and often very warm. Jack recounts,

> We were right across the street from the beach, so many students swam before or after the meetings and wore bathing suits during our two- to three-hour meetings. They were sunbathing. A major issue arose when a couple of the younger women wanted to remove their bra tops to get an even suntan. Older members objected because it would be undignified. I stopped the action, we held hands in a circle, asking the Holy Spirit to guide us, and after fifteen minutes of meditation, addressed the issue specifically in *ACIM* terms. We had a great discussion covering ego, judgment, fear, true vision, equal treatment of both sexes, and our true nature. At the end of that discussion, a young lady said, "If 'I am not a body. I am free' [one of the workbook lessons], what can a mere strip of

cloth mean to me?" We then took a vote and decided that if, in the privacy of our meetings, any woman wished to be topless like the men, she could, but it was not required. This went on for a while—some did, some didn't—it actually wasn't a big deal.

Some of the 60,000 attendees that came to teach us [the *Course* states that we are all teachers to one another] were lawyers, doctors, ordained ministers, Catholic priests and nuns, La Jolla matrons, university professors, nurses, teachers, businessmen, airline pilots, military—both active duty and retired—the luminaries of *ACIM* except for Helen, working people and retired ones, people living in their cars, and patients sent by psychologists. Out of this stimulating mix, no one ever questioned the early days' practice of some girls going topless. In the 2,160 consecutive meetings with thousands of participants, not allowing smoking was a much larger issue.[7]

Although the truth is not as exotic as the fiction about the Garden groups, the meetings certainly were a vast leap from his days at Columbia and a marvelous opportunity to be part of the *Course*'s influence as it spread across the country and throughout the world. In addition, Bill attended a number of other *ACIM* groups in the area and made a host of new friends in the process. He was presented with other opportunities for friendly outreach beyond the *Course* community. How could it be otherwise with Jack and Layle as guides? They took him everywhere. Almost every night they went to restaurants, movies, dinners, and entertainment of every conceivable kind. Jack commented on his preferences:

Bill loved films; he preferred foreign and art films and also liked drama, historical pieces, and adult comedies. Under no circumstances would he attend sci-fi, action, war, western, or vampire flicks, or stupid comedies. His favorite movie was *Amadeus*, which he viewed several times. We had season tickets to most live-theater houses. Bill liked the theater but had hard and fast rules about going. He insisted on an aisle seat and the play had to have an intermission (he opined that having no intermission meant the play was no good and everyone would leave if given a chance). In addition to opera and classical concerts, Bill also loved the circus, ice shows, and jazz concerts. We all had annual tickets to Sea World and often attended their night spectacles.

As you know, Bill was very well read. During our time together he read the *New York Times* front to back, but he was done with his book and magazine reading. We lived very close to the La Jolla library (Layle and I always had books out) and had several excellent bookstores nearby, but Bill wasn't interested. He read the *Course* daily, usually with me, and that was it.[8]

They soon realized that Bill was not used to interacting with others in a restaurant, despite all his years of eating out. (Regarding food preferences, Bill would eat anything; no special diets for him. His colleagues at Columbia said he routinely ordered cake and ice cream for lunch!) Layle tended to engage with the wait staff, and following her lead, Bill started talking with them more and thoroughly enjoyed becoming acquainted with them. At his favorite places, the staff began to call him by name, and he would chat away with them. Pretty soon word went out that he was available for socializing and that the best venue for this was to invite him to breakfast. I can personally attest to his greater participation, because my husband and I went many places with him on our last visit to La Jolla, and he was well known at all the restaurants we visited.

To continue broadening his range of experience, the Lucketts took Bill to a nightclub, where he had never been before. For most of his life, he might have felt that was somehow beneath him and not necessary for his growth, but by the mid 1980s he was up for anything! They also took him to improv places with stand-up comedians. Jack remembers one occasion:

So here we were sitting in this Improv, talking about *ACIM*, and the girl who had seated us said that she had been in the *Course*. Two other waitresses came over and one of them was part-time in Hare Krishna, while the other was a born-again Christian. . . . Layle was pinning these tiny hearts on people. We all came together and I had everyone hold hands. This is a nightclub, mind you! We all said a prayer, asking that everybody who was going to be on the stage that night would provide healing for everyone in the audience, that they would heal something in us that we didn't understand or had rejected. And they all joined in, very willingly. It was not inappropriate at all, and Bill said, "You know, one of the things I have learned from being with you, Jack, is that the spiritual movement is happening everywhere if you take it with you, if you let the light shine."[9]

They also took him to a late-night version of the *Rocky Horror Picture Show*, where devotees come dressed as the characters. Knowing the lines, they stood down in front acting out the parts and the entire audience spoke the words as the movie unfolded. Some might call the diehard participants outcasts, certainly not the kind of folks Bill would have encountered in his sophisticated New York or northern California worlds, but here was a place where they could fully join and participate. Bill was fascinated; remember he was unused to participating and Layle said they all felt like fifteen again. Bill just laughed and laughed, having one of the best times of his life. Jack observed,

> He had a marvelously developed sense of humor and the quality I'm certain all masters have, of not being pretentious and of being able to see the beauty in all forms of life. He could see the kids joining. He could see them in costume, letting the other sides of themselves come out. He could see all of us laughing together at the silliness of the whole thing. He caught it. Some people are full of religiosity and they fully approve of everything that seems to fall within their scope of standards, but are certain that anything that falls outside that scope has some evil attached to it. That was not Bill's way. His way was to be like Jesus, as I understand Jesus. He saw the beauty in all aspects of humanity.[10]

Another sign of his freedom was when we went to see an *ACIM* "gardener" [a participant in the *ACIM* Garden group] in a home-grown play. It turned out to be held in the back room of a biker bar with the toughest-looking guys you can imagine! Billy just walked through smiling and waving to everyone as if this were his usual routine. Also, around Bill's birthday in 1988, a handsome young sailor came to the Garden. They struck up an instant relationship, one so close that Billy actually acceded to driving up to Los Angeles with this guy in his red Jeep just for lunch! Can you imagine him so loose? This was a big deal; he wanted everyone to see him riding around in a Jeep.[11]

And the loosening continued. Late one night as the three of them were returning from the theater, Bill, out of the blue, started to sing parodies about the *Course*, changing the lyrics of the first lines of well-known songs. Jack also knew a lot of music, so he chimed in immediately with the next line. They alternated singing these lines from songs, creating an abbreviated, funny version of the *Course* history. For fifteen minutes, they invented hilarious new words, feeding off each other's creativity. Jack said Bill got so tickled and laughed so hard, it was just wonderful, another great release for him. Bill had made up some musical parodies with Helen in New York, but this was the expanded version and yet another marker of his disappearing barriers and inhibitions. Jack referred to his time in LaJolla as "an out-reaching, people-oriented, heart-opening experiential phase. To his credit he participated with verve and charm."[12]

My husband Bob and I saw Bill for the last time on a visit to La Jolla in April 1987. For several nonstop days, we attended *ACIM* Garden meetings with him, a daily routine, and it was great seeing him in his new "natural habitat." We went to some of his favorite haunts, spent much time at his home, walked through the nearby park, and accompanied him to the first public viewing of the video, *The Story of A Course In Miracles*; it was scheduled, "by coincidence" for its premiere one evening while we were there. He was a bit nervous about everyone else watching him on film while he, too, watched but it seemed a relatively minor issue. This video documents the history of *A Course In Miracles* with Bill's firsthand narration and skillful use of pictures of Helen, including excerpts read from her diaries. It was an unexpected treat for Bob and me to observe Bill watching himself on screen. Afterward, he asked for feedback about several aspects of the production, and we assured him that both the video and his presentation were right on. It was a delight to be with him as he jumped another hurdle about being publicly noticed. I thought he had grown so much and was more casual, relaxed, and open than ever before. He was more expressive generally and seemed very happy. In the year following our visit, we spoke periodically on the phone, and I was deeply satisfied to know that all was right with his world and getting better all the time.

Our last time together in La Jolla 1987

In April 1988, when asked how he would like to celebrate his upcoming sixty-fifth birthday, Bill replied that he wanted absolutely nothing, no party; he was still a little shy about people focusing attention on him. The Garden group paid no attention and had one anyway. On short notice, word of this momentous birthday celebration spread, and around seventy people bearing covered dishes and cakes decorated all sorts of ways—several sporting the *ACIM* cover—showed up to honor him.

He received meaningful gifts from the Foundation for Inner Peace. Judy Whitson had assembled sections from all the foreign translations then in progress and put them in a black thesis binder identical to those that held the early typescripts of *ACIM*. In addition, Judy created a large scrapbook filled with cards, greetings, and photos from his friends. These displays of affection meant so much to him, and he was touched and thrilled by the scrapbook, also a bit embarrassed and overwhelmed (rather than "under-whelmed" as he liked to joke).

Someone suggested that Bill circle the garden and allow each person to express gratitude for his presence and for bringing *ACIM* into being. Jack reminisced,

> Well, there is no way he would have allowed it before that day, because he would have disappeared. He would not have put up with it. So the first person really poured out his heart, "Billy, thank you for this and this and this." Billy reached over and just melted him in a hug that lasted for at least a minute, just pulled him into him . . . and held him silently. Then he went to the next person, and we spent the day doing this, each person acknowledging him fully. He put up with it, and he gave a one-minute, or longer, hug to everyone.[13]

When it was Jack's turn, he joked with him as was their custom, and put a large crown of blown-up balloons on Bill's head, calling him the "crown prince" of *A Course In Miracles*. Remarkably, he surrendered to it.

And so he could accept this rather foolish and bizarre-looking crown, and he laughed, smiled, and said again, "I'm too old not to be flexible," and that was his great lesson. And always the great punster, he often said later, I am, "flexi-Bill." [That name derived from a song written by Libby McGuire entitled, "Flexi-Billy-T."] . . . And he later confided that he had had the fullest experience of love, beyond anything he had ever allowed himself with anybody on this planet. He felt completely loved. He would not have accepted that before this time in his life. He would not have understood it, . . . but he finally got it.[14]

65th birthday with gift of ACIM translations
from Foundation for Inner Peace 1988

In response to Bill's joyful pronouncement about his flexibility, Whit Whitson wrote,

I believe he was saying that he had finally torn down the psychological boundaries by which he had defined himself for a lifetime. In so doing, he had forgiven himself for all the judgments with which he had imprisoned his closest friends and colleagues in his own perceptions. It was as if he had finally liberated himself from the crises of his long journey of self-definition. Finally, he was free.[15]

When I asked Jack about Bill's evolution once he moved to La Jolla, he replied:

> As far as I could see, Bill had full spiritual depth the day I met him and that did not change. His social skills, his relaxing, his ease with others changed considerably, even dramatically, after he moved to San Diego, becoming part and parcel of the wild group we had down there. He really felt at home. When he was up in the Bay area, they called him Dr. Bill. Who the hell wants to be a Dr. Bill, anyway? We stopped that right away. He was just Bill [or Billy] and a member of the group.[16]

> Secondly, Bill, the human, took the *Course*, turned his life around, and became the humble, modest, perfect, enlightened teacher of the *Course* by his conduct, by his being, and by his grace, gentleness, and love. Even if he had never helped bring us the *Course*, and I had just met this man, I would still honor his most beautiful life. And he's still operating because his energies are still with us, surrounding us.[17]

While basking in the glow of his newfound freedom and finally allowing himself to be fully loved, remnants of his past tugged at him. In March 1988, out of the blue, Bill contacted his old friend Jo, his girlfriend from college days, to wish her happy birthday and to invite her out for a birthday dinner. She was recently widowed and they rekindled their old friendship. They had met only twice since college, once in the late 1970s when Bill was in San Diego, her home at that time, and once when she was in Tiburon about four years later. According to Jo, they had a truly marvelous time and got together several times during the following three months. In midsummer, with an extended business trip to New Zealand coming up, Jo had to make arrangements for her rental property out in the desert while she was gone; she invited Bill to drive out with her and he happily accepted. Jo reminisced about all the fun they had had together as pals, before Bill gave her his fraternity pin:

> We used to sit on the bench at his piano, which he could play beautifully. He could sing beautifully, too.... We used to sing things like *Danny Boy* and *The Desert Song*.

> So it was funny some fifty years later when we were driving up to the desert and he broke out in this song and we sang together. It was really neat, just like old times, . . . a delightful weekend. There was nothing [romantic] between us, yet he seemed so much at home. It was like he was really at peace with himself. . . . So we agreed we were just really great old friends, and I realized at that time, that's it. It was kind of interesting because on that trip he gave me a copy of his book, *Choose Once Again*, and I think there's a message there. Like I had to choose once again, somebody, but not him.

> But I have to say that even though I'd known Bill since kindergarten, he was still somewhat of an enigma to me. Yet he really opened up to me, more than ever before, that last time we were together in the desert. We were closer than ever before as just good friends.

> The one thing that was interesting, too, and he was almost secretive about this, is that he said, "I'm really going to be more of a risk taker," although he didn't explain what that meant. . . . "I've got a lot of plans and I've made up my mind. I think I've protected myself too much all my life; I'm going to be more of a risk taker." That last week he was so relaxed and confident. It was like, "I've finally arrived and I really have it all together now." I was really looking forward to seeing him again.

> When we parted [two days later], he told me he was going to try to get to New Zealand while I was there, since I was going to be there a whole year. I said, "Great, as soon as I get there and find out what my address

is I'll write you." [Soon after], I left for New Zealand and he left for San Francisco that same day.[18]

Jo indicated they each knew, though didn't say, that this was really the last good-bye.

By all accounts from many witnesses, by the end of his earthly life Bill had become playful, participating, flexible, light, joyous, and free—aware of his true identity. Many people had served him throughout his life as he owned his shadow side, and ownership allowed his fears to fade away. Much of his humor stemmed from recognizing fear's lack of substance and the absurdity of taking ourselves so seriously. "This is the way salvation works. As you step back, the light in you steps forward and encompasses the world. It heralds not the end of sin in punishment and death. In lightness and in laughter is sin gone, because its quaint absurdity is seen. It is a foolish thought, a silly dream, not frightening, ridiculous perhaps, but who would waste an instant in approach to God Himself for such a senseless whim?"[19]

At long last, Bill became aware that he no longer needed to escape from anyone or anything, but could simply set aside any upset as a nightmare without appeal. He chose not to be imprisoned. In all ways, large and small, his loving presence eclipsed his fearful, self-serving thoughts. He reached the point where there was little more for him to say, because knowing was so deeply embedded in his psyche. He had allowed grievances and old habit patterns to be dissolved, and now *experienced* the truth of his being. Talk would only trivialize it. In adopting the goal of a better way to live, he instantly found himself on a path with no exit point, leading straight to the heart of love itself. What he had admired in Mother Teresa, he had become.

Now, many years later, with so many sharing their unique perspectives of him, no more hiding is possible. The enigmatic, secretive, and compartmentalized Bill finally stands revealed for all to see.

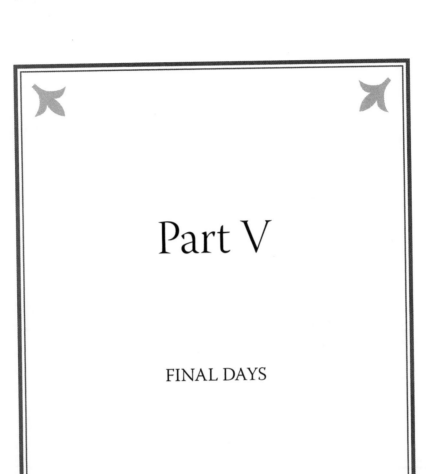

Part V

FINAL DAYS

On the last weekend Bill and Jo spent together, he had declared his intention to take more risks, expand his reach, and be ever more true to himself. The time for wearing a mask was over. My favorite mantra is, "When all else fails, tell the truth," and Bill now adopted this fully. We have been conditioned to do everything else but that, having learned our manipulating and negotiating skills at a very early age. As with all of us, Bill's imprisonment began in childhood; with each grievance he collected, another imaginary bar was installed, creating the subjective experience of an unshared, lonely prison. But with each choice to change his mind, a bar vanished, and he felt more powerful, integrated, secure, confident, and able to access his inborn wisdom. He was in charge of the prison doors and could use his talents to gain his freedom.

> Abilities must be developed before you can use them. This is not true of anything that God created, but it is the kindest solution possible for what you made. In an impossible situation, you can develop your abilities to the point where they can get you out of it. You have a Guide to how to develop them, but you have no commander except yourself. This leaves you in charge of the Kingdom, with both a Guide to find it and a means to keep it. You have a model to follow who will strengthen your command, and never detract from it in any way. You therefore retain the central place in your imagined enslavement, which in itself demonstrates that you are not enslaved.[1]

Bill was always forthright about needing help with wanting to forgive. Lukewarm to the idea at first, he developed a zeal for leaving no grievance unaddressed as the years passed and his understanding grew. When he recognized that his own ego thoughts enslaved him, his final biggest "risk" was deciding to let them all go. He often said that his major prayer was "Help!" or the expanded version, "Help me do this!" It was no more specific than that, regarding either the subject or object of his prayer. The Lucketts said that occasionally, while they shared a home with Bill, they could hear him earnestly praying, "Help me do this!" His deepest desire was to completely forgive everyone and everything. In her book, *You Are That*, the American teacher Gangaji describes what we set in motion with the simple prayer, "Help":

> Help is here. You are never separate from help. Anytime you ask for help, help presents itself. It is beautifully humbling to ask for help. It is good to give up your idea of independence. Just say "Please help," and you will see instantly that every enlightened being in every realm, known and unknown, from all the dimensions, charted and uncharted, is immediately supporting, helping, reminding, pushing, pulling, embracing, holding, shaking or doing whatever is needed. Your plea for help cuts through all past arrogance. You are helped immediately because you are calling to the truth of yourself.[2]

A Course In Miracles echoes this:

> Everyone here has entered darkness, yet no one has entered it alone. . . . For he has come with Heaven's Help within him, ready to lead him out of darkness into light at any time. The time he chooses can be any time, for help is there, awaiting but his choice. And when he chooses to avail himself of what is given him, then will he see each situation that he thought before was means to justify his anger turned to an event which justifies his love. He will hear plainly that the calls to war he heard before are

really calls to peace.[3]

Asking for help turns out to be the best insurance policy around!

In February 1988, Bill experienced some bronchial difficulty, which required postponing a planned trip to Tiburon. For several years, he had had occasional incidents of atrial fibrillation, an arrhythmia of the heart not uncommon in older people but more dangerous for him, as his heart had been compromised by the rheumatic fever he developed as a child. Throughout his adult life he had irregular heartbeat episodes that he basically ignored; he was very casual about body-related issues except for the carotid artery blockage in 1981, which demanded attention and, ultimately, two surgeries. Jack noted Bill's flu-like symptoms and, aware of his chronic heart condition, asked if his affairs were in order and/or if he would like help with his will or other related paperwork. Bill thanked him and laughed, reassuring him, "Don't worry, it's all done and, by the way, when my time comes, I'm going to Judy. Judy's in charge and will know what to do." Jack commented about his health:

> After his near fatal heart attack in 1981, Bill was always aware that the angel of death was on his left shoulder. He had constant heart fibrillations. We took him to the emergency room at Scripps Hospital more than once for fibrillations. He was having some signs that his work was done. He did not make a big thing of this publicly, but he knew his life was in danger at all times. This was one reason he asked Layle and me to live with him; he wanted others around if help was needed. He strove to live fully and experience all he could before he left. He was very brave.[4]

Although many were completely surprised at Bill's passing, others were apparently prescient close to the end. Driving around a bend in the road (in April, his next-to-last trip to Tiburon), Diane Cirincione was surprised to see Bill standing there. He smiled, she stopped the car and got out to visit with him.

When I first saw him, I had this strange feeling—it was so wonderful to see him there, but in a very special way. As I got in the car at the end of our conversation, he leaned through the window and gave me another hug. I pulled away slowly, looking in the mirror as he stood there watching the car. I was amazed to find myself thinking, very consciously, "If this is the last time I ever see Bill, that will be okay." I felt so good, totally fulfilled, and when I heard that he had died, that picture of him looking at me through the window, accompanied by that strange thought, immediately flashed through my mind.[5]

Pat Hopkins also had a very telling dream three weeks before Bill's passing. Excerpts cited from that dream reveal the magnitude of Bill's transformation and the universal availability of that information in the one mind we all share.

In the dream, his friend, Calvin Hatcher, the only other administrator at Columbia who knew at the time what he and Helen were up to, had taken Bill and me to an opera in New York City. For whatever reason, our tickets were split and Bill was sitting two or three rows in front of me; Calvin and Judy were in my row and farther down the line was Frances [Vaughan]. About the time people would be reading their program notes, some ladies came through; if you were at a ballgame you would say they were hotdog and beer hawkers. But these were very straight, ethereal-looking, ballerina-type ladies and they were handing out chocolate sundaes, for which Bill had a particular fondness. Not only were there chocolate sundaes, but those coffee-crunch things you could put on top, which he also loved. I thought this was very strange, but they were very good and I noticed that he was eating his. About the time you would expect the overture to begin, Bill stood up from his chair, turned around to face us, and said, "I have come full circle in my life. All the things that I didn't understand, all the things I was afraid to say, I now want to share with you." He proceeded to give the most exquisite, simple, eloquent speech that moved absolutely everybody. Knowing how he hated to speak in public and the anxiety it caused him, the relaxation with which he delivered this truth of his life was an incredible thing to behold. When he was finished, Frances, Judy, Calvin, and I looked at each other and said we thought we knew Bill, but this was a totally new dimension of this person that we all loved so much. Nobody applauded but when he finished, everybody stood up with tears running down their cheeks. The house was filled and people started to gather in small clumps or groups and began to tell each other the truth of their lives with the same utter defenselessness, vulnerability, and trust that he had exhibited when he stood and talked with us. I saw Bill beaming down on absolutely everyone at what he had set in motion. That was the end of the dream. The next morning when I awakened, I was in a joyful state. I knew that Bill had come to something in his life that was totally freeing, absolutely new, and the achievement of a lifetime. Naturally, my ego got involved and wondered if it was my own projection, so I waited eagerly for his next visit to share the dream with him, to see for myself whether or not it was true. As we now know, it was a dream but it was also true.[6]

Hugh noted that, although he never talked to him about this specifically, he thought Bill understood that the greatest thing we can do for the world is to awaken individually. He and Gayle strongly felt he did awaken by the end of his earthly life, and accomplished it in a relatively short period of time. He observed:

At the end of his life, Bill was going around telling everybody not to take this *Course* so seriously, not that one doesn't revere or appreciate it, just don't make it into such a rigid, deadly thing. He still had his little soap operas with extensive travel plans on the drawing board, other relationship and living arrangement offers on the table, and then there was the real Bill. Toward the end, he got into that wonderful state of mind where he could awaken; you could see it all so clearly. He was smart enough not to get involved back in the world, a perfect time for him to leave.[7]

After he passed, I asked Gayle what confirmed for her that he really had awakened. She answered, "A great burst of joy came to me during his memorial service."[8]

As the daily *ACIM* transcription process stretched into months, then years, Bill and Helen had mused about whether it would ever end, and if so, how they might know that. At first, they thought it would be only a few pages long, but as it continued to unfold, it became clear it was a much longer work. Now, four decades later, we can say offhandedly, "Oh yes, the *Course* consists of a text, a workbook, and teacher's manual," but they had no way of knowing that early on. When they inquired, the inner Voice told them they would recognize the end of dictation (of the text) when they heard the word *Amen.* I am consistently moved to tears, imagining that October morning in 1968, when Helen slowly read the words, "And now we say *Amen,*" the first sentence in the final paragraph of the text.

And as for Bill, now we say *Amen.* Those who knew and loved him during the California chapter of his life watched his steady transformation unfold—sometimes barely perceptible, sometimes in sudden leaps, occasionally with some discomfort, but always modestly—as his initial small willingness to practice forgiveness grew into a serious commitment. Once he made that commitment to practice complete forgiveness, he never really wavered. Everyone noticed the steady dissolution of his ego, that process markedly accelerating after he moved to La Jolla. His prayers for help, indeed, were granted, and one day Bill simply woke up, walked out of "prison," and declared his own independence on July 4, 1988. No one who knew him believed the date was a coincidence; in retrospect, everyone laughed about it, affirming the perfection of his last few days. Bill, who so loved to play with words, was playing with dates. In the end, all grievances were healed and "flexi-Bill" was free.

For what would be his final visit to Tiburon, Bill planned to arrive on July 3rd to join the holiday festivities at the Whitson household. Just before leaving, he and Catherine Prescott discussed getting together, as was their custom on his occasional trips up from La Jolla. With uncharacteristic fervor, Bill insisted that they have dinner with Jerry the night of the third. Since she planned to leave for Hawaii the next day, she responded, "No, it's not worth it, Bill; I'll see you when I get back." In retrospect, she found it amazing that he kept saying, "No, no, I have to see you before you go!" She agreed to dinner, somewhat reluctantly, because she had an early morning departure and many last-minute chores still to do.

Jerry picked Bill up at the San Francisco airport the morning of July 3, and on the drive north to Tiburon, they found themselves ensnarled in a huge traffic jam. The drive usually takes about an hour but on this day it was closer to three and a half hours, which Jerry later recalled as a real blessing. Spending that much time with Bill was such a treat for him. "Bill was in a very playful, joyful mood, very light. I never saw him so exuberant; his humor was amazing. He was walking very lightly and kind of playing. You know how he liked to play on words. I was really happy to see him lighter, not taking life seriously. I absolutely remember telling him how wonderful it was to see his joy and what a great decision it had been to go down there [to La Jolla]."[1]

Judy Whitson recounts, as if it were yesterday, the sequence of events that unfolded in Bill's astonishing final days:

> The whole story of his last two days was all one piece. I was expecting him for the weekend, as it was the Fourth of July, and I had invited thirty-six people to greet him and have an outdoor meal on the deck with fireworks and all. Jerry picked him up at the airport to bring him to our house for lunch, which I had ready about 12:30, expecting them by 1:00 p.m. It passed, then 1:30, 2:00; they weren't there and I was getting a little miffed! This was before cell phones. Finally, around 3:00 they walked in and what I saw was so unexpected. Jerry looked kind of sheepish and Bill was smiling as if he were onstage. He was lifting up his arms in the air with grace—I never thought of Bill as a graceful person—and doing a little jig as he walked in the door. Then he kissed me and said, "You won't believe what happened, you won't believe what happened!" I said, "What?" still a little miffed. He said, "We had terrible, terrible traffic and Jerry didn't get angry once!" I looked at Jerry and he sort of shrugged, smiling his little embarrassed smile because that remark meant that he usually did get annoyed at traffic. But Bill felt something had happened and was commenting on the difference, "We had such a wonderful talk, a really wonderful connection." He was very much aware that it was different with Jerry, and oh, my goodness, he was dancing, literally dancing into our house![2]

The *Course* states unequivocally that as we change our thoughts, their outer counterparts—the details of our daily lives, including others' behavior—will change automatically. Since Bill had clearly made a major shift in his thinking, he naturally saw things differently, experiencing everyone around him—in this case Jerry—as more loving, open, and intensely satisfying. Of course, such healing is mutual—the ultimate win/win situation! Jerry and Bill made their arrangements for the evening and Jerry left. Judy continued,

Bill was still "tripping the light fantastic" all around the living room, though there was no music playing. I asked what he was doing and he answered, "Oh, I feel so flexible, I feel so flexible!" I asked if he would like to sit down to have lunch and he replied, "Alright," but he was blithe, that is the only word I can think of. It was a very different Bill. He was just happy, but the happiness was not "good mood" happiness, rather a joy that was radiating through the body. His spirit was transcendent. Watching him as I served him lunch (there was the watcher part and the doer part of me), the watcher thought something strange was going on here. I wondered if he was on something, thinking some medication had him stoned. I asked him what he was taking these days and he laughed, saying, "No, no, I'm just feeling so good, so free, so complete!" When I asked if he meant "relationship complete," he answered that he was. So, playing the role of the sister, I started quizzing him about them, beginning with Ken. Bill said he had spoken with Ken a few months before, telling him that anything he had ever held against him was his own misperception and how terribly sorry he was. He was honest with Ken about the times he had resented him, his judgments about him, and his resistance to being friends with him. He said the grievances were all gone, absolutely gone in his mind, that he didn't see him that way anymore and asked for forgiveness.[3]

The conversation with Ken took place, to be precise, in February on Ken's birthday. Jack Luckett confirmed the circumstances from his own perspective, as he had overheard Bill's side of the phone call.

Bill normally got up earlier than I did, and he would have clippings from the newspaper set out on the coffee table for us to talk about when I joined him. On this day, as every morning, Layle was out doing her yoga and Bill and I were drinking coffee, chatting about those articles. Unexpectedly, he got up in the middle of a discussion, dialed the phone, and spoke to Ken, among other things wishing him a happy birthday. When he hung up I told him I was listening to the tone of his voice and that it was so clear to me he had totally forgiven Ken. He answered that it was, indeed, true.[4]

Ken corroborated the story. He said the conversation was a short one, but Bill was very warm and sincere and that it felt genuine to him. He didn't remember the exact words, but Bill did apologize, saying something like he had no right to judge or know what Ken should be doing or might do, that anything he did was fine with him. A month or so after the call, Ken spoke with him again, asking Bill to attend the grand opening in August of the retreat center in Roscoe, New York, which he and his wife Gloria were starting. Bill agreed to join them there.

Judy continued questioning Bill about his relationships:

> Then I went through a list of about eight people where I knew the relationships had been sticky ones and with every one of them he was beaming. I got to the one I thought might be extremely embarrassing, asking about Jo, his first girlfriend. He knew what I meant and said they had gone away together two weekends before to her condo out in the desert [near San Diego]. When I inquired, he said he had finally told her and it was clear, although they discussed his visiting her in New Zealand once she got settled. Bill and I never actually discussed the fact that he was homosexual. It wasn't as if I didn't know, we just didn't discuss it.

> Then I asked him about Helen, because that was the big one. "Funny you should ask that," he answered, "because the other night I had a dream where I saw her as the priestess [representing an important aspect of Helen's nonphysical function, one she had many dreams and visions about]. She was holding out her hands to me and glowing, with such a sweet smile on her face." It seemed that, indeed, there was nothing left undone, so I gave him a hug, saying, "Well, you *are* free, you've done your homework." He smiled, just a big grin, and said, "Yes, I have!"[5]

As planned, Jerry came for Bill later that evening, then they collected Catherine to join them for dinner. "Bill was so happy and excited," she recounted. "He played out this romantic thing with me even though there was nothing to it. I was his 'girlfriend,' but not really. Nothing ever happened, but I think he liked to play this knight in shining armor and be kind of chivalrous."[6] She said he was ebullient and joyful as he danced around; his dancing apparently hadn't stopped when he left the Whitsons' home.

The trio ordered fish, and when it arrived already filleted, Catherine said, "I looked down at it and had a feeling, a psychic hit, right then that something was going to happen because it looked like a dead body!"[7] Often throughout the meal Bill would hug her, saying, "Well, there must have been some reason I was supposed to see you tonight, right? It had to be tonight."[8]

Meanwhile, Catherine noted,

I had this fish and a feeling in the pit in my stomach, but never did I think it was related to Bill, never. His energy, his frequency, was vibrating at such an incredibly high rate he swept me into it, like going up in a hot-air balloon. He was saying all the way home from the restaurant, "There's no baggage; I'm cleaned out, in and out; I'm complete with everyone." On arriving home, while Jerry waited in the car, he kissed me, danced around in the street, and the last thing he said was, "See, there had to be a reason that I saw you tonight. Tonight's the night." But I had this clutching feeling, and the tape playing on my stereo when I walked in was called "Walk and Talk Like Angels."[9]

While Catherine pondered her strange feelings, Jerry returned Bill to the Whitsons,' where the three of them talked a bit about the evening, and then, still playful and elated, Bill retired to bed. Whit corroborated Judy's accounting of the day, "On that last night he was very light, literally dancing around, and I'd never seen him do that. He was very joyful, up on tiptoes as if he were going to lift off."[10] He noted, as did everyone else who saw him those last couple of days, that a substantive shift had occurred. Bill seemed to have cut loose all the anchors—professional ones related to his scientific persona, as well as his personal ones, the struggles and disappointments.

The next morning, while serving Bill breakfast, Judy commented about its being the Fourth of July, and he said, "Yes, it's my independence day!" She asked if he still felt free, and he reiterated, "Yes, I'm so flexible!" He and Whit had talked about the meaning of *flexible* as a term from the PAS-flexibility not of the body but of the personality. He had gone from being restricted, reserved, and inflexible to expansive, flowing, and inclusive. He also offered his private conviction to Whit that the PAS was still the most powerful and advanced psychological tool for describing human behavior and that only a few people really understood it. Judy's chronicle continues:

Bill knew I was having a large group over for the holiday; the tables were all set up and I had a refrigerator full of food. After breakfast I decided, however, that I had to go to the market and get some more chicken. Bill insisted I already had enough, but I said, "Yes, but I'm a Jewish mother and have to have extra." He then announced that he was going for a walk [as was his daily custom], would meet me at the supermarket, and then drive home with me. Since I didn't really have time to shop, needing to tend to the barbecue and other last-minute details, I must have responded with a funny look. He apparently noticed that because he said, "Don't worry, dear. If I'm not there when you're ready to leave, go home without me." I put my arms around him, hugged him really tight, and said, "Bill, I'm never going home without you!" thinking only from the *Course* frame of reference of our returning Home together. He seemed perfectly fine, and I didn't connect his comment with any feeling of foreboding, certainly nothing like death! He just patted me on the head.

Bill walked out the door to take his stroll while I went downstairs, collected my shopping list, and maybe five minutes later, got in the car and drove a few feet. And there was Bill, lying on the ground, the paramedics already there. My next-door neighbor, a surgeon—God bless him—had been clipping his bushes in the front yard. He saw Bill go down, ran to his car maybe three yards away, grabbed his medical kit, called the paramedics, and in seconds was by his side. The whole idea of Bill dying right then and there—my mind raced thinking about his being alone, all that one thinks when something like that happens. If I had come out three minutes earlier, could I have saved him? But the doctor was in total control, and I'll never forget his kindness. He wanted to know what medicines he might have been on, so I ran to the house, brought out his shaving kit, and he started going through it while still holding Bill. The paramedics wanted to give him oxygen, but the doctor said he was already gone, dead before his head hit the road. There was considerable blood because he hit the ground so hard, but the doctor thought the cause of death was his heart "blowing out." That, of course, is not a medical term, but it did describe the situation.[11]

The autopsy later confirmed that part of Bill's heart had, indeed, exploded and that he had left suddenly and painlessly.

Whit and I accompanied Bill's body to the hospital, where he was placed in a room to be checked over. I called Jerry, Pat, Roger and Frances, and after they arrived, we all stayed in the room with him for about an hour just saying good-bye, reciting some of our favorite quotes from the *Course*, touching and petting and loving him. The only picture I carry in my mind is one of love, his face showing total peace, as he lay on that table. After all, it was Bill's independence day.

On the way back, I had to go by to tell my mom, who lived a few minutes away. She loved Bill, and they were very, very close. Of course, she had to know. "Does this mean we aren't going to have his party?" she inquired. We looked at each other and only then did I realize people would be at our house in an hour. Some lived far away and there was no way to stop them from coming, so we agreed we would celebrate Bill, as that's what he would have wanted. As they arrived, I told each guest about his sudden passing, and of course, all were tremendously saddened. But we did, indeed, celebrate Bill. After dinner, with ringside seats from the deck of our house, we watched those remarkable Fourth of July fireworks, especially gorgeous that night all over San Francisco, no fog or anything. And all I could think of was Bill going out in a blaze of glory![12]

Despite their surprise and grief, many were so amused that Bill left on the Fourth of July—so like him to take even his own dying process light-heartedly. Some might have found Bill's friends a curious lot, as amid the shock of his sudden death, one could hear expressions of elation and delight; "Oh, my God, he did it! He did it! He's the first person to finish the *Course*, really finish the *Course*!"—not unlike adoring fans cheering their star quarterback over the goal line.

Bill's memorial service was held outdoors on July 8, 1988, at the Congregational Church in Tiburon. "Panis Angelicus," one of his favorite pieces, commenced the program. Then followed a passage from a tape Bill had created a short while before, perhaps not consciously aware it would be used as his last good-bye. Listening to his beautiful voice, everyone was deeply moved by his final blessing. Tammy, Judy's daughter, chose to be at the crematorium rather than at the church so he would not be "alone"; she later confirmed that his body was cremated at the exact moment his taped reading was played. An intuitive, tuned-in young woman, she testified that she and Bill "watched" the service remotely and that he was laughing the whole time.

Thus ends the earthly sojourn of Bill Thetford. The calling card found in his wallet had only Bill Thetford printed on it. Just plain Bill. He asked for the *Course*; he received it and used it, willingly stripping himself of his persona, psychological armoring, prestige, unhelpful habits, and presumptions. Throughout the process, he danced, laughed and struggled, joked, despaired and supported, loved, feared and prayed, and steadily forgave his way to the end, soaring to a glorious finale worthy of the grandest of operas he so adored. And memories of Bill have settled with everlasting comfort into the hearts of all who knew, loved, and were touched by this most gracious friend.

Epilogue

While in this world, Bill finally wanted only to be ordinary and to find sameness with everyone. Only if we *are* the same does his story have meaning for us. If we change just a few details, we recognize our own journey in his and can see that his answers are also ours. It is true that Bill possessed talents and assets that many of us don't have, making many facets of his life easier than for most. However, those assets of privilege were paired with challenges that would have broken the spirits of many. He was an amazing human being, but he *was* human. As I am sure he would earnestly want to convey, the traits he cultivated, the ones that led him home, are well within everyone's reach: a daily, steadfast determination to let go of conflict—the ego's sustenance—and willingness to make peace of mind the primary goal for each encounter. We need his human example to see that we're not asked to sacrifice in practicing forgiveness. His life demonstrates that it is worth it. We do need to relinquish our defenses, attachments, and valueless investments, though not necessarily our worldly possessions if they aid with our gifts of service. We cherish our grievances rather than each other, as if they were precious heirlooms, but we *can* change our minds. If Bill had a profound mission, so do we. As he liberated his light, presence, and joy, so will we.

After Bill's passing, Pat Hopkins took on the administrative duties, sorting out and determining the final disposition of his possessions. He lived a simple, uncomplicated life, so after all archival material—personal correspondence and other written material, pictures, and books—was safely in the Foundation's keeping and his clothes and household goods disposed of, not much was left. Pat asked each of Bill's close friends what we wanted as a keepsake. He always had a single crystal hanging from the window or sliding glass door of his bedroom wherever he lived, and that was my choice. I love the sparkling clarity of beautiful crystal and glass, and it is the perfect reminder of the light he brought and still brings to the world.

> Without defenses, you become a light which Heaven gratefully acknowledges to be its own. And it will lead you on in ways appointed for your happiness according to the ancient plan, begun when time was born. Your followers will join their light with yours, and it will be increased until the world is lighted up with joy. And gladly will our brothers lay aside their cumbersome defenses, which availed them nothing and could only terrify.[1]

The Epilogue from the workbook reminds us that *A Course In Miracles* is a beginning, not an end. It invites everyone to renew the promises of the ancient plan and lay aside all that hurts and confounds us. At Bill's memorial service, Roger Walsh's concluding remarks conveyed that spirit of growing brotherhood, which is humankind's birthright,

> And finally, Bill gave us the priceless gift of each other, this community of practitioners gathered here together and around the world trying to embody, to incarnate this material, to remember that we are one in love and that in your brother you but see yourself, that it is impossible to overestimate the worth of your brother. How could we possibly overestimate the worth of Bill? Truly, we've been blessed by him.[2]

And in contrapuntal response, one can almost hear Bill's voice read from the text,

> In joyous welcome is my hand outstretched to every brother who would

join with me in reaching past temptation, and who looks with fixed determination toward the light that shines beyond in perfect constancy. . . . I give You thanks for what my brothers are. And as each one elects to join with me, the song of thanks from earth to Heaven grows from tiny scattered threads of melody to one inclusive chorus from a world redeemed from hell, and giving thanks to You.[3]

And now, I invite you to take a brother's or sister's hand, find the song in your heart, and step forward to join "Bill's chorus." The best of this musical comedy of life is yet to come, and never again will we forget to laugh.

Afterword

The profound effect the *Course* has already had in its first four decades is incalculable, starting with those who birthed it. It has entered into manifestation not just because Helen and Bill wanted to find a better way, but through willingness and desire on the part of human consciousness to come of age. It manifested in accordance with the deepest urgings of our common mind to move through the fog of egocentricity into the clear and wordless experience of unity.

Bill and I spoke about the *Course's* longevity shortly before his passing. We agreed it would doubtless reach many more people before its zenith and that we simply couldn't imagine its ongoing influence. Both of us believed that those who had encountered the *Course* up to that point (in 1988) were the pathfinders, psychological pioneers who had volunteered to challenge the old precepts on which most of human experience has been based. In every era, various seers and masters have comprehended the hypnotized state of the human condition and offered Truth as its remedy, but this modern group of pioneers represents a grassroots movement. These are "ordinary people" questioning the status quo and claiming their right to be free of psychological bondage.

In time, I believe *ACIM* will be recognized as one of the foundational writings of this century, if not this millennium, a standard against which other writings are measured. Perhaps it won't be known in the form of the blue book we recognize, but through variations that countless numbers can comprehend and embrace. Its future lies in the people who are changed by it now as it informs their lives and work, resulting in the inevitable expansion of collective consciousness. There will always be a recognizable response to mankind's growing desire to be whole and at peace, and as the last sentence of the workbook states, "His Love surrounds you, and of this be sure; that I will never leave you comfortless."[1]

Appendix One

William Whitson and another PAS-savvy colleague, who also knew Bill for many years, jointly reconstructed a simple version of Bill's most likely PAS profile based on years of observations. Excerpts from their conclusions are as follows:

Years one to seven: Self-sufficient and relatively inactive, he was probably an "Internalizer" to whom ideas were real because he discovered he had a facility for abstract and symbolic reasoning. As a consequence, he would have been relatively passive, preferring to withdraw into an inner world to think rather than do and to shun the concrete, the specific,. and the practical. His emotions would also have been directed inward. Primarily self-contained, he would have sought major psychological satisfactions in the privacy of his own experiences.

Nevertheless, he was probably sensitive to a wide range of confusing subtleties, signals, and stimuli around him. Working from diffused impressions, his intuition and active imagination would have been quick to grasp the "atmosphere" of a new situation. Thus, his process for finding meaning would have been "Flexible," perceiving his world in shades of gray, never completely logical or black and white. His major problem was probably his need to restrict his awareness and responses sufficiently to enable him to concentrate and organize his experiences with the external world. Learning new activities might have been frustratingly slow for him because he first needed to understand the meaning and purpose of a task or a situation. That is to say, he probably was not inclined to rote learning but preferred trial and error.

Although he was externally passive and demanded little attention, he was highly "Adaptive" socially. Blessed with a chameleon-like personality as a child, he could mask his confusion and true feelings by his ability to play any congenial role called for by the occasion. By the age of seven, he should have discovered that he could be "all things to all people." Despite his surface social warmth, his confusion and his fantasies may have fostered caution, imaginary playmates, and terrors such as nightmares, hypochondria, and inner tensions that he could mask by a seeming empathy for others, even though he would not often understand them.

Years eight to fourteen: Forced to associate with older children, he must have learned how to exploit his continuing social adaptivity, his charm and empathy, to find practical application of idealistic impulses with adroit creativity and imagination. Thanks in part to his "coming out" (after years of seclusion) into society, he probably was experientially curious, enjoying a wide diversity of sensual stimulation, including responsibility, authority, and carefully controlled heterosexual activity in school. Inclined to enthusiasm and advocacy, he would have enjoyed argument, persuasion, and discussion, usually being tolerant while he tried to make classmates understand and accept his own ideas and beliefs.

On the other hand, when he recognized that another person could not or would not accept his beliefs, he could have been quite unfeeling in the way he rejected or rebuffed them. Although attracted to group feelings, he would have even abandoned a group if it failed to live up to his ideals. In other words, instead of adjusting to a group's identity, armed with the courage of his convictions and a low tolerance for disillusionment, he would have searched for other people who might fulfill his unchanging values, ideals, and expectations. Setting very high standards, by the time he entered high school he had probably become something of a social snob, situation-oriented, role versatile, and fickle in his choice of friends.

Years fifteen to twenty-one: In sum, at the intellectual level he ended his development poised between "humanitarian, striving for the common good, loyal, sincere, and persevering" and "needing external activity but developing relationships that were more likely to be superficial than deeply involved." . . . He learned to control his childhood tendency toward warm empathy and excessive personal involvement.

With respect to his social behavior, his school years must have fostered a highly developed social conscience. In consequence, he shifted from his role as a social chameleon to a stronger sense of responsibility, with a well-defined set of personal values and greater concern about the impression he was making. In conventional social relations, he would have been impatient with indifference, incompetence, lassitude, and irresponsibility. Instead, he had committed himself to understanding and bringing improvement and progress to conventional methods, systems, and society. Indeed, his zeal for improving the world probably made it difficult for him to relax.

Appendix Two

Curriculum Vitae — William N. Thetford

EDUCATION:

A.B., DePauw University, 1944

Ph.D., University of Chicago, 1949

POST-DOCTORAL TRAINING:

Institute for Psychiatric and Psychosomatic Research and Training,
Michael Reese Hospital, Chicago, 1949–1951
Washington School of Psychiatry, 1951–1954

PROFESSIONAL EXPERIENCE:

Professor of Medical Psychology, College of Physicians and Surgeons,
Columbia University, 1971–1981

Associate Professor of Medical Psychology, College of Physicians and Surgeons,
Columbia University, 1958–1971; Department of Psychology,
Columbia University, 1966–1970

Director, Division of Psychology, Presbyterian Hospital, 1958–1978

Assistant Project Director (Psychology), Study Program on the
Pathogenesis of Cerebral Palsy, Columbia University, College of
Physicians and Surgeons, 1959–1968

Senior Psychological Consultant, Study Program in Human Ecology
and the Health of Man, Cornell University Medical College, 1962–1968

Special Consultant, U.S. Public Health Service (NINDB), 1961

Assistant Professor of Psychology, Department of Psychiatry,
Cornell University, 1955–1958

Chief Psychologist, Study Program in Human Ecology, Departments of
Medicine and Psychiatry, Cornell University Medical College, 1955–1957

Director, Department of Psychology, Institute of Living,
Hartford, Connecticut, 1954–1955

Senior Psychologist, U.S. Government, Washington, D.C. 1951–1954

Research Consultant, Foreign Service Institute, U.S Department of State, at American University, Beirut, Lebanon, 1953

Research Psychologist, Michael Reese Hospital, Chicago, Ill., 1949 –1951

Clinical Psychologist, Roosevelt College, Chicago, Ill., 1948–1949

Research Psychologist, Psychological Corporation, New York, N.Y., 1947

Research Assistant and Counselor, Counseling Center, University of Chicago, 1945–1946

Administrative Office, University of Chicago, Metallurgical Laboratory, (Atomic Research Program), 1944–1945

PROFESSIONAL SOCIETIES:
Fellow, American Orthopsychiatric Association
Fellow, American Psychological Association
Fellow, International Council of Psychologists
Fellow, Society for Projective Techniques
American Association for the Advancement of Science
American Association on Mental Deficiency
American Association of University Professors
American Federation for Clinical Research
American Psychosomatic Society
Association of American Medical Colleges
Eastern Psychological Association
Inter-American Psychological Association
New York Academy of Sciences
New York Society for Projective Techniques
New York State Psychological Association
Sigma Xi
World Federation for Mental Health

OTHER:

President, New York Society for Projective Techniques, 1963–1966

Who's Who in the East, 1960 on

American Men of Science, 1956 on

Member, Committee on Orthopsychiatry in Pediatric Settings, American Orthopsychiatric Association, 1963–1965

Member, Columbia University Seminar on the Role of the Health Professions, 1961 on

Member, Professional Standards Committee, ACCEPT (New York Council on Alcoholism), 1970 on

Certified by the State Education Department, University of the State of New York

RESEARCH GRANTS:

Principal Investigator on following research grants awarded by Human Ecology Fund:

Investigations of the Personality Assessment System in Patients with Psychosomatic Symptoms (1960–1961)

Personality Assessment System and Learning Behavior (1961–1962)

Formulation of a Personality Theory (1961)

Learning Behavior and Personality Traits (1962–1963)

Prediction of Overt Behavior by Means of the Personality Assessment System (1963–1964)

Principal Investigator on grant awarded by the Geschicter Foundation:

Prediction of Overt Behavior by Means of the Personality Assessment System (1965–1966)

Principal Investigator on research contract awarded by Psychological Assessment Associates:

Brief Procedures for the Personality Assessment System Evaluation (1967–1968)

TRAINING GRANT:

Co-Director, Training Program in Clinical Psychology (with H. Hunt, |Director), National Institute of Mental Health, 1965 (continued support from 1958 on)

PUBLICATIONS AND PAPERS:

Thetford, W. N. The measurement of physiological responses to frustration before and after client-centered psychotherapy. *American Psychologist,* 1948, 3, 278 (ab.).

Thetford, W. N. & Molish, H. B. Aspects of personality development in normal children. *American Journal of Orthopsychiatry,* 1950, 20, 866 (ab.).

Thetford, W. N. Developmental aspects of fantasy in normal and schizophrenic children. *American Psychologist,* 1950, 5, 295 (ab.).

Beck, S. J., Thiesen, W., Rabin, A., Molish, H. B. & Thetford, W. N. The normal personality as projected in the Rorschach test. *Journal of Psychology,* 1950, 30, 241–298.

Thetford, W. N. Childhood schizophrenia and the Rorschach test. *Human Development Bulletin.* University of Chicago, 1951, 10–14.

Thetford, W. N., Molish, H. B. & Beck, S. J. Developmental aspects of personality structure in normal children. *Journal of Projective Techniques,* 1951, 15, 58–78.

Thetford, W. N. The development of fantasy perceptions in children. *American Journal of Orthopsychiatry,* 1951, 21, 860 (ab.).

Thetford, W. N. An Organismic approach to frustration. *Personality: Symposia on topical issues.* New York: Grune & Stratton, 1951, 1–19.

Thetford, W. N. & DeVos, G. A Rorschach study of clinical groups by means of Fisher's maladjustment index. *American Psychologist,* 1951, 6, 505 (ab.).

Thetford, W. N. Fantasy perceptions in the personality development of normal and deviant children. *American Journal of Orthopsychiatry,* 1952, 22, 532–550.

Thetford, W. N. An objective measurement of frustration tolerance in evaluating psychotherapy. In W. Wolff & J. Precker (Eds.), *Success in Psychotherapy.* New York: Grune & Stratton, 1952, 26–62.

Thetford, W. N. Personality characteristics of schizophrenic children. *American Psychologist,* 1952, 7, 301 (ab.).

Thetford, W. N. Educational therapy as an integral part of the psychotherapeutic process. *Proceedings of the Inter-American Psychological Association,* Mexico, 1954, 24–25.

Thetford, W. N. (Chm.). Diagnostic techniques in clinical psychology. *Proceedings of the International Applied Psychology Association,* London, 1955, 56.

Nicholas, Alma & Thetford, W. N. The use of the Hewson ratios in the diagnosis of cerebral pathology. *American Psychologist,* 1955, 10, 563 (ab.).

Thetford, W. N. & Goldberger, L. Personality features and reactions in a group of Chinese. *American Psychologist,* 1956, 11, 385 (ab.).

Thetford, W. N., Goldberger, L. & Wolff, H. G. A cross-cultural approach to the study of personality and illness. *American Psychologist,* 1957, 12, 375 (ab.).

Chapman, L. F., Berlin, L., Guthrie, T. C., Thetford, W. N. & Wolff, H. G. Human cerebral hemisphere function. *The Physiologist,* 1957, 1, 4.

Chapman, L., Thetford, W. N., Berlin, L., Guthrie, T. & Wolff, H. G. Impairment of cerebral hemispheric functions following prolonged life stress in man. *Transactions VIth International Congress of Neurology,* Brussels, 1957, 203–218.

Thetford, W. N., Goldberger, L., Hinkle, L. & Wolff, H. G. Personality features and their cultural interrelationships in a group of Chinese. Brussels: *Proceedings of 15th International Congress of Psychology,* 1957, 541–542.

Hinkle, L. E., Christenson, W., Kane, F. D., Ostfeld, A., Thetford, W. N. & Wolff, H. G. Some relationships between health, personality and environmental factors in a group of adult Chinese. *Psychosomatic Medicine,* 1957, 19, 159 (ab.).

Chapman, L. F., Thetford, W. N., Berlin, L., Guthrie, T. C. & Wolff, H. G. Studies in human cerebral function: Prolonged stress and the highest integrative functions of man. *Excerpta Medica, Free Communication 24, VIth International Congress of Neurology*, Brussels, 1957.

Chapman, L., Thetford, W. N., Guthrie, T., Berlin, L. & Wolff, H. G. Studies in human cerebral hemisphere functions. *Transactions of American Neurological Association*, 1957, 95–96.

Hinkle, L. E., Plummer, N., Metraux, R., Richter, P., Gittinger, J. W., Thetford, W. N. et al. Studies in human ecology: factors relevant to the occurrence of bodily illness and disturbances in need, thought, and behavior in three homogeneous population groups. *American Journal of Psychiatry*, 1957, 114, 212–220.

Chapman, L., Thetford, W. N., Berlin, L., Guthrie, T. & Wolff, H. G. Highest integrative functions in man during stress. *The Brain and Human Behavior.* Baltimore: William and Wilkins, 1958, 491–534.

Hinkle, L. E., Christenson, W., Kane, F. D., Ostfeld, A., Thetford, W. N. & Wolff, H. G. An investigation of the relation between life experience, personality characteristics, and general susceptibility to illness. *Psychosomatic Medicine*, 1958, 20, 278–295.

Thetford, W. N. The place of projective techniques in the medical curriculum. *American Psychologist*, 1958, 13, 346 (ab.).

Thetford, W. N. & Carr, A. C. The role of clinical psychology in medical education. *Journal of Medical Education*, 1960, 35, 62–66.

Thetford, W. N. Theoretical formulations in personality evaluation. *American Psychologist*, 1961, 16, 431 (ab.).

Schucman, H., Saunders, D. R. & Thetford, W. N. An application of syndrome analysis. *American Psychologist*, 1962, 17, 359 (ab.).

Thetford, W. N. & Schucman, H. *The personality assessment system.* Human Ecology Fund, 1962. (Preliminary monograph)

Thetford, W. N. Principles of administrative development: technical developments. Presented at Psychology Conference, *New York State Department of Mental Hygiene*, 1962.

Thetford, W. N. Psychodynamics of intelligence: a projective approach. Address as president-elect, *New York Society for Projective Techniques*, 1962.

Thetford, W. N. Theoretical formulations underlying research. *Measurement of personality traits resulting from the interaction of ability and environment.* New York: Human Ecology Fund, 1962, 1–3. (Foundation monograph)

Thetford, W. N. (Chm.). Symposium: Approaches to integrated concepts of personality theory and assessment. *New York Academy of Science,* June, 1964.

Thetford, W. N. (Ed.). *Multitrait, multilevel personality assessment.* New York: Human Ecology Fund, 1964 (Foundation monograph)

Thetford, W. N. (Chm.) Symposium: Multitrait, multilevel personality assessment: theory, measurement, evaluation. *American Psychologist,* 1963, 18, 411 (ab.).

Hunt, H. F. & Thetford, W. N. Editorial. *Journal of Abnormal Psychology,* 1965, 70, 1.

Thetford, W. N. The Holtzman inkblot test. In O. Buros (Ed.), *The sixth mental measurements yearbook.* Highland Park, N.J.: The Gryphon Press, 1965, 442–444.

Thetford, W. N., Schucman, H. & Farmer, C. Psychological testing of children with headaches. In A. P. Friedman & E. Harms (Eds.), *Headaches in children.* Springfield: C. C. Thomas, 1967, 82–114.

Thetford, W. N. Problems of assessment and evaluation of the mentally retarded and the culturally deprived (symposium discussant). *Excerpta Medica,* International Congress, Series No. 153, 1967, 33–34.

Hinkle, L. E., Plummer, N., Metraux, R., Richter, P., Gittinger, J. W., Thetford, W. N. et al. Studies in human ecology. In L. Y. Rabkin & J. E. Carr (Eds.), *Sourcebook in Abnormal Psychology.* Boston: Houghton Mifflin, 1967, 342–350.

Schucman, H. & Thetford, W. N. Expressed symptoms and personality traits in conversion hysteria. *Psychological Reports,* 1968, 23, 231–243.

Thetford, W. N. & Schucman, H. Personality patterns in migraine and ulcerative colitis patients. *Psychological Reports,* 1968, 23, 1206.

Thetford, W. N. & Schucman, H. Self-choices, preferences, and personality traits. *Psychological Reports,* 1969, 25, 659–667.

Schucman, H. & Thetford, W. N. A comparison of personality traits in ulcerative colitis and migraine patients. *Journal of Abnormal Psychology,* 1970, 76.

Thetford, W. N. & Schucman, H. Conversion reactions and personality traits. *Psychological Reports,* 1970.

Thetford, W. N. & Schucman, H. Motivational factors and adaptive behavior (Chapter 17). In J. A. Downey & R. C. Darling (Eds.). *The physiologic basis of rehabilitation medicine.* Philadelphia: W. B. Saunders, 1971.

EDITORSHIP:

Associate Editor, *Journal of Abnormal Psychology,* 1965–1970 (with Howard F. Hunt, Ed.)

Endnotes

All page references to *A Course In Miracles* are from the Third Edition published by the Foundation for Inner Peace, Mill Valley, CA, 2007. A new archival website created by the Foundation for Inner Peace and the Foundation for *A Course In Miracles* is under construction. It will contain articles, pictures, videos, interviews, and other *ACIM* memorabilia not heretofore available to the public. The interviews and some excerpts from the biographies referenced in this book will be included.

PREFACE

1. *A Course In Miracles* is a self-study course in three parts: a text, a workbook, and a manual for teachers. Its basic hypothesis is that we are cond itioned from birth to a limited way of perceiving and our "understanding" of life is a product of past conditioning. Practicing the workbook lessons undoes our negative, unhelpful, inaccurate view of people, situations, and events, resulting in a different perception of the world. As *Course* practice proceeds, the fearful ideas we have learned are systematically replaced with an alternative viewpoint—happier, more spiritual, and all-encompassing. Later lessons are designed to evoke a direct spiritual experience and greater love for self and others.

INTRODUCTION

1. *A Course In Miracles* Text, 517.

PART I

CHAPTER ONE

1. *A Course In Miracles* Text, 586–587.

2. Helen Schucman: Autobiography, in "Origins of *A Course In Miracles*," 3:49, Foundation for Inner Peace Archives, Tiburon, CA (cited hereinafter as FIPA).

3. William W. Whitson, "William Newton Thetford and the Central Intelligence Agency," manuscript, FIPA, 28.

4. This phrase is a shortened version of the complete sentence from the Introduction to *ACIM*: "It does aim, however, at removing the blocks to the awareness of love's presence, which is your natural inheritance."

5. William N. Thetford, "I Live Again," personal essay written in 1938 as a class assignment in high school. Foundation for Inner Peace, Tiburon, CA, 6–14.

6. *A Course In Miracles* Workbook, Lesson 136, 258.

7. Thetford, "I Live Again," 15–16.

8. Catherine Prescott interview by Tamara Cohen, in "Origins of *A Course In Miracles*," ed. James Bolen, 24:3, FIPA.

9. Thetford, "I Live Again," 20–21.

10. Edna Jo Hunter-King interview by Tamara Cohen, in "Origins of *A Course In Miracles*," ed. James Bolen, 11:4, FIPA.

CHAPTER TWO

1. Robert Skutch, *Journey Without Distance: The Story Behind A Course In Miracles* (Berkeley, CA: Celestial Arts, 1984), 3–4.

2. Gardner Murphy, *Personality: A Biosocial Approach to Origins and Structure* (New York: Harper and Brothers, 1947), Foreword.

3. Ibid., 919.

4. David Keirsey, *Please Understand Me, II* (Del Mar, CA: Prometheus Nemesis Books, 1998), 26.

5. Ibid., 118.

6. Ibid., 123–124.

7. Ibid., 144.

8. *A Course In Miracles* Workbook, Lesson 135, 255.

9. *A Course In Miracles* Text, 172.

CHAPTER THREE

1. *A Course In Miracles* Workbook, Lesson 158, 298.

2. Jack and Layle Luckett, email message to author, August 2007.

3. William W. Whitson, "William Newton Thetford and the Central Intelligence Agency," manuscript, FIPA, 3–4.

4. Alice Stephens telephone interview by author, March 2007.

5. Whitson, "Thetford and the CIA," 19.

6. David Goodrich telephone interview by author, February 2008.

7. Internet site www.pasf.org

8. *A Course In Miracles* Text, 656.

9. Ibid., 659.

10. Whitson, "Thetford and the CIA," 11.

11. David Keirsey, *Please Understand Me, II* (Del Mar, CA: Prometheus Nemesis Books, 1998), 130.

12. Goodrich interview, February 2008.

13. David Keirsey, *Please Understand Me, II,* 121.

14. Goodrich interview, February 2008.

15. William Thetford: Life Story, in "Origins of *A Course In Miracles*," 4:9, FIPA.

16. *Personews*, an in-house publication of the Institute for Living, Hartford, CT, March 1956, 10.

17. Thetford: Life Story, 4:10, FIPA.

18. Ibid., 12.

19. Neal Vahle, *A Course In Miracles: The Lives of Helen Schucman & William Thetford* (San Francisco: Open View Press, 2009), 60.

CHAPTER FOUR

1. Helen Schucman: Autobiography, in "Origins of *A Course In Miracles*," 3:27–28, FIPA.

2. Ibid., 28.

3. Ibid., 29.

4. Dorothy Ulmann interview by Tamara Cohen, in "Origins of *A Course In Miracles*," ed. James Bolen, 8:4, FIPA.

5. *A Course In Miracles* Text, 18.

6. William Thetford: Life Story, in "Origins of *A Course In Miracles*," 4:29, FIPA.

7. *The Story of A Course In Miracles*, DVD, Tiburon, CA, Foundation for Inner Peace, 1987.

8. Charles Lehman interview by Tamara Cohen, in "Origins of *A Course In Miracles*," ed. James Bolen, 9:2, FIPA.

9. Calvin Hatcher interview by Tamara Cohen, in "Origins of *A Course In Miracles*," ed. James Bolen, 7:11, FIPA.

10. *A Course In Miracles* Text, 354–355.

11. Ibid., 223.

12. Ibid., 22.

13. Schucman: Autobiography, 3:30, FIPA.

14. Ibid., 31.

15. Ibid.

CHAPTER FIVE

1. Helen Schucman: Autobiography, in "Origins of *A Course In Miracles*," 3:35, FIPA.

2. Introduction by Tamara Cohen, in "Origins of *A Course In Miracles*," 1:2, FIPA.

3. Schucman: Autobiography, 3:37, FIPA.

4. Ibid., 46.

5. William Thetford: Life Story, in "Origins of *A Course In Miracles*," 4:18, FIPA.

6. Schucman: Autobiography, 3:50, FIPA.

7. Ibid., 51.

8. Thetford: Life Story, 4:21, FIPA.

9. Schucman: Autobiography, 3:52, FIPA.

10. Thetford: Life Story, 4:58, FIPA.

11. *A Course In Miracles* Manual for Teachers, 58.

12. Ibid., 87.

13. Kenneth Wapnick, "The History of the Manuscripts of *A Course In Miracles*," manuscript, Foundation for A Course In Miracles, 9–10.

14. *A Course In Miracles* Manual for Teachers, 60–61.

15. Transcription of Thetford personal reading, Paul Solomon, Spring 1976.

16. Ibid.

17. Ibid.

18. Ibid.

19. Jaison Kayn telephone interview by author, February 2007.

20. Transcription of Thetford personal reading, author's copy, LeRoy Zemke, February 1980.

21. William Whitson interview by Tamara Cohen, in "Origins of *A Course In Miracles*," ed. James Bolen, 21:3–4, FIPA.

22. Kenneth Wapnick telephone interview by author, February 2009.

23. *A Course In Miracles* Text, 587–588.

24. *The American Heritage Dictionary of the English Language,* Fifth edition, s.v. "urtext."

25. Urtext, 98 (second).

On Dec. 10, 1965, Bill began to renumber the pages of his typed notes to date; therefore, page references for the Urtext will be followed by "first" or "second" to denote the set of pages referred to. Because there is an on-going controversy concerning the Urtext itself, here included is an excerpt from Kenneth Wapnick's manuscript, "The History of the Manuscripts of *A Course In Miracles*": "Under false pretenses, the notebooks [Helen's] and the Urtext were taken from the Library of Congress and copied, a violation of federal law. We talked to legal authorities at the Library, who were outraged. . . . The people who were now in possession of the illegally obtained material—the notebooks, Urtext, and Hugh Lynn Cayce version—had it scanned or retyped and have made it available on the Internet and elsewhere for purchase."

26. Thetford: Life Story, 4:28, FIPA.

27. Ibid., 29.

28. Judith Skutch Whitson interview by author, January 2008.

29. Thetford: Life Story, 4:30, FIPA.

30. Ibid.

CHAPTER SIX

1. William Thetford: Life Story, in "Origins of *A Course In Miracles*," 4:39, FIPA.

2. Kenneth Wapnick telephone interview by author, February 2009.

3. Thetford: Life Story, 4:40, FIPA.

4. Wapnick interview, February 2009.

5. Ibid.

6. Kenneth Wapnick, *Absence From Felicity* (Roscoe, NY: Foundation for *A Course In Miracles*, 1991).

7. Wapnick interview, February 2009.

8. The Hugh Lynn Cayce version is the text partially edited by Helen and Bill and given to Cayce as a gift for his help and support with their project.

9. Judith Skutch Whitson, email message to author, December 2008.

10. Thetford: Life Story, 4:40, FIPA.

11. Robert Skutch, *Journey Without Distance: The Story Behind A Course In Miracles* (Berkeley, CA: Celestial Arts, 1984), 88.

12. This cave is the one Helen saw in her vision that preceded the scribing of *ACIM*.

13. Skutch, *Journey Without Distance,* 88.

CHAPTER SEVEN

1. William Thetford: Life Story, in "Origins of *A Course In Miracles*," 4:46, FIPA.

2. Wapnick telephone interview by author, February 2009.

3. Judith Skutch Whitson telephone interview by author, February 2008.

4. Judith Skutch Whitson interview, January 2008.

5. William Congreve, *The Mourning Bride*, 1697. Incorrectly attributed to Shakespeare, the full quote is "Heaven has no rage like love to hatred turned/ Nor hell a fury like a woman scorned."

6. Judith Skutch Whitson interview, January 2008.

7. Thetford: Life Story, 4:50, FIPA.

8. *A Course In Miracles* Text, 530.

CHAPTER EIGHT

1. *A Course In Miracles* Text, 295.

2. Author's transcription of Thetford Memorial Service, William Whitson, July 1988.

3. Thetford: Life Story, 4:33, FIPA.

4. *A Course In Miracles* Text, 346.

PART TWO

CHAPTER NINE

1. William Thetford: Life Story, in "Origins of *A Course In Miracles*," 4:11, FIPA.

2. Julius J. Finegold and William N. Thetford, Eds., *Choose Once Again* (Millbrae, CA: Celestial Arts, 1981).

3. For more information on Rolfing, see www.rolf.org

4. Jaison Kayn telephone interview by author, February 2007.

5. Judith Skutch Whitson telephone interview by author, January 2008.

6. Hugh and Gayle Prather interview by author, October 1993.

7. Thetford: Life Story, 4:52, FIPA.

8. Robert Skutch, *Journey Without Distance: The Story Behind A Course In Miracles* (Berkeley, CA: Celestial Arts, 1984).

CHAPTER TEN

1. Transcription of Thetford personal reading, author's copy, LeRoy Zemke, February 1980.

2. *A Course In Miracles* Text, 433–434.

3. Thetford personal reading, LeRoy Zemke, February 1980.

4. Jack and Layle Luckett telephone interview by author, September 2007.

5. Ibid.

6. William Thetford: Life Story, in "Origins of *A Course In Miracles*," 4:48, FIPA.

CHAPTER ELEVEN

1. Bob Howe interview by author, March 2007.
2. Robert Rosenthal interview by Tamara Cohen, in "Origins of *A Course In Miracles*," ed. James Bolen, 16:2, FIPA.
3. Jaison Kayn telephone interview by author, February 2007.
4. *A Course In Miracles* Text, 649–650.
5. *A Course In Miracles* Workbook, Lesson 166, 315–316.

CHAPTER TWELVE

1. *A Course In Miracles* Workbook, Lesson 185, 348.
2. Ibid., Lesson 134, 248.
3. *A Course In Miracles* Text, 568.
4. Ibid., 569.
5. Robert Rosenthal interview by Tamara Cohen, in "Origins of *A Course In Miracles*," ed. James Bolen, 16: 2–3, FIPA.
6. Roger Walsh interview by Tamara Cohen, in "Origins of *A Course In Miracles*,"ed. James Bolen, 25:5–6, FIPA; and personal communication to author, August 15, 2009.
7. Helen Schucman: Autobiography, in "Origins of *A Course In Miracles*," 3:52, FIPA.
8. *A Course In Miracles* Text, 37.
9. www.circleofa.org
10. Jaison Kayn telephone interview with author, February 2007.
11. Ibid.
12. Bob Beale telephone interview with author, February 2007.
13. William Thetford: Life Story, in "Origins of *A Course In Miracles*," 4:51, FIPA.
14. Jaison Kayn interview, February 2007.
15. Ibid.

CHAPTER THIRTEEN

1. Gerald Jampolsky, M.D., *Love Is Letting Go of Fear* (Millbrae, CA: Celestial Arts,1979).
2. James Bolen, "Interview: Judith R. Skutch," *New Realities* (April 1977), 19.
3. Introduction by Tamara Cohen, in "Origins of *A Course In Miracles*," ed. James Bolen, Introduction: 4, FIPA.
4. Gerald Jampolsky, M.D., Diane Cirincione, Ph.D., *To Give Is To Receive: An Eighteen Day Mini-Course on Healing Relationships* (Sausalito, CA: Mini-Course Publishing, 2007).
5. *A Course In Miracles* Text, 314.

CHAPTER FOURTEEN

1. *A Course In Miracles* Text, 28.
2. William Thetford: Life Story, in "Origins of *A Course In Miracles*," 4:24, FIPA.

PART THREE

CHAPTER FIFTEEN

1. Catherine Prescott interview by Tamara Cohen, in "Origins of *A Course In Miracles*," ed. James Bolen, 24:7, FIPA.

2. Transcription of Thetford personal reading, author's copy, LeRoy Zemke, February 1980.

3. Jack and Layle Luckett, email message to author, August 2007.

4. Ibid.

5. Ibid.

6. *A Course In Miracles* Text, 456.

7. *A Course In Miracles* Workbook, Introduction, 1–2.

8. *A Course In Miracles* Text, 666.

9. Thetford personal reading, LeRoy Zemke, February 1980.

10. Dante Alighieri, *The Vision of Hell*, Purgatory, and Paradise (New York: D. Appleton & Co., 1852), 484.

11. Maurice Baring, *Royal Flying Corps Headquarters* (publisher and date unknown), translation of Dante's quote noted above.

12. *A Course In Miracles* Text, 565–566.

13. Jaison Kayn telephone interview by author, February 2007.

14. Bruce Gregory telephone interview by author, January 2008.

15. Judith Skutch Whitson telephone interview by author, January 2008.

16. Hugh and Gayle Prather interview by author, October 1993.

17. Catherine Prescott telephone interview by author, August 2008.

18. Diane Cirincione telephone interview by author, July 2007.

19. Carlagaye Olson telephone interview by author, September 2007.

20. Gregory Howe interview by author, January 2009.

21. Frances Vaughan interview by Tamara Cohen, in "Origins of *A Course In Miracles*," ed. James Bolen, 19:8, FIPA; and personal communication to author, August 13, 2009.

CHAPTER SIXTEEN

1. Kenneth Wapnick, "The History of the Manuscripts of *A Course In Miracles*," manuscript, 9–12.

2. Urtext, 23–24 (first).

3. Ibid., 47 (first).

4. Ibid., 60–61(first).

5. Carlagaye Olson telephone interview by author, September 2007.

6. *A Course In Miracles* Text, 220–221.

7. Jerry Jampolsky telephone interview by author, July 2007.

8. Ibid.

9. Jaison Kayn telephone interview by author, February 2007.

10. Bob Beale telephone interview by author, February 2007.

11. Bruce Gregory, personal communication to author, March 2008.

12. Ibid.

13. Frances Vaughan interview by Tamara Cohen, in "Origins of *A Course In Miracles*," ed. James Bolen, 19:7, FIPA; and personal communication to author, August 13, 2009.

14. *A Course In Miracles* Manual for Teachers, 10.

15. Urtext, 122 (first).

16. Ibid., 42–43 (second).

17. Ibid., 55 (second).

18. Ibid., 77 (first).

19. Ibid., 87 (first).

20. Ibid., 119 (first).

21. Ibid., 120 (first).

22. Ibid., 48 (second).

CHAPTER SEVENTEEN

1. Urtext, 155 (first).

2. William Whitson interview by Tamara Cohen, in "Origins of *A Course In Miracles*," ed. James Bolen, 21:2, FIPA.

3. Transcription of Thetford personal reading, author's copy, LeRoy Zemke, February 1980.

4. Jack and Layle Luckett telephone interview by author, September 2007.

5. Jack and Layle Luckett, email message to author, August 2007.

6. Hugh and Gayle Prather interview by author, October 1993.

7. William Whitson telephone interview by author, February 2008.

CHAPTER EIGHTEEN

1. Urtext, 170–171 (first).

2. Ibid., 103–104 (second).

3. Ibid., 15–16 (second).

4. Jack and Layle Luckett telephone interview by author, September 2007.

5. Author's transcription of Thetford Memorial Service, Frances Vaughan, July 1988.

6. Sarah Whalen-Kraft, Thetford essay, personal communication to author, March 1994.

7. Edna Jo Hunter-King interview by Tamara Cohen, in "Origins of *A Course In Miracles*," ed. James Bolen, 11:7, FIPA.

8. *A Course In Miracles* Text, 236.

9. Catherine Prescott interview by Tamara Cohen, in "Origins of *A Course In Miracles*," ed. James Bolen, 24:2, FIPA.

10. This event took place while Bill was still in Chicago, either while a graduate student with Carl Rogers or at Michael Reese Hospital. He apparently told Helen about it and she suggested he let it go. Although Ken knew about the incident, he did not recall details. I questioned all others with whom he might have discussed this event and no one knew anything about it.

11. Urtext, 165–167 (first).

12. Ralph Blum, *Little Book of Runic Wisdom* (London: Connections Book Publishing, 2001), 21. A rune is one of the letters of an alphabet used by ancient Germanic peoples, especially by the Scandinavians and Anglo-Saxons. In modern usage, it refers to a poem, a riddle, or a secret writing related to determining right action in any given situation.

13. *A Course In Miracles* Text, 243.

14. Ibid., 565.

15. Catherine Prescott, telephone interview by author, February 2008.

16. Ibid.

17. Ibid.

18. *A Course In Miracles* Text, 651.

19. Prescott interview, February 2008.

CHAPTER NINETEEN

1. Jack and Layle Luckett telephone interview by author, September 2007.

2. *A Course In Miracles* Text, 577–578.

3. Hugh and Gayle Prather interview by author, October 1993.

4. Luckett interview, December 2007.

5. Jerry Jampolsky telephone interview by author, July 2007.

6. Carlagaye Olson telephone interview by author, September 2007.

7. Ibid.

8. *A Course In Miracles* Text, 202.

9. As cited on daily AHAM email message to subscribers. (Association of Happiness For All Mankind, Asheboro, NC 27205, ahamcntr@asheboro.com)

10. Luckett, email message to author, August 2007.

11. Transcription of Thetford personal reading, author's copy, LeRoy Zemke, February 1980.

12. Jampolsky interview, July 2007.

13. Judith Skutch Whitson telephone interview by author, January 2008.

14. *A Course In Miracles* Text, 172–173.

15. Bob Beale telephone interview by author, February 2007.

16. Hugh and Gayle Prather interview by author, October 1993.

17. Thetford personal reading, LeRoy Zemke, February 1980.

18. Catherine Prescott telephone interview by author, February 2008.

19. Author's transcription of Thetford Memorial Service, William Whitson, July 1988.

CHAPTER TWENTY

1. Author's transcription of Thetford Memorial Service, Frances Vaughan, July 1988.

2. Jaison Kayn telephone interview by author, February 2007.

3. Pat Hopkins interview by Tamara Cohen, in "Origins of *A Course In Miracles*," ed. James Bolen, 20:5, FIPA.

4. Bob Beale telephone interview by author, February 2007.

5. William Whitson telephone interview by author, February 2008.

6. Hugh and Gayle Prather interview by author, October 1993.

7. Roger Walsh telephone interview by author, March 2008.

8. Thetford Memorial Service, Roger Walsh, July 1988.

9. Jaison Kayn interview, February 2007.

10. Catherine Prescott telephone interview by author, August 2008.

11. Prather interview, October 1993.

12. Jaison Kayn interview, February 2007.

CHAPTER TWENTY-ONE

1. *A Course In Miracles* Text, 157.

2. Hugh and Gayle Prather interview by author, October 1993.

3. Jim Bolen, "William N. Thetford, Ph.D," New Realities (September/October 1984), 20.

4. William Thetford: Life Story, in "Origins of *A Course In Miracles*," 4:50, FIPA.

5. Bob Beale telephone interview by author, February 2007.

6. Thetford: Life Story, 4:48, FIPA.

7. Transcription of Thetford personal reading, author's copy, LeRoy Zemke, February 1980.

8. Thetford: Life Story, 4:34, FIPA.

9. Ibid., 34–35.

10. Ibid., 36.

11. Ibid., 37.

12. Ibid., 38–39.

13. Calvin Hatcher interview by Tamara Cohen, in "Origins of *A Course In Miracles*," ed. James Bolen, 7:8, FIPA.

14. Jim Bolen, "William N. Thetford, Ph.D," New Realities (September/October 1984), 20.

15. Roger Walsh interview by Tamara Cohen, in "Origins of *A Course In Miracles*," ed. James Bolen, 25:7, FIPA.

16. Jack and Layle Luckett telephone interview by author, September 2007.

17. Patricia Hopkins interview by Tamara Cohen, in "Origins of *A Course In Miracles*," ed. James Bolen, 20:6–7, FIPA.

18. Luckett interview, December 2007.

19. Prather interview, October 1993.

20. Thetford: Life Story, 4:51, FIPA.

PART FOUR

CHAPTER TWENTY-TWO

1. Patricia Hopkins interview by Tamara Cohen, in "Origins of *A Course In Miracles*," ed. James Bolen, 20:2–3, FIPA, Tiburon, CA.

2. William Thetford: Life Story, in "Origins of *A Course In Miracles*," 4:52, FIPA.

3. Hopkins interview, 20:6,4, FIPA.

4. *A Course In Miracles* Text, Introduction.

5. Bob Howe interview with author, March 2007.

6. Pat Hopkins telephone interview with author, December 2007.

7. Jaison Kayn telephone interview with author, February 2007.

8. Robert Rosenthal interview by Tamara Cohen, in "Origins of *A Course In Miracles*," ed. James Bolen, 16:4, FIPA.

9. Sherry Ruth Anderson & Patricia Hopkins, *The Feminine Face of God* (New York: Bantam Books, 1991).

10. Rosenthal interview, 16:4, FIPA.

11. Hopkins interview, 20:9, FIPA.

12. Pat Hopkins interview, December 2007.

13. Hugh and Gayle Prather, interview with author, October 1993.

14. Ibid.

15. Ibid.

CHAPTER TWENTY-THREE

1. Pat Hopkins, telephone interview with author, December 2007.

2. Jack and Layle Luckett, email message to author, January 2008.

3. Jack and Layle Luckett telephone interview with author, December 2007.

4. Ibid.

5. Luckett interview, March 2008.

6. Ibid.

7. Luckett email, January 2009.

8. Jack and Layle Luckett, email message to author, September 2009.

9. Luckett interview, December 2007.

10. Ibid.

11. Luckett email, January 2009.

12. Luckett email, September 2009.

13. Luckett interview, December 2007.

14. Ibid.

15. William Whitson interview by Tamara Cohen, in "Origins of *A Course In Miracles*," ed. James Bolen, 21:11, FIPA, Tiburon, CA.

16. Luckett interview, September 2007.

17. Luckett interview, December 2007.

18. Edna Jo Hunter-King interview by Tamara Cohen, in "Origins of *A Course In Miracles*," ed. James Bolen, 11:7, FIPA.

19. *A Course In Miracles* Workbook, Lesson 156, 294–295.

PART FIVE

CHAPTER TWENTY-FOUR

1. *A Course In Miracles* Text, 102.

2. Gangaji, *You Are That* (Boulder, CO: Sounds True, 2007), 105.

3. *A Course In Miracles* Text, 524–525.

4. Jack and Layle Luckett, email message to author, October 2007.

5. Diane Cirincione telephone interview by author, July 2007.

6. Author's transcription of Thetford Memorial Service, Pat Hopkins, July 1988.

7. Hugh and Gayle Prather interview by author, October 1993.

8. Ibid.

CHAPTER TWENTY-FIVE

1. Jerry Jampolsky telephone interview by author, July 2007.

2. Judith Skutch Whitson telephone interview by author, January 2008.

3. Ibid.

4. Jack and Layle Luckett telephone interview by author, March 2008.

5. Judith Skutch Whitson interview, January 2008.

6. Catherine Prescott telephone interview by author, August 2008.

7. Ibid.

8. Ibid.

9. Ibid.

10. William Whitson telephone interview by author, February 2008.

11. Judith Skutch Whitson interview, January 2008.

12. Ibid.

EPILOGUE

1. *A Course In Miracles* Workbook, Lesson 135, 255.

2. Author's transcription of Thetford Memorial Service, Roger Walsh, July 1988.

3. *A Course In Miracles* Text, 668.

AFTERWORD

1. *A Course In Miracles* Workbook, Epilogue, 488.

Acknowledgments

I t is a simple fact that this book is possible only because of extensive and heartfelt input from many of Bill's closest friends, and to them I am grateful beyond measure. Although I already possessed many documents and much information about Bill, the Foundation for Inner Peace kindly made their archives available to fill in the gaps. Without Judy and Whit Whitson, who along with Bob Skutch and Kenneth Wapnick are the centers of the original *ACIM* family, it would be a decidedly less complete work. They have generously shared their time, their memories of Bill, and their enthusiasm for the project. Nor would it have come together without the excellent suggestions and expertise of my dear, lifelong friend and professional editor, Sarah Whalen-Kraft. She has skillfully assisted in turning my memories poured out on paper and my transcribed conversations with more than thirty people into a more graceful document. I extend sincere thanks also to Julie Ruffo, who provided specialized editorial services and assisted with publishing decisions. My treasured friend, Alice MacMahon, served as reader, unofficial editor, and cheerleader for the project. So too, my sons Greg and Nelson were wholeheartedly in favor of my writing Bill's story and encouraged me to persevere when the mountain of details and information seemed daunting. Last but certainly not least, Cathy Sanders and Kathryn Van Aernum brought their extensive graphic design experience and good will to the layout design and cover respectively.

Those interviewed in person or by phone, some more than once, include

Bob Beale, Diane Cirincione, Dean Clyde (now deceased), Jules Finegold, David Goodrich, Bruce Gregory, Patricia Hopkins, Bob Howe, Greg Howe, Jerry Jampolsky, Jim Jeffries, Jaison Kayn, Jack and Layle Luckett, Carlagaye Olson, Hugh and Gayle Prather, Catherine Prescott, Bob Skutch, Alice Stephens, Roger Walsh, Kenneth Wapnick, Sarah Whalen-Kraft, Judith Skutch Whitson, and William Whitson.

From the archival records of the Foundation for Inner Peace, I gathered excerpts from interviews with Art Carr, Tammy Cohen, Calvin Hatcher, Edna Jo Hunter-King, Charles Lehman, Robert Rosenthal, Frances Vaughan, and Dorothy Ullman.

Angie Mills responded to my letter to her sister Harriet, and both corroborated Bill's story of Harriet's retrieval from Hong Kong as told in his autobiography and added new material. Paul Solomon (now deceased) and LeRoy Zemke provided valuable insights into Bill's psyche through their in-depth readings given for him in 1976 and 1980 respectively.

Thank you one and all for making Bill's story available for everyone, and may we all learn to emulate "flexi-Bill!"